CW00796585

PATAGONIA WILD AND FREE

PATAGONIA WILD AND FREE

Memories of William H. Greenwood

COMPILED AND EDITED BY:

Duncan S. Campbell and Gladys Grace-Paz

ILLUSTRATIONS: Julieta Fernández Cánepa

Patagonia Wild and Free
Memories of William H. Greenwood

Copyright © 2015 by Duncan S. Campbell and Gladys Grace-Paz
email: dg@patbrit.org

Registration Nº: 257,013 (Chile)
ISBN: 978-956-358-993-1
First edition: November 2015

Original articles: William H. Greenwood

Compilation, editing and publication:
Duncan S. Campbell and Gladys Grace-Paz

Illustrations: © Julieta Fernández Cánepa

Translation of Preliminary Study: Duncan S. Campbell

Book composition: Mirko Vukasovic
Cover design: Cristian Haase
Map design: Neil Campbell
Photo credits: (Editors) Peter Carey; (Greenwood) Perran Newman;
(Steinman) Hans Joachim Schmid

❧ CONTENTS ❧

✿ ACKNOWLEDGMENTS ✿

We wish to thank all who have accompanied and assisted us on our journey of discovery and publication of the reminiscences of William Greenwood (alias *Don Guillermo*).

The following persons deserve special recognition:

ROBERT LÉMAIRE, great-grandson of Henry L. Reynard, Cañadón de las Vacas, Santa Cruz (Argentina), permitted us to study the family's old documents and manuscripts — key to our investigation — and guided us to locations associated with Greenwood's presence on the *estancia*; his generous hospitality was in the best Patagonian tradition.

MATEO MARTINIC, Professor Emeritus, University of Magallanes, Punta Arenas (Chile), has consistently encouraged our research into Patagonian history. We have benefitted from his enthusiastic support and pertinent suggestions, and are particularly fortunate to include his detailed PRELIMINARY STUDY, prepared specially for this edition.

ALFREDO PRIETO, University of Magallanes Centre, Puerto Natales (Chile), convinced us of the importance of Greenwood's memoirs, and encouraged us to conduct the search; and, once the materials were found, helped us to find the means to publish them.

JUAN MAC-LEAN, partner and Manager of *Hielos Patagónicos S.A.*, Puerto Natales, demonstrated his commitment to regional culture by generously underwriting and supporting this project.

ANDRÉS FERNÁNDEZ, of *Ediciones Skyring*, Punta Arenas, provided tangible support and practical advice; his patient help guided us through the complexities of book production.

JULIETA FERNÁNDEZ CÁNEPA, our illustrator, has successfully captured the "look and feel" of a 19th-century publication, which was ably complemented by MIRKO VUKASOVIC's book composition and CRISTIAN HAASE's cover design. NEIL CAMPBELL, graphics designer transformed our rough sketches into clear and professional maps of Greenwood's areas of activitiy.

PERRAN NEWMAN, great-grand-nephew of William Greenwood, kindly shared family portraits of our author, lifting a corner of the curtain of mystery surrounding his life in Cañadón de las Vacas.

ROBERT RUNYARD placed at our disposal his archive of maps, photographs and information on Southern Patagonia, which served us well on numerous occasions; he also generously shared his experience in the field of publication and provided sound counsel.

FERNANDO CORONATO kindly translated for us a Welsh language text by the colonist Lewis Jones, that mentioned the visit of Greenwood and his friend Leesmith to Chubut.

WULF STEINMANN and HANS JOACHIM SCHMID, descendants of the German geologist Gustav Steinmann shared information and family photographs. Together with ILSE SEIBOLD, GERHARD EHLERS and ISABELLE CASANOVA, they helped us to identify materials relating to the 1883 scientific expedition in Southern Patagonia.

WILLIAM EDMUNDSON, author of "*A History of the British Presence in Chile*", ARNOLD MORRISON and NEIL MORRISON reviewed parts of Greenwood's text. ELVIRA PAZ and SYLVIA GRACE provided insightful comments on the translated narrative.

We also wish to express our thanks to:

Hugo Aguilar, Clare Baylis, Pablo Beecher, Francisco Busolich, Reiner Canales, Peter Carey, Kate Child, Paola de Smet d'Olbecke, Marcelo Gavirati, Armando Iglesias, Carlos Nuevo, Michael O'Byrne, Milagros Pierini and Norma Sosa; and to all the family members and friends who helped us in one way or another, not least of these being the difficult task of choosing an appropriate title for this book.

A special debt of gratitude is due to the Max von Buch Library of the UNIVERSITY OF SAN ANDRÉS, Buenos Aires, for archiving and conserving the former newspaper *"The Standard"*, in which Greenwood's articles were originally published. Their Special Collections and Archives staff were helpful and efficient.

We also wish to record our appreciation for the assistance provided by staff of these institutions in the following countries:

ARGENTINA: Santa Cruz Province Historical Archive, Río Gallegos

CHILE: National Archive and the National Library, Santiago; Historical Archive and Library, National Maritime Museum, Valparaíso; Magallanes Regional Museum and the Centre for Studies of Southern Man (University of Magallanes), Punta Arenas

ENGLAND: Natural History Museum, South Kensington, London

GERMANY: Steinmann Institute, University of Bonn.

WILLIAM H. GREENWOOD, 1872

CARTE DE VISITE

(Dedication)
George & Emma
W. G.
August 1872

(Photographers)
Hamilton y Cía
Calle Potosí N° 106
Buenos Aires

❧ FOREWORD ❧

"What do you know about William Greenwood?"

This question was asked repeatedly by our historian friends. As investigators of the British presence in Southern Patagonia, we owed them an answer, but … who was he, and why so much interest?

Don Guillermo (as he became known locally) was one of the first English settlers of the 19th century in Southern Patagonia, living for years in remote and unexplored parts of the Interior. It was known that he had kept daily "notes", which some believed had been published. As late as 2013, these had not been found: understandably, interest was high to find them and learn their contents.

Our hunt for the missing papers became a fascinating challenge and a story in its own right (see ANNEX ONE, PROCESS OF DISCOVERY). Suffice it here to say that we finally discovered the answer: a long series of articles had been published in an English-language newspaper in Buenos Aires. Taken as a whole, they convey the wisdom accumulated by its author over a quarter of a century of tribulations and adventures, "on the trail" in wild Patagonia.

It was the range of his themes, and the novelty of some of the information he brought to light, that convinced us of the relevance of this material for the region. It ought to be shared, not only with historians but also with the general public: and so, this book was born.

We are pleased to offer the reader this important collection of articles written by a *true Patagonian author*. Greenwood's memoirs of old Patagonia open a window on a lost world.

DUNCAN S. CAMPBELL and GLADYS G. GRACE-PAZ
Editors

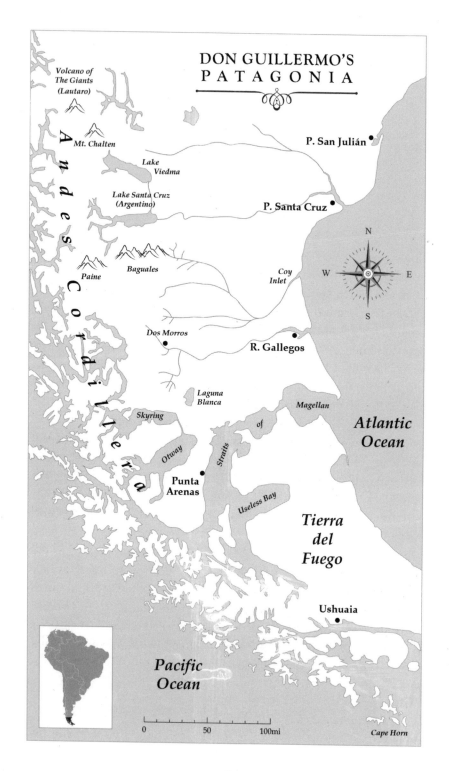

DON GUILLERMO'S
P A T A G O N I A

Volcano of
The Giants
(Lautaro)

Mt. Chalten

*Lake
Viedma*

*Lake Santa Cruz
(Argentino)*

P. San Julián

P. Santa Cruz

Andes

Paine

Baguales

*Coy
Inlet*

N

W   E

S

Dos Morros

R. Gallegos

Cordillera

*Laguna
Blanca*

Magellan

Skyring

of

**Atlantic
Ocean**

Otway

Straits

**Punta
Arenas**

Useless Bay

*Tierra
del
Fuego*

Ushuaia

**Pacific
Ocean**

0   50   100mi

Cape Horn

❧ INTRODUCTION ❧

William H. Greenwood arrived in South America around 1870 and, whether intentionally or not, he stayed. What followed were three decades of extraordinary adventures: it comes as no surprise, therefore, that he felt compelled to describe what he saw and the life he led. For a better understanding of his memories, we shall look briefly at the world that he found, how his life developed in it and what his writings tell us about that world and about himself.

Southern Patagonia's slow Awakening

The year 1520 was a milestone for Patagonia: that was when Ferdinand Magellan discovered the passage that led his expedition to the Pacific Ocean. However, it was more than three centuries before a permanent settlement was established on the Strait that now bears his name — not until 1848, in fact, when the young republic of Chile founded the town and penal colony of Punta Arenas.

Initially, living conditions were primitive: there were chronic shortages, and communications with the rest of the world were sporadic. As for the vast expanse of the Patagonian Interior, and its pampas, little or nothing was known. These "uncivilised" lands were the home of nomadic natives, followers of the herds of guanaco which formed the mainstay of their life and economy. Across the Strait, the large island of Tierra del Fuego was likewise almost unknown: some people even thought that it was populated by cannibals!

The new settlement on the Strait progressed steadily, but slowly, due to its geographical isolation and small population. By 1872, when our author arrived, things had begun to look up: there was trade with the native groups, maritime traffic had increased and small businesses were flourishing. Industrious families had migrated from Chiloé (Chile) and the first immigrants were arriving from distant Europe. Predictably, these groups included a few young adventurers, and others attracted by the "glint of gold".

For a brief period (barely two decades), a handful of hardy frontiersmen — William Greenwood among them — enjoyed a primitive lifestyle, ranging freely through the Patagonian *hinterland*, hunting, trading, exploring and acting as guides. These were the so-called *baqueanos*, and this was their Golden Age.

The Man who became "Don Guillermo"

William Greenwood had left behind a comfortable English home environment, arriving in Punta Arenas after visiting Buenos Aires and Chubut *en route*. Well educated, 22 years of age and filled with youthful optimism, he saw opportunities in the small community and started various business ventures. Three years later, he was bankrupt. This unforeseen situation was a decisive moment in his life, leading him to abandon "civilisation" and set up home in the almost unexplored "wild" lands of the Interior. In this new life, William had the good fortune to associate himself with the most respected *baqueano* of the region, Santiago Zamora. A consummate horseman, knowledgeable about the natural environment and an expert guide, Zamora was to become William's mentor and business partner. Together, they enjoyed several fruitful years, at times hunting and exploring in the Last Hope district (Última Esperanza, Chile), at others in the Santa Cruz valley or around Lago Argentino. This freewheeling existence gave rise to the character *Don Guillermo*.

Nearing 40 years of age, William was still active, but his tough way of life was beginning to take its toll. Eventually, in a move designed to draw him back to "society", his trusted friend Henry Reynard proposed a partnership: the invitation was to establish a new sheep ranch at Cañadón de las Vacas, in the Argentine province of Santa Cruz. William accepted. However, by 1896, seeing that the frustrations of this new responsibility were demoralising William and undermining his health, Reynard convinced him to return to England and recuperate. There, in 1898 (close to 50 years of age), William got married; yet, in December that same year, he was to return alone to Argentina. Later (in 1900), he fell seriously ill and his wife Alice came out to Buenos Aires to care for him and take him home.

THE MAN BEHIND THE PEN

Before returning to England for good, Greenwood published a series of 59 articles about Patagonia. Through these writings, the personality that emerges is pragmatic, self-sufficient and optimistic. Life's difficult moments are described as matter-of-fact. He takes pleasure in simple things, such as tending his vegetable garden or reading a book. At times he confides his foibles: the conviction that one day he will "strike it rich" by gold prospecting; and a recurring irresponsibility with money, which slips through his fingers like grains of sand. In the same way as the native Patagonians, whose traditional territory he travelled for many years, he is satisfied to live in the present moment, happiest when alone with Nature. By contrast, he resents the concerns and constraints of the civilised world.

Paradoxically, although our author chose to live for many years far from organised society, he seems to have been a sociable person. He devotes entire chapters to certain individuals, and comments about several more at various points in other articles. He shows empathy with the Indian groups whose access to their original tribal grounds is being curtailed by the need for sheep pasture, and feels disgust for the traders who prey on their weakness for alcohol; he respects his companion Zamora, and cares for him compassionately when he is seriously injured; he sees the outlaw Brunel as a victim of circumstances, and regrets his falling into criminal ways.

Greenwood admires those who live by the moral values he holds dear. His gallery of worthy characters includes: his gentlemanly friend Henry Reynard; the kind Doctor Thomas Fenton; the generous Tehuelche Chief Pedro Major; the well-disciplined Navy officer Rogers; and the conscientious scientist Steinmann. He accepts a degree of weakness in others, provided it is counterbalanced with positive traits — for instance, the dedicated, but rather opportunistic, Governor Viel. However, Greenwood has no qualms about criticizing those who transgress his ethical norms — men such as the Governor Dublé Almeida, whose despotism and unbridled use of corporal punishment contributed to the disastrous mutiny of 1877 in Punta Arenas; or Navy officer Del Castillo, who incited Brunel to steal horses as a means of satisfying his personal vendetta. He even lightly chides the authoress Lady Dixie for her occasional less-than-accurate descriptions of Patagonia's reality.

Greenwood seems to feel a close bond between himself and the other inhabitants of the animal kingdom: how else to explain his keeping skunks as pets! There is one exception to this rule — the puma — which he sincerely detests, mostly because it was found in great numbers at the time and caused countless headaches on the sheep ranch: eradicating it became his speciality. Hunting, setting fire to clear the land or poisoning wild animals — all these behaviours mark *Don Guillermo* as a man of his time rather removed from the ecological sensitivities of the 21st century. However, he respects Nature "in his own way": hunting not for sport but rather for survival, for trade and to protect his own animals.

As his friend Reynard once remarked, Greenwood is "*a most witty and amusing fellow!*" On occasions, he also shows a mischievous streak, shocking his "civilised" readers (*anno* 1900) with plainspoken descriptions of the cruelty of life in the wild. This notwithstanding, *Don Guillermo* loves Southern Patagonia dearly: the reader feels tempted to visit the natural beauties that he so poetically describes; and might even decide to go and work there because (according to Greenwood) the person who wants to get ahead can and will do so.

His Texts

Coming from a Victorian religious family, Greenwood adds a moralistic touch to his stories. Also, as a good storyteller, his style is conversational (rather than literary), and his texts sometimes wander off the point in the search for dramatic effect. Meanwhile, on the subjects dearest to his heart, such as his favourite animals, *Don Guillermo* provides lengthy anecdotes and explanations, asking the reader to make allowance for his indulgence. The articles convey his special ability to portray people, places and events. As his memories come to life, we participate in soirées with the Governor, experience the passion of the hunt and the dangers of the blizzard, and smile at the surprising abilities of wild and domesticated animals.

As he admits, Greenwood is not a trained naturalist or geologist; nevertheless, his texts contain interesting information for those in the field.

He mentions having spotted (around 1880), a very scarce water bird, white with a scarlet head, which may be the hooded grebe, a species not recorded for science until 1974; there are also admiring remarks on the abundant wildfowl at Laguna Nímez, close to the present-day town of El Calafate. And again, in his piece about the sea lion rookery at Monte León (Santa Cruz Province), he anticipates the ecological value of that district, which was awarded National Park status in 2004. Especially noteworthy is the reference to a prolific deposit of fossils, including "huge masses of fossilised wood and bones of every description", whose location he unfortunately does not disclose. There are also two intriguing references in the vicinity of Lago Argentino: one to a mountaintop strewn with regular-shaped clear crystals (nowadays, Cerro Cristal), and another to a mysterious stone structure, presumably of human origin. Furthermore, as Mateo Martinic explains in the following PRELIMINARY STUDY, Greenwood is a unique source of information concerning the eruption of the Volcano of the Giants (Volcán Lautaro) in 1883; and, he appears to be among the first to specify its exact location. While on the subject of toponyms, the texts also show that Greenwood and Zamora "baptised" such (nowadays) well-known locations as Baguales and Centinela. (Another source also credits Greenwood with naming the river Turbio [Rogers 1878: 76]).

A UNIQUE PATAGONIAN WRITER

Two important factors qualify Greenwood as one of a select group of writers about Patagonia: his texts describe personal experiences, and these occur at an early time in its colonisation. There are few of whom one can claim so much.

Among the better-known Spanish-language writers of this period are the Chilean explorers Rogers and Ibar Sierra, and the Argentines Moreno, Lista and Del Castillo; acting in a largely official capacity, they informed their respective governments of the diverse range of information (geographical, scientific, etc.) collected during their expeditions. Another writer, the Argentine journalist Payró, travelled down the Atlantic coast of Patagonia, describing for his readers what he saw and what others told him.

Contemporary 19th-century English-language authors include: Musters, who gives an impressive, polished description of the

Patagonians, with whom he lived and trekked extensively for a year; Beerbohm, who spent several weeks in the company of a group of *ostrich* hunters, providing a vivid description of his wanderings and adventures; Hudson, the great naturalist, who takes an intellectual view, because his "idle days" were spent more in observation and reflection than in action; Lady Dixie, whose impressions of travelling "across Patagonia" are those of a tourist, gathered during her only visit; likewise, the US journalist Spears, who combines interviews and personal observations in what he called "a collection of facts about the coasts of Tierra del Fuego and Patagonia", with emphasis on the pursuit of gold.

Although, at times, William Greenwood and the above-mentioned authors deal with similar topics (for example, Musters gives descriptions of an incident with a wild bull and a traditional *ostrich* hunt), he stands out in contrast to all of them: his accounts are those of a man of action, writing from half a lifetime of personal experience in Southern Patagonia, with all the diversity that this had entailed.

In summary — The depth, variety and authenticity of Greenwood's narrative make him the Patagonian writer *par excellence* for the early period of colonisation. His memories provide a rich, new source of first-hand historical information.

UNCOVERING
DON GUILERMO

PRELIMINARY STUDY BY

Mateo Martinic B.

RECIPIENT OF THE CHILEAN NATIONAL HISTORY AWARD, 2000

Uncovering Don Guillermo

More than half a century ago, when we were working on the investigation that would bear fruit in our first important historical publication, *Chilean Presence in Southern Patagonia 1843–1879*[†], one of the aspects that awakened greater interest was the rescue of all available information concerning life in the rural districts of South Patagonia. The Colony of Punta Arenas, especially from the governorship of Oscar Viel (1868–1874) onward, had begun to stimulate and drive that development, albeit timidly. It was at this period that the Chilean presence in the region of the Magellan Strait was consolidated, especially northward — a vast district known at that time by the general term *pampas*. It was then that we learned of — and greatly enjoyed — the tales of backcountry hunters, adventurers and wild horses lost in the recesses of the east Patagonian Cordillera and its foothills; and of the surprising wildlife, its attractive landscapes and varied resources; but that did not seem sufficient.

The subject was fascinating, and we felt tempted to learn more about it; but there was little solid information at hand. Our interest was so enduring that over the years we deepened and enlarged the knowledge at our disposal, transforming ourselves into conveyors of historical facts, which were practically unknown at the time. We published numerous articles and books on the subject, thereby increasing the available information dealing with the district of Última Esperanza and environs during the period preceding its colonisation.

[†] Published by Editorial Andrés Bello, 1963 and 1971.

Notwithstanding this work, we were not satisfied, because we knew that there were still loose ends and some gaps in the history. We were convinced that something was still awaiting discovery: important data on the period prior to the arrival of the first colonists in the Andean foothills, the deepest recesses of Última Esperanza and southwest Santa Cruz (Argentina). This conviction was based on some sentences in the account published by the explorer Agustín del Castillo of his journey to the aforementioned region. Specifically, naming William Greenwood, an adventurer whom he had known during his visit to the upper reaches of the River Gallegos, he wrote: *"During his long presence in Patagonia he has not missed a single day in enriching his notebook. He has written much and is profoundly indifferent to all that some foreigners have said against Patagonia."*[‡]

We thought that those papers, if they still existed, must hold a hidden treasure of new information about the pristine state of Patagonia, prior to its colonisation. How to locate them, allegedly in the form of a personal diary, became a pending task. On various occasions we discussed the subject with Alfredo Prieto, an archaeologist and colleague at the Centre for the Study of Southern Man (Patagonia Institute, University of Magallanes), and tried to find at least a clue which might lead us to our objective, namely to discover the cherished document which we imagined hidden in some old family attic in England, or published and likewise forgotten in some old newspaper of unknown date — in any case, very distant — knowing, as we did, that Greenwood had been a news reporter at one point in his life. After fruitlessly trying here and there, we came to believe that the memoirs of the famous *Don Guillermo* had been lost forever.

Then, all of a sudden, a miracle! — one of those discoveries which occur from time to time while searching for old papers! That this was possible was thanks to the research skills and sixth sense of Duncan S. Campbell and Gladys Grace P., through the creation and management

---

[‡] Agustín del Castillo. "Exploración de Santa Cruz y las Costas del Pacífico", Marymar, Buenos Aires 1979, p.63.

of their websites (patbrit.org and patlibros.org). First, one day about two years ago, Alfredo Prieto informed us that these two researchers had found a trustworthy lead; and then, later, that they had located what we had been looking for, namely Greenwood's narratives, which had appeared in "*The Standard*", an English-language newspaper published in Buenos Aires, during 1900 and 1901. We shall leave it to Campbell and Grace, now The Editors, to tell us in ANNEX ONE how they carried out their search, and what happened after it proved successful. What matters most is that these *notes*, penned by the almost-legendary *Don Guillermo*, have proved to be as valuable a *treasure trove of historic information* as we had originally believed.

And what treasure! Thanks to their diligent and careful work, these researchers have now placed before us a book, accessible to all who enjoy reading about Patagonia, and especially its history. The following pages present the complete set of newspaper articles dealing with different subjects, all duly set in their historical context. These articles were the fruit of Greenwood's notes and reflections on a quarter century of authentic, true-life adventures while residing in Southern Patagonia (approximately from 1872 to 1896). His were unique experiences, set deep in an unspoiled natural world, which would shortly disappear. We know of no other civilised man in the region, neither before nor since, who went through such extreme challenges as those that he experienced.

Add to this Greenwood's simple, easy-flowing writing, which is presented in an agreeable style and with a truly British sense of humour. These qualities reflect his background and level of education, enriched by an excellent ability for observation and analysis, and a remarkable memory. In summary, what we have is a historical narrative that should be accepted unhesitatingly as true, coherent and impartial. Its expression must have answered the author's need to repay a debt of gratitude to the vast and remote land that had accepted him – a land still free of the hand of civilisation, and a source of strong spiritual meaning. Greenwood considered himself fortunate to have enjoyed all this; and so, seeing that, on balance, the satisfying memories of his existence far

outweighed its difficulties, extreme though some of them had been, he
decided to share these events with his contemporaries.

✤

We believe that it is worthwhile to emphasise those parts of the
content and subjects which we find most interesting. To begin with,
we draw attention to the valuable new information which he presents
concerning the INDIGENOUS PEOPLE who were living at the same
period in the Magellan territory; and even more so, the Patagonians
(CHAPTERS 6 and 10, plus mentions in various others), because it comes
from someone who lived alongside them and as one of them. For this
reason, Greenwood can be considered a reliable informant, in the same
way as Theophilus Schmid and George Musters before him, and James
Radburne afterwards. His observations of the ancestral culture of the
native people of Southern Patagonia enrich our (forever incomplete)
body of knowledge about that world.

The author deals repeatedly with the NATURAL WORLD in its various
forms (CHAPTERS 17 to 21, with several additional mentions, plus
isolated facts). His agreeable presentation and specialised knowledge,
accompanied by a descriptive accuracy characteristic of naturalists of
earlier times, provide a comprehensive view of the animal world as
it existed before *economic man* began to interfere with it. His unique
information about WILD HORSES AND CATTLE (principally CHAPTERS 3
and 4) is equally valuable, given that these animals became the primary
source of economic activity of the Punta Arenas colony; and moreover,
the horses provided the justification to explore the mountainous district
of Última Esperanza.

Particularly interesting are his recollections of acquaintances and
dealings with PERSONS OF HISTORICAL SIGNIFICANCE such as Ascencio
Brunel, the legendary bandit (CHAPTER 14); Oscar Viel, corvette captain
of the Chilean Navy and Governor of the Magallanes colony, with
curious and surprising information about his use of local power and his

personal character (CHAPTER 2, and mention in CHAPTER 1); the German scientist Gustav Steinmann (CHAPTER 12) and, especially, Santiago Zamora, the archetypal hunter/guide of former times (CHAPTER 5). Likewise, he deals with EXCEPTIONAL EVENTS, such as the mutiny of the Punta Arenas artillerymen in 1877 (CHAPTER 9) and the eruption of the Volcano of the Giants (CHAPTER 13). Whereas the author provides valuable evidence that helps to complete the existing biographies of such interesting personalities as Brunel and Zamora, in the case of Professor Steinmann his information about the little-known scientific excursion is certainly novel and has real historical importance.

Two striking events are mentioned. First, his account of the mutiny and its regrettable consequences confirm and complement known information on the subject. Secondly, in the case of the volcanic eruption, his information is both unique and valuable because, exceptionally, it comes from an eyewitness. Proper identification of this mysterious Andean volcano would not occur for a further half-century. In this case, we are surprised that Greenwood uses the term *Volcano of the Giants*, which was not employed by others in reference to its activity, neither at that date nor subsequently. This volcano, whose existence was for long presumed rather than proven to be real, we find mentioned for the first time in the *Map of South America*, published in 1775 by the Spanish geographer Juan de la Cruz Cano y Olmedilla. We stress our surprise at the Englishman's knowledge of this term, which we attribute to his high degree of culture and education.

His statements and reflections on the origins and conduct of the SHEEP-RAISING ACTIVITY, during the final two decades of the 19th century, are interesting. So too are his well-expressed remarks on *sheep fever*, which he accurately describes, using his first-hand knowledge of the subject (CHAPTERS 15, 16 and 22).

In our judgment, although what has been rescued of Greenwood's writings is a treasure-house of historical information — and it truly is — the most valuable part of his written legacy is found in CHAPTERS 7, 8 and 10 (and even 11). Here, in colourful detail, and at times with dramatic

touches, we have an account of the events that occurred in DEEPEST
SOUTHERN PATAGONIA BETWEEN 1877 AND 1882, approximately. It was
in this period that the author of these narratives had his richest and
most varied rural experiences, which, without a shadow of doubt, left
an enduring imprint on his character: it was these events which were
presented in a suggestive summary by the explorer Agustín del Castillo
in his travel report. These chapters should be savoured: in the author's
words and sense of motivation, one finds — for the first time ever —
detailed, complete and irreplaceable first-hand information about the
way of life on the frontier of colonisation. That natural environment
and the few people who lived in it are now consigned irreversibly to
the realm of history.

These writings, now rescued at last for posterity, are what we once hoped
they would be — and perhaps more than that. Therefore, we are deeply
pleased to prepare this Preliminary Study for their publication, and we feel
ourselves participants, albeit secondary ones, in a successful search effort.

It was a sound move for the region to use the term *Don Guillermo* —
as Greenwood was known and respected by his contemporaries — and
better still was the subsequent decision to perpetuate it in the name
of a stream and an area through which he passed so frequently in his
Patagonian travels. Our recognition of his memory is amply justified:
for the valuable evidence that he preserved about Nature and his fellow
human beings; for what he revealed as an explorer, for the common
good and for science; and for what he has handed down to us as a
writer. In this sense, the publication of his memoirs is, at one and the
same time, both a significant revelation and a well-deserved tribute to
his memory.

Such an evaluation might strike the readers as excessive, but they
would be incorrect: it comes from one who has dedicated his life to

the knowledge of regional history. Across the years and on the specific subject that concerns us — the eastern foothills of the South-Patagonian Andes — we have seen how the corpus of knowledge has built up little by little; and now, with the addition of *Don Guillermo* Greenwood, it is virtually rounded out. It is an opportunity to recognise and give thanks to the early British immigrants and travellers in Patagonia, who, as a group, have provided us such extremely useful information, thus advancing the knowledge of history.

Duncan Campbell and Gladys Grace deserve a particular mention here for their creativity and persistence in researching and preserving that part of Patagonia's historical memory which relates to the British presence in the territory: the book you hold in your hands is one example of their relevant and satisfying results.

Additionally, we wish to draw attention to their skilful translation for the Spanish version of this book, which faithfully retains the meaning and style of the original English content, sacrificing neither accuracy nor comprehension. Their work reads easily and comfortably.

Due to the force of circumstances, this material is late in appearance; but, from this moment on, by its own merit, it joins the select group of classic books about our old dear Southern Patagonia.

Mateo Martinic B.
Punta Arenas, 2015

Don Guillermo

❧ ARTICLES ❧

by WILLIAM H. GREENWOOD

❧ EDITORIAL NOTES ❧

The richness of the information present in Greenwood's texts led us to pursue two objectives: to publish his complete series of newspaper articles, and to translate them all into Spanish (published separately).

COMPILATION

While some of the themes in the newspaper collection were published in a single issue, others appeared over several issues. These latter articles have been combined, reorganising the material for clarity and removing obvious repetitions. The original 59 articles have been arranged into 22 chapters. Since they cover a wide range of loosely related themes, the reader can "dip" into any of them, without fear of losing the flow of the narrative.

Throughout, when needed, we have organised the text into paragraphs and made minor editorial corrections, including punctuation. The text is faithful to the original wording, respecting its recurring grammatical complexity and occasional outmoded vocabulary.

TERMINOLOGY

Foreign-language words (Spanish, Latin and French) and usages local to Patagonia (*e.g. ostrich, station*) have been set in italics and are defined in the GLOSSARY. One special case is the word "*camp*", which appears in italics only when used in the local sense of "open country". Some early place-names used by Greenwood have been retained: noteworthy examples are "The Colony" or "Sandy Point" for Punta Arenas and "Lake Santa Cruz" for Lago Argentino.

ADDITIONAL MATERIALS

In the course of verifying Greenwood's material, we have gathered additional background information, some of which is provided as brief footnotes. In a few instances, these have also been used to correct his memory lapses (typically found in personal accounts written years after the events described).

Titles, subtitles and illustrations have been created especially for this edition. Sketch maps provide a rough guide to the routes followed by Greenwood and the expeditions mentioned in the text. Lists of persons, locations, flora and fauna named in the text have been included as APPENDICES.

All misinterpretations, errors and omissions are our sole responsibility.

THE EDITORS

The 🦁 Standard

BUENOS AIRES, TUESDAY, JULY 17, 1900

"We propose giving our readers a most interesting description of the *Great Lone Land in the Far South*, of which the following is the first chapter. The writer has an unique store-house to draw upon, of personal experience, and we can safely say that no white man living or dead knows more about Patagonia than he does, his sojourn there covering an uninterrupted period extending over 30 years. This in itself is a record and cannot fail to give added interest to his narrative. — Editor."

❄ 1 ❄

First-Hand Information

*Trustworthy information about Patagonia—Climate—Soggy arrival—
Hospitable Governor—Wind and crops—Opportunities for raising
livestock—Illnesses of sheep—Pumas, the main predator—Guanacos
stupid but abundant—Aristocratic sportsmen—Lady Dixie and the
geographic complexity of Patagonia—Baguales are the best kind of sport*

Patagonia is a country of which much has been said and much has
been written; but I do not think that anyone has hitherto given a
really correct idea, either of this territory or of its resources.

First of all, as regards the climate: the idea that existed till a few years
back was that the country was a desert, and the winters so severe that
the bare idea of living there frightened everyone before they ever gave
it a trial. When I first went down to Sandy Point in the year seventy[1],
everyone imagined that it was a complete wild goose chase; and, to
speak the truth, when I landed in Sandy Point the prospects did not
appear very brilliant.

There being no mole and a heavy surf on the beach, the first adventure
I experienced was the overturning of the boat. Myself and three companions in adversity found ourselves distributed on various portions
of the shore, mixed up with our baggage, stores, etc.; moreover, it was
pouring with rain and blowing a gale of wind. After picking ourselves
together and collecting all we could of our traps, our first enquiry was
where we could stop for a few nights, until we could make arrangements
for starting on a voyage of exploration. But no place was to be found, as

---

[1] Year of arrival — Indirect evidence points to Greenwood arriving in Punta Arenas in
December 1872. Published sources provide dates ranging from 1870 to 1873.

all the fifty or sixty houses which constituted the town of Sandy Point were occupied; or, if not, in such a state of dilapidation that they were quite useless to us as a shelter. At last, however, the Governor (Señor Oscar Viel) came to our assistance, and very kindly allowed us to occupy one of the Government sheds, and also gave us meat and firewood; so, we managed to make a huge fire and to dry most of our things.

First impressions are everything, and ours were far from pleasant ones; but, after a good sleep we woke up to find a glorious morning except, as usual, a very strong wind from the West. I may mention that during the spring and summer months these strong westerly winds are almost incessant, and very often of extraordinary violence, so much so that one can often hardly sit on horseback. For this reason, it is almost impossible to grow either fruit or corn except in the most sheltered places, as all the blossoms are blown off the trees before the fruit is set; and the corn, just when the ears are green and heavy, is completely levelled to the ground: but, where good shelter can be obtained, both fruit-trees and corn thrive wonderfully.

Every kind of root can be grown and, if carefully planted, you may be sure of a good crop — also lettuces, cabbages, cauliflowers, etc. I have frequently seen potatoes weighing two and three pounds each, and I remember one cabbage or cauliflower that weighed eighteen pounds: so, you can see the ground is not (as reported) useless for cultivation. Both alfalfa and clover will grow anywhere, so long as a moist spot is chosen. The country is so broken that there is no difficulty whatever in selecting sheltered places for small crops for the use of your establishment; but, for agriculture on a large scale, the country is practically useless: both on account of the strong winds, and the impossibility of finding sheltered spots on the high *Pampas*.

Now for the stock prospects: the gigantic increase in the prosperity of the territory during the last fifteen years tells its own story. When I first arrived, there were just one hundred and fifty sheep in Sandy Point and its vicinity; in Gallegos none, not even a house had been erected; and in Santa Cruz there were only three or four houses, and a few hundred sheep, cattle and horses, all of which belonged to the late Captain Luis Piedra Buena. At the present moment [1900], the stock on the different farms can be counted by hundreds of thousands, not only in the Straits of Magellan, but right up the coast nearly to the Río Chubut. Sheep, especially, thrive well in all this district, and anyone starting with a moderate capital can be sure of doing well if he sticks to business.

There are, however, three great drawbacks: first and foremost, the great prevalence of scab[2] (owing principally to the damp weather during the winter months); secondly, another disease which we call inflammation[3], which is most fatal and kills the sheep in a few hours, and for this we have found no remedy; thirdly, the immense damage caused by the *lions* — or, I should say, pumas — which are so numerous in these districts. I think during the eight or nine years I was sheep-farming, these pests killed on my farm alone at least five thousand sheep, and all the other farmers suffered — and still suffer — in the same manner.

Another great nuisance to the farmers are the guanacos, which come down in thousands in the winter season, breaking down the fencing and devouring everything they can get hold of. Sometimes I have seen herds of three or four thousand head altogether, but this is exceptional; they generally run in flocks of from two or three hundred to a thousand. The animals are so stupid that they will go straight for a fence or river or lake or anything else in the way, and either get through the obstacle or kill themselves. I believe that, like sheep, they take a pleasure in committing suicide: if one falls over a cliff, all the rest must go and tumble after him, to see what it is like; and if there is a hole or a boggy place which they can fall into, they will invariably do it. Far from seeming to decrease, they appear to become more numerous. Formerly, the

Indians used to keep them down, but now Indians are almost things of the past. The two or three hundred that remain in this part of Patagonia are only allowed to hunt in certain places: they made themselves very obnoxious to the settlers — when the latter were first commencing sheep-farming — by killing sheep, breaking fences and doing all sorts of mischief.

---

[2] Scab — Infectious disease, caused by skin mites, which affects sheep, goats and cattle.
[3] Inflammation — Greenwood does not provide sufficient information to identify this condition.

Having disposed of sheep, guanacos and pumas, I think I can move on to the more interesting subject of hunting, and the general sport to be found in the country. To any stranger arriving there for the first time, it will appear that (with the exception of wild fowl shooting and guanaco and *ostrich* hunting) there is little or nothing to be done to amuse oneself. This is a great mistake: I know of no country where you can get more fun and amusement in the way of sport, if people will only take the trouble to look for it.

In truth, Patagonia offers as fine a prospect of real good sport, both in hunting and shooting, as the greatest enthusiast could desire. Admittedly, the variety of the game is not excessive, at least the variety of "big animals"; but, of the few different species that exist, there are such quantities as are rarely found in other parts of the world.

We have had many distinguished visitors at one time or another, and many keen sportsmen: to wit, the Marquess of Queensberry and Lord Howard de Walden; not to mention Lady Florence Dixie's party, who certainly appeared to have enjoyed themselves — to judge by the tone of her Ladyship's book "*Across Patagonia*". How on earth her party managed to get "across" Patagonia in so short a time, I can hardly imagine. I can only say that I have for many years tried to arrive at that climax (as have other, far better men than myself), but without success. If one had wings, it would doubtless be very easy to accomplish the feat and pass *canals*, glaciers and ranges of mountains without trouble, and tumble over into the Chilean Republic; but, without such appendages, I do not see how it can be managed.

Everyone knows that to arrive at the *Cordillera* of the Andes is only child's play, and is done by hunters and traders every month in the year; but, to get across, except by the one or two well known passes far to the north, is a very difficult matter. To pass even the small low ranges of the *Pre-Cordillera* is no easy task; and when that is accomplished, there are the hundreds of *canals* with which the mountains are intersected; and, after that, there is the main range of the Andes; and then more *canals* and rivers; and then the *Pre-Cordillera* on the Western side. Of course, the farther north one travels, the easier the passage becomes, there being no *canals*; and, moreover, the woods and *bosques* are nothing nearly so dense as in the south — and the *Pre-Cordilleras* are very low.

It is, however, quite unnecessary for the sportsman to go so far afield to obtain his heart's desire; he will soon get tired of potting guanacos, *ostriches* and *deer*, and look for some other diversion. This can be easily found in the chase of the wild horse or *bagual*, which to me is the acme of all sport in Patagonia, and has its spice of danger with it to give it a zest. Later, I shall describe several of the other animals to be found in the region, with a description of the best mode of finding where they live; and, after that, the best way to hunt them[4].

---

[4] Other animals suitable for hunting — See 21, LESSER GAME.

❧ 2 ❧

Cattle and Horses

A man's worth measured by his animals—Power structure in the Colony—Change of Governor—Meat supplied from the wild—Without fences, domestic cattle wander off—Qualities needed in a horse

Some years ago, when sheep farms were not even dreamed of, the acquisition of cattle and horses occupied everyone's attention. I really believe people were measured — and liked or disliked — exactly in proportion to the quantity of these animals which they happened to possess. If there is a trifling quarrel or petty jealousy existing at present between the various farmers, as regards the amount of each one's possessions in the sheep line, it is nothing to compare with the fierce feuds previously carried on between the various cattle and horse owners.

Everyone took his standing, credit, and general status in Sandy Point society according to the number of cattle and horses he possessed. If a man owned an old walleyed[1] horse and a cow or two, he was regarded as a rising man, and one whose future prospects were looking up. As for another man, who happened to own eight or ten animals, his fortune was considered as secured; and, as previously he was denominated Dick or Tom or Harry, now not even his most intimate friends would dare to mention him except as *Don* Ricardo, *Don* Tomás, etc.

---

[1] Walleyed — Having large, staring eyes; eyes showing more than normal amount of white (*divergent strabismus*). Greenwood is being humorous.

Very few people did own animals at this time (I refer to the years 1871 to 1874), except the Governor and his pet crony and toady who, next to our chief (who, of course, as Governor had feathered his own nest very well) was the richest man in the little colony. There was also a Secretary who, I believe, owned eight or ten cows and a few horses, and he stood third on the list as a reigning power.

I was very much amused on my first arrival to watch the proceedings of the three great and all-powerful men. The Governor was really a capital fellow, and was most kind and attentive to us on our first arrival, and gave a general invitation to his evening levees. These, of course, we made a point of attending: first, out of pure gratitude for his kindness; and, secondly, because the reception saloon was the most comfortable room in the place, and the Governor's whisky and cigars were not to be despised in a town where no one could buy anything but the most ordinary *wachakai* (*caña*) and very bad  cigarettes. At any rate, we attended the receptions regularly: in fact, we were expected to do so, and were rather amused to watch the behaviour of the three potentates.

The Governor always occupied, of course, the big armchair in the most comfortable place before the fire, supported on either hand by the two lesser lights. The conversation was mainly conducted by these three and ourselves. There were several other far lesser lights generally present; but these (being only owners of four or five animals) kept respectfully in the background and said nothing, and did less — unless any of them observed that his Lordship required a light, or a cigar, or something else: in which case, there would be a general and frantic rush to see who could serve him first. Of course, it would have been quite *infra dig* for a man in his position to ask for anything; so, he would only stretch out his hand in a vague, uncertain manner and glance appealingly round … and then you should have been present to observe the excitement which ensued.

The two right and left hand supporters of the great power would actually rouse up a little and make some slight movement, as if they thought they ought to do something, but did not exactly know what.

The others, however, vied with one another in their endeavours to serve the Governor first: I have actually seen two of them, each with a lighted match in his hand, bang themselves together in their efforts to be first in the field. During the confusion, a third would quietly step in and supply the required article, much to the *chagrin* of the other two. This is really not exaggerated: I have actually witnessed the scene I described on more than one occasion.

Please do not think that the late *Don* Oscar Viel was unaware of all this, or that he did not appreciate this eagerness to serve him at exactly its true value; neither, it must be imagined that he was a man in any way devoid of energy when circumstances called it forth. I have on occasion seen this same man ride all the way to Port Gallegos and back (a distance of 180 miles) in two days, to have a look at a strange vessel which was loading guano there without permission[2]. But, he had passed so many nights in exactly the same position, and with the same companions, that he knew that it was utterly useless for him to try and help himself when any of his satellites were present.

At this time the Colony of Sandy Point was full of convicts — many of them desperate characters — who required most careful management; and it required a most judicious man and a clever one to handle them properly. See what took place when Governor Viel was superseded, and another strict and far less intelligent man was appointed in his place. I refer to the well-remembered mutiny[3] in the Colony of the year 1877, when convicts and soldiers — indignant at the extreme severity and injustice with which they were treated — joined together in one great rising; reduced the greater part of the Colony to a pile of ashes; killed the Captain of the troops, and many others who could not manage to escape; and had a general good time of it.

I have as usual gone straight off at a tangent from my original subjects, cattle and horses, but it is astonishing how one thing leads to another when one is retailing events of the past.

[2] Governor Viel's horse-ride — The incident mentioned by Greenwood has not been corroborated; his figures for the distance covered and the duration of the journey are insufficient.
[3] "well-remembered mutiny" — See 9, SANDY POINT MUTINY.

To return to the reunion at Señor Viel's house: of course, what conversation took place generally referred to the absorbing topics of the
day: "cattle" and "horses". At this time, the wild horses (*baguales*) had
not been discovered; but the wild cattle had, and a great portion of
the few inhabitants dedicated themselves to the work of catching and
taming them; and also killing them to supply the Colony with meat. At
this time, the main meat supply was from the wild cattle in the woods,
and from guanacos, *deer* and *ostriches* killed and brought in from the
Pampas.

You can judge how scarce the meat supply was when I mention that
guanaco, *deer* and *ostrich* meat was never sold at less than fifteen cents
gold per lb., and beef or mutton generally fetched 25 cents gold, and
sometimes more. It is not, therefore, to be wondered at that every one
was anxious to have plenty of cattle, and also horses, with which to
hunt the wild animals.

For more than a year, I did nothing but hunt game and bring the
meat into the Colony: it really paid remarkably well, as far as making
one's living was concerned. As for saving money, that was impossible,
as everything was so exorbitantly dear in the Colony at that time. Very
often, the commonest necessaries could not be obtained at any price.
There used to be periodical times of famine and plenty, according to
the arrival of vessels from the North; but this was only during the first
two or three years of my residence there. Now the whole country is
literally inundated with stores and, of course, meat of all kinds is at a
discount.

Cattle became so plentiful that the difficulty was to find a sale for
them; and, both at the present moment and for years past, people have
been killing them for their hides alone. A *grasería* was started on two
different farms, and many thousands of superfluous sheep and cattle
were rendered down; but, I do not fancy the business paid particularly
well, or perhaps the supply was not sufficient to make it pay: at any rate,
none of the rendering-down establishments worked regularly — only
for a few months in the year.

※

When I first started farming in the Cañadón de las Vacas, I commenced with cattle alone, more with a view to clearing out the pumas

than anything else; but, directly I brought up the first sheep, I found that the cattle would not remain on the ground. They gave me so much trouble that I eventually let them go; I doubt not they are at present wandering about the *camp*, in company with hundreds of other animals which have escaped from — or been let go by — other farmers.

At first, mine did not go very far from my *camp*; but, little by little, they retired inland; and, when I left Patagonia, if we wanted beef we had to go at least eight or ten *leagues* before we could find any to kill. Of course, we held on to the tame milk cows: not only for milking purposes, but because we found our working bullocks (one of the most necessary adjuncts to a farm, when one has to cart his produce sixty or seventy miles) would not stay on the ground unless they had some cows with them.

From the large mobs of semi-wild cattle, which I have seen from time to time in the outer and unpopulated *camps*, I do not doubt they will increase enormously, and in the next few years perhaps become as great a nuisance as the guanacos. However, if a man keeps a tolerably large *point* of milk cows, he will get sufficient increase from them to supply himself and farm with occasional banquets of beef, to change the monotony of eating nothing but mutton.

The quantity of horses to be found is now very great; large numbers of colts are shipped to the Falkland Islands, and many mares have been sent to the *graserías* to be rendered down. Of course, it is necessary to have a few tame mares on every farm, to keep up the strength of your troops of working horses from their colts: each *tropilla* requires constant renewing and strengthening, because the ground is very rough and hilly, which makes it very hard to work.

The reasons of the enormous increase in the number of working horses now existing are as follows.

First: A great number of animals have been imported from the North. For years, several parties of Englishmen and *gauchos* made it a regular business to go up by steamer to Bahía Blanca, Río Negro and Chubut, to purchase large troops of horses, both wild and tame. These they brought down overland, calling at the various farms on the road, and disposing of their animals at very reasonable rates. This was a very paying business for some years, but now it is completely played out, there being amply sufficient horses and mares bred in the country to supply all demands.

Second: The *baguales* or wild horses, formerly so numerous in the *Cordilleras*, were captured in great numbers and brought down for sale[4]. These animals themselves did not serve for hard work, unless very carefully tamed and very tenderly treated. But, crossed with tame studs in the Colony and different farms, they gave a splendid result: they are literally not to be tired, can live on almost anything, and are splendid on hilly ground. In boggy or soft ground, they are not of very much use; but, give them hills to climb and they are all there.

This race appears to be blessed with unusual powers of longevity. For example, in 1878, I brought down several pure-bred *baguales* from the mountains. One was at least seven years old, and the others at least three or four years. To the best of my belief these animals are still alive on Mount Observation Farm — my first establishment in the north — and are still giving yearly increase.

To anyone going down south to start farming, I can confidently recommend the purchase of this breed of horses. They do not generally run more than 13 *hands* high, are not at all coarse looking, but particularly wiry and strong. Remember, you don't want a thoroughbred horse for sheep work: they are no good to you, and won't stand climbing hills (which is indispensable in all these *camps*) for any time at all; you want something sturdy and untireable — never mind the looks.

---

[4] Discovery and capture of wild horses — See 4, Baguales (Wild Horses).

Although they are, of course, cheaper than in former years, good horses are not sold cheap in Patagonia: you can't expect to buy at Bahía Blanca or Río Negro prices. Moreover, you may be perfectly certain that, if a troop is offered to you particularly cheap, there is some reason for it. I should advise everyone who is new to the country to mount and try every horse before he buys it — don't be taken by appearances. At the same time, you need not go in for showy or expensive *tropillas*.

$\cdot \frac{\star}{}$ 3 $\frac{\star}{}\cdot$

Last of the Wild Bulls

*What became of the wild cattle and horses?—Greenwood and Zamora
kill 8 of 9 wild bulls—Pursuit of the last survivor—Vandalous attack
by bull and horse—Unexpected and near-fatal encounter—The chums
die together*

I t appears strange that, whilst there were so many wild cattle found in
the forests and mountains near Sandy Point, and also on the shores of
Otway and Skyring Waters (which animals were constantly hunted and
disturbed), so few found their way further north to the forests lying to
the west of Laguna Blanca. It is true that there are hundreds of leagues
of dense *monte,* quite unexplored, which may contain thousands of
animals, for aught anyone knows.

Yet, one would think it would not be possible for animals to winter
in these mountains which, however mild it may have been on the coast
and *pampas* are, in the winter months, completely covered with snow
and ice. Yet, where do they go to? And, where did all the wild horses go
after they were once disturbed? They must have some refuge, right in
the Interior, and the wild cattle doubtless did the same.

I can't tell you the amount of time old Zamora[1] and I wasted in looking
for cattle; and yet, we never found but one small *point* of 9 bulls. These
were in the mouth of the Canyon of the Vizcachas, right in front of our
pass to Lake Santa Cruz; they had evidently only just arrived there, as

---

[1] Old Zamora — More information in 5, Homage to Santiago Zamora.

there were very few tracks about; and, what there were, were all quite recently made. These 9 bulls, Zamora and I pursued relentlessly, and killed 8 of them. The only way was to watch and shoot them, as they were all thoroughly vicious; and even Zamora, old *vaquero* though he was, did not care about *lassoing* one of them without a competent companion: which I certainly was not. I always considered it advisable and discreet, when we were looking for these animals (unless I had my rifle with me), to keep as far from my old friend as possible. I should infinitely have preferred an entire family of Bengal tigers rather than one of these demons. I knew the old man was literally spoiling for a set-to; but, beyond standing behind a big bush or rock and taking pot shots, I did not feel inclined to render him any assistance.

As I said, we managed to pot 8 out of the 9 bulls; the ninth, a huge *tordillo*, disappeared completely, nor was he seen again for 3 or 4 years. But, when Captain Rogers was exploring near the Sierra Paine with Señor Yáñez and Zamora, they suddenly came across him on the coast of the Rapid River[2]. They only had revolvers with them, and I believe they fired all the bullets they had with them at the brute, but he appeared rather to enjoy the proceedings. Eventually, finding them rather monotonous, he executed a series of charges and cleared the country of his tormentors, and was no more seen till the day of his death, many months afterwards[3].

It was in this wise. At the time of the great gold craze, I and a German fellow were looking for gold in the neighbourhood of Paine; we had had very hard luck, only finding about 170 grammes during 3 or 4 months' hard work. One night, over the campfire, the conversation turned on this said wild bull; and Zamora, in whom the instincts of the *vaquero* were still keen, said he would never be contented till he had found the animal and killed him. The German, who wanted a *lasso*, caught at the idea and proposed looking for him at once. Of course, the old man desired nothing better; and, naturally, I had to appear delighted at the idea; but, internally, I cursed both the bull and the

[2] Rogers' encounter with wild bull — Occurred in March 1879. (Rogers 1880: 144).
[3] Death of the last bull — Another source gives a date of 1886. (Del Castillo 2007: 62).

man who proposed looking for him — my strong point was not wild cattle hunting. Moreover, we were all hard up, and looking for the brute meant loss of time and no profit. However, there was no remedy, and in the morning we started off at daybreak to see if we could find any tracks. We took a rifle and all the dogs, and left the bell-mare hobbled.

Of course, because I hoped we should not find anything, we must needs come across tracks about a month old, before we had gone a mile; and, following them up, found them fresher and fresher. It is quite certain we must have passed quite close to him at one time: at any rate, he evidently saw us or found our tracks, as what happened afterwards will show. What was curious was that, wherever we picked up the bull's tracks, they were closely followed by the tracks of a very large horse; where one went, the other went, but we could see nothing of them; and finally, tired and disgusted, we returned home.

Following the road we had come, we were surprised to see that both the bull and the horse had picked up our tracks, and gone straight back on them towards our camping place. On arriving there, what was our disgust to find our 3 tents levelled to the ground, and our things distributed all over the place. We had left a lot of clothes hung out to dry on the bushes; these were all knocked down and trampled under foot. Also, a big sack full of books I had left in my tent was torn to pieces, and the leaves of the books blown all over the place. The bull and the horse were evidently partners in the outrage, as the ground was literally ploughed up with their tracks.

Well, after this, we all swore a solemn oath of vengeance: we would either kill that bull and that horse, or die in the attempt. Fortunately for us, the ground was very moist, and tracking was very easy: so, early in the morning, we started and easily picked up the tracks. Right in front of us was a perpendicular mountain or hill, with no woods on it except at the extreme summit, where there was a thick bunch of *roble* wood, formed like a horseshoe with the entrance facing downhill. The tracks led us straight up this hill towards the front of the *monte* at the top. The ground being full of holes, the two animals left a regular road, which we followed till we came to the entrance to the woods.

I was well mounted, and some way in advance of the other two. When I got there — to my delight — I saw that the tracks led straight into the entrance before-mentioned. I also knew that the other side of the mountain was perpendicular, with a sheer fall of a thousand or more feet to the *canal* below: so, I felt pretty sure we had got our friend safe this time. I unstrung my rifle, let the reins of my horse fall on his neck, and fumbled about for a cartridge with which to load. I found one, and had my hands fully occupied in loading when, without the least warning, the enemy, closely followed by his adjutant, a huge *raking rosillo bagual*, charged straight down upon me.

Fancy the situation. I was perched on the almost perpendicular side of the mountain, with both my hands occupied, loading my rifle. Of course, my horse immediately took fright and turned sharp round. I flew over his head about 10 yards down the hill, and my rifle went heaven knows how far. My horse made tracks for home as if *Old Nick* were after him; and the bull — followed by the big horse — passed right over the top of me, one of them even treading on my left hand and breaking a finger. Of course, the bull could not check himself to do me any harm on such an incline, or he would otherwise most assuredly have finished me. The beast passed close to my two companions, about 20 yards below me, and ran downhill till he got to the bottom, where he entrenched himself in a large bunch of *calafate* bushes, completely blown. My companions took no notice of my misfortune, but followed the bull till he stopped.

Meanwhile I picked up what was left of me, found my rifle, and tramped slowly down the hill after them. I found them impatiently awaiting my arrival with the rifle: the bull was still stuck in the bushes about 20 yards off, and his chum the horse was standing nearby, waiting on him. A couple of Comblain[4] bullets soon squared the account, and our enemy was *non est*. As the horse, on missing his companion, might take it into his head to interfere with our *tropilla*, I wasted another bullet on him. So, the two strangely assorted chums died together.

The bull was an enormous creature; he had, from old age, changed from *tordillo* to pure white, and his teeth were worn right up to the gums. Strangely enough, he was still very fat and gave us two large biscuit-sacks full of *grease*. The meat was splendid when hung for a few days.

This was the last wild bull I saw in Patagonia; but, I doubt not there are large mobs of cattle somewhere in the mountains which, if they have not already been discovered must, as civilisation progresses, undoubtedly be so.

---

[4] Comblain rifle — Invented in Belgium, where it was used from 1870 onward; a variant of this design was later supplied to the Chilean armed forces.

⁂ 4 ⁂

Baguales (Wild Horses)

Rumours about their Existence

Theories about baguales—Sprung from similar stock—Palique remembered what his father told him—Casimiro told Zamora— Domain of Gualicho

Where the original stock (which formed the race of wild horses called *baguales*) sprang from, is difficult to determine; it is also difficult to account for the presence of those animals in such quantities on all the slopes of the *Pre-Cordillera*; and it is still more strange that until a few years ago even the Indians had no idea that they existed.

The common belief is that these animals are descendants of horses let go by the Spanish explorers, when they were on these coasts, in the days when Patagonia was an unknown country. It is well known that these adventurers constantly left animals wherever they touched with the view to their utility when (in future years) these territories should be populated. Or else, they may have originated with some few animals landed by the old Spanish settlers in San Julián, at the same time they commenced the settlement in that port (which was afterwards abandoned).

The *baguales* may also be descended from the animals left in Port Famine when that ill-starred colony was abandoned. It is quite certain that from thence sprang the breed of wild cattle, which still exist (although in small quantities) in the woods and mountains of South Patagonia. I have never heard that the Spaniards landed any horses to the south of Port San Julián; and, from thence, it would be almost impossible for them to have travelled so far south — unless they were

53

driven there — as the Rivers Chico and Santa Cruz would certainly stop them on the road. So, I think we may stick to the original theory: that this race sprang from the few animals left in Port Famine[1].

In any case, very few animals must have been lost; and more or less the same colour, as all have a white star on the forehead and one or more white hocks. When we first discovered their existence, with the exception of a few strayed *Christian* or Indian horses (which had mixed with them), all were of only two or three different colours. Anyone with half an eye can recognise one of the breed! The colour never varies: it is either *rosillo* or *rosado*; and, with very few exceptions, the white marks on each animal are almost identical.

Rumours had been afloat for many, many years that there existed a race of wild horses somewhere in the recesses of the *Cordilleras*. I think the first to start this report was an old Indian witch doctor, called Palique, who said that his father, a very old Indian, had told him that there were large quantities of horses — and also a large number of white settlers — in the interior of the mountain where the wild horses were originally discovered. Also, several strange horses of these colours had from time to time been captured far out on the plains; as no one had lost any animals of this description, it is natural to suppose they must have come from somewhere or another.

The old Chilean hunter, Santiago Zamora, said that he remembered having been told by the old Indian Chief Casimiro (the same mentioned in Captain Musters' celebrated work "*At Home with the Patagonians*"), that in the recesses of the *Cordillera* there were many wild horses and cattle; but, that no one could go to look for them, because these animals lived in the woods and mountains, far to the west, in almost inaccessible places. Moreover, the said animals were the particular perquisite and property of the great devil spirit *Gualicho*, who would most assuredly exterminate any living soul who ventured to interfere with his rights over them, or in any way interrupt the harmony of the said *Gualicho*'s peculiar precincts and property. For this reason, the old Chief said all the Indians carefully avoided the *monte* and the neighbourhood thereof;

---

[1] Origin of the wild horses at Port Famine — Greenwood's theory is highly debatable.

he said that the Devil loved bushes and woods, but detested the open *camps*, which he left exclusively for the benefit of the Indians, so long as they did not in any way interfere with his "manorial rights" over them.

The Great Discovery

Herd discovered by Greenwood and Zamora—A happy camp—Baguales unfamiliar with humans—Organising the capture

Perhaps it may be interesting to describe how we first discovered these wild horses, so I will do it as briefly as possible.

Many years ago (say 18 or 20 years)[2] all hunters, traders and Indians had a perfect dread of approaching the vicinity of the mountains, for fear of being snowed up (by the way, I was snowed up once for four months); and, therefore, carefully avoided the mountains, till the spring was far advanced. As I have said, the Indians had never searched these districts, because they never camped (in those days) near woods, being in terror of the aforementioned evil spirit *Gualicho*, who is supposed to take his pastime in woods and forests.

Directly the spring was well set in, we used to move from the lower *camps* towards the mountains, following in the tracks of the migrating animals. Every year we found tracks of large troops of horses on the plains below the mountains. At first, we thought that they were animals which had strayed from either the Indians or from traders. But, at last, it struck us, from noting the quantity of tracks, that it was an impossibility that such a quantity of animals could be lost.

Anyway, some of us — including the ever adventurous Zamora — determined to have a search expedition; if we did not find horses, we might find something else. We informed some Indians, whom we met on the road up, whither we were bound; they prognosticated much evil fortune for us in this unknown land of evil spirits, and wanted us to abandon the idea.

I think five of us started on this expedition[3], including the old man and myself. The two of us were determined to go on at all costs; the others, fearing that we should make a strike without them, accompanied

---

[2] Discovery of wild horses — Although the precise date is not known, these events occurred some years before 1879. (Rogers 1880: 135).
[3] Size of group — Elsewhere, Greenwood refers to four individuals, not five.

us (though with a very bad grace), as there appeared to be some doubts in their minds as to the advisability of tempting the Devil's wrath. But, as everyone was very hard up, and most anxious to make a strike — somehow or other — we determined to brave *Gualicho*'s wrath and follow the adventure to the bitter end. Therefore, we marched straight for the *Cordillera* (due west), following as far as we could the tracks of the strange animals.

By good fortune, we struck it right in front of the great Baguales Valley, as we afterwards baptised it. At the end of the third day, we arrived at the foot of the first ranges of *Cordillera*, always encountering tracks — more and more numerous — as we neared the first slopes. I think it was on this third night that we camped in front of the valley, and prepared to enter the mysterious country.

On the plains below it, we found tracks of large mobs of horses, which had evidently passed the winter there. This was cheering for Zamora and myself; but not so to the others, who declared that so many animals could not be running wild, but must belong to some unknown race of Indians, who would kill and devour us if we attempted to intrude on their privacy or in any way interfere with their domestic arrangements. At the last moment, two of them threw up the sponge: they said it was tempting Providence to go any further, and they absolutely declined to accompany us on our voyage of discovery to the Interior. Nevertheless, they agreed to await us on the outside until our return, or till we made them a fire signal — as a sign that all was well, and as a summons to join us with the horses.

Zamora and I would gladly have parted from the men altogether; but, on this occasion, it was useful to have them: it was impossible for us to take all our horses with us, as we did not know what kind of road we had to travel or what we should encounter; therefore, they could look after them till we either returned, or signalled them to join us.

All being agreeable to this plan, old Zamora and I, mounted on our best horses and well equipped with both *campañistas'* arms and provisions, determined to brave the evil spirit alone: early the next morning, we started up the wide and feared valley.

Passing into the valley, we found it getting narrower and narrower as we advanced. A swift rocky stream ran through the middle of it and occupied the greater part of it; and, on each side of this, broad roads ran straight up the canyon — although no track appeared very fresh, we followed. The further up we went, the wider became the track; we could now plainly see that it had been formed by large bodies of animals, passing up and down from time to time.

We could not determine at first whether this road was formed by guanacos or horses; but, our doubts were soon set at rest by our finding a dead mare lying across the track. It was quite entire and perfectly dry — like a mummy — so we set it up against a rock in the middle of the track. A mile or two farther up, we found a dead foal on the track, and shortly afterwards a big *rosillo* horse — completely sun-dried and hard. This too we propped up against a rock, exactly in the middle of the tracks, as a sight to our companions, and to astonish their weak minds (if such were possible). Having arranged with our companions that, if we made a signal fire, they might be sure we had "struck oil", and might follow us with all security, we immediately made a fire of the thick *mata negra* brush, and proceeded on our way, rejoicing in the almost certainty that we were in a fair way to reap the reward of our labours.

The canyon now became wider and wider, and at last opened out into a big flat of about three or four *leagues* in extent — all surrounded by woods — with several small streams running into the main stream at the mouth of the valley. All this flat appeared beautifully well grassed, and was dotted with bunches of *roble monte,* like an English park. What was more to the purpose, spread all over it were troops of horses — nearly all, as far as we could see, of two colours, viz. *rosado* and *rosillo.* However, I noted, in the mob nearer to us, a fine-looking black stallion and several darker coloured animals, probably the offspring of the same. We afterwards caught this black horse, and found he was an escaped Indian horse, and was marked on ears and flank.

We had been advancing very cautiously, to await the arrival of our recreant friends, and sat down and had some breakfast and a smoke meantime.

Very soon, our men arrived, in a great state of excitement, which was not decreased when we took them to the mouth of the valley and showed them our discovery.

Of course, it was determined to open the campaign at once. The only question was, how to do it to the best advantage; we finally determined to make a general rush into the midst of them, and *bolear* and *lazar* as many as we could. So, fixing all our gear so as to be in perfect readiness for action, we all four dashed into the valley and bore down upon the nearest lots of mares and horses.

We expected that, on our appearance amongst them, the whole lot would clear out at once; but, far from this being the case, they only appeared perfectly astounded at our appearance. Far from running away, they came circling round us within a very few yards, snorting, pawing the ground, neighing and rearing, apparently wondering who and what we were. They most certainly had not the slightest idea of what Man was (at least, nearly all of them), but we noted that some few of different colours — amongst whom was the black horse before-mentioned — kept at a most respectful distance: these were, of course, escaped Indian horses, and well knew their old enemy and master, Man.

They were so thick and near to us that we had not space to work and, although we all discharged two or three pairs of bolas at the mobs, no one "*bolear-ed*" anything; but this was sufficient to frighten them, and they broke up into numerous *points* and sped off towards the woods. We now somewhat recovered from our astonishment and, after collecting our *bolas*, each one of us followed in pursuit of a different *point* of animals.

They were all so fat that they could not run fast or far, and the mares, being very heavily in foal, were dead-beat after a few hundred yards' race; before sundown, we caught eight or nine animals and secured them. By the time we had fixed off our captives with *maneas* and *trabas*, it was nightfall; we retired to a *point* of *monte* in the entrance of the canyon we had come up, and made ourselves snug for the night. I

never remember passing a happier night in the *camp*: we had plenty to
eat with us, every man had his *tacho* (a small kind of kettle used by all
Chilean *campañistas*) and a good supply of *yerba*. Late we sat by the
fire, and many a good yarn was told. Everyone was in a good temper,
having the almost certain prospect of making a really good thing out
of our discovery.

Next morning, after due consideration, we came to the unanimous
conclusion that we had better try and work our El Dorado on a whole-
sale system. We resolved to explore the different passes into the woods,
which the *veld* horses evidently frequented; to build a large *corral* or two
in the most convenient track; and to see if we could shut in a large mob
at once. Three of us remained to do this, whilst we sent the other man
to fetch our axes and other gear, and also to see that our own horses
had not strayed.

We were pleased to see that the wild horses had returned to their
feeding-ground, and appeared as quiet and contented as if they had
never been disturbed. Carefully skirting the woods, we soon arrived at
an opening, following which we came to a lovely little glade, about two
hundred yards in circumference; from its tracks and trodden-down
appearance, it appeared to be a favourite sleeping place of at least a
considerable portion of the mob of wild horses.

Nothing was easier than to shut this place securely in, and turn it
into a capital little paddock. Even without axes, it could easily be done,
as there were hundreds of fallen trees lying in all directions. An opening at the other side of the glade, about twenty yards wide, evidently
led to some other resort of the *baguales*; this we carefully stopped up
with logs, building a wall of at least six feet high, and strong enough to
hold elephants. The undergrowth was so thick all round our paddock
as to be almost impervious, and any weak place we fortified with logs.
By nightfall we had all fortified and ready, except the entrance, which
fortunately was only about ten yards wide and, to make matters more
convenient, had a big tree growing in the middle.

We now returned to our camping place, passing on the road several
small *points* of our friends, who only stared at us. They ran a little distance, others retreated again: they were evidently yet quite unscared by

our arrival, and unaware of their impending trouble. Our friend had duly returned, bringing with him all the necessary articles; and, reporting our own troop safe, he also brought a fresh horse for each of us.

Although we had our wild horses shut in, that was only the beginning of the business: the next thing to be done was to secure them and then get them into the Colony. To take in the whole lot would be useless, as many of them were old studs and utterly worthless; these we should have to let go, or kill: what we required were the good-looking mares and young animals.

One thing was quite certain: we must first starve them into a state of submission, or we should never be able to handle so many. We therefore stopped there for two whole days, paying only occasional visits to the *corral*, to see how they were getting on. The mares and young animals appeared tame enough; but the old studs (especially the black one) were as furious as ever whenever we came near the place. There were 9 very old horses, which would really never be any use to us: so, I resolved to shoot them in the *corral*, as the brutes would go for you in a moment if you went near them or the mares. One of them did actually get hold of my coat and tore it right down the back, and another tore Zamora's *poncho* right off him. Nine bullets soon put an end to this difficulty, and we could then go into the *corral* and work with safety.

First of all we caught the oldest mares, turned all their ears in and made them perfectly stupid, and collared them in threes and fours. There were 5 or 6 nice young colts of 3 or 4 years old — these we caught and collared to our tame horses — besides about a dozen of the youngest and best-looking mares. We killed 5 or 6 of the oldest and most intractable mares, as they were no good for either breeding or training. After this, there only remained young animals, yearlings and foals, which followed the older animals; and the 5 or 6 escaped tame horses, either *Christian* or Indian, which we soon secured and put to active service.

We were almost ready, with the exception of taking the *potro boots* from the dead animals, and also some *lonjas* for plaiting gear, both of which articles were invaluable to us. We also resolved to *charquear* a couple of the fattest animals, as provisions for the voyage, as we knew we should have no time to hunt on the road; it was very hot weather, and in 24 hours the meat was dry enough for our purpose. Now we were ready for a start.

Delivery to the Colony

Difficulties in driving the animals—Keeping watch at night—The Governor's welcome—Business ruined—Persecution and disappearance of the wild horses—Advice on taming them—Tribute to "Dangerous"

Our idea was to drive the animals in as hard as we could to the Colony, keeping them all the time in a more or less tired state, as otherwise they would be sure to give us a great deal of trouble. I shall never forget the work we had to make a start. Some of the *colleras* would not move at all, while others would only go round and round in a circle; and others would dash about all over the place. However, by dint of swearing and whacking, we managed to start them down the canyon.

I forgot to say that the previous day we had collared the 5 mares we caught first to tame horses; they were now used to the collar, so we put them in front and one of us drove them down the valley as an advanced guard. The others followed tolerably well, and before nightfall we were at our old camping ground on the plains below. We found it would be absolutely necessary to keep a watch over them at night: we had omitted to do so the first night, and in the morning they were all over the country. There were 5 of us, so 2 hours' guard every night was not a very great hardship; and in this way we managed to get the lot safely into the Colony, with the exception of 2 or 3 foals which got tired and had to be abandoned, and one *collera* of 4 animals which disappeared in an extraordinary manner.

I think, when we arrived in the Colony, there were about 50 animals left, big and small. We duly presented ourselves at the Government House with these, and made our report to the Governor, who happened to be in a particularly good humour; after complimenting us on our energy and adventurous spirit in making the discovery, he accepted the 2 best-looking mares as a present, and gave us permission to continue our labours.

Not content with these proofs of his amiability, he and one or two of his principal traders organised an expedition on their own account, sending out a lot of soldiers, convicts and *campañistas* — armed with brands — with orders to catch everything they could and mark it. They would have no difficulty in finding the animals as, of course, all our party had been talking and everyone knew exactly where to go. If we could have kept the affair dark, it would have been a most lucrative business for us; as it was, the entire thing was ruined. Even the Indians took heart and ventured into the mysterious territory.

The poor *baguales* were so persecuted that the whole lot disappeared — no one knew where. Perhaps 2 or 3 hundred might have been caught and killed, but certainly not more; and small *points* of 20 or 30 were (and are, from time to time) found in different parts of the mountains and plains; but, where the main body of them went is a mystery. My theory is that they found some pass through the mountains, and are now enjoying the peace and tranquillity that was denied to them in the Canyon of the Baguales.

✻

A few more words about the *baguales*: they are sturdy little animals: in fact, one might almost call them ponies. However, they must be most carefully tamed and taught by degrees — not hurriedly, or they turn out useless. Once well tamed, and accustomed to their work, no animal is hardier or capable of more endurance. Moreover, they appear to have the privilege of an exceptionally long life.

For example, the first of these *baguales* which I caught had two foals at her feet, and was then certainly six or seven years old (this was in the year 1879). I called her "*Dangerous*", and dangerous she always was, and no one ever cared to ride her but myself. She was such a perfect demon and so cunning: you had always to mount her on a steep hillside, and keep her head well up the hill at first go off. If once she got her head downhill then, heaven help you; for, if she could not buck you off, she would throw herself down and roll over you; and if she got a chance to bite or kick you, did not ever lose it — and yet, I loved her; and if she is alive, I love her still.

After some years of quarrelling and many sore bones on my side, we came to a perfect understanding. No one could catch her but myself without a *lasso* or *boleadora*; but, even in the open *camp*, if I called out to her by name, she would stand perfectly quiet; and, when mounted bare-backed, would only give five or six playful jumps and then go off like a lamb — and no power on earth could tire her out.

She was still alive when I left Patagonia, but well stricken in years, being then, I should imagine, about thirty years old. Two years previously, she presented me with a very fine colt foal, exactly like herself. I left him on my late farm at Cañadón de las Vacas when I came away, and only trust he will prove a worthy scion of a noble mother.

Perhaps I may bore most of my readers with this tribute to the memory of my dear old friend; but, I think any lover of horses and dogs will not wonder at it, and pardon me for my indiscretion.

⁂ 5 ⁂

Homage to Santiago Zamora

Beginnings in Patagonia

Tribute to one of the pioneers of South Patagonia—Chilean or Argentine?—Son of a muleteer from San Juan—Hunter of wild cattle in Punta Arenas—Meeting at Otway Water—Active and intelligent man—Zamora and Greenwood work together—Many lucrative activities—Rise in the price of feathers—Winter spent hunting ostriches—Bonanza beside River Santa Cruz—Relative prosperity

It is quite impossible that I should keep on writing about Patagonia, and not pay some tribute to the memory of one who, although poor, ignorant and superstitious, was one of the pioneers of South Patagonia, and perhaps the most useful and energetic man I ever met — Santiago Zamora. He travelled with me for four years before his death[1], so I had ample time during our wanderings to learn all he knew and could remember about himself. I wish to give a detailed account of his life, which I think cannot fail to interest.

I could never quite make out whether he was a Chilean or an Argentine; he thought he was born in San Juan (Argentina). His father was a well-known mule train-driver, taking charge of large mule trains

---

[1] Zamora's travels with Greenwood — This chronology presents problems. Greenwood was probably with Zamora in 1888 (4 years before the latter's death); but they first met in 1873, and were associated for approximately 7 years, as Greenwood indicates later in the text.

journeying between the two Republics from year's end to year's end[2]. His first remembrances were serving in his father's mule train as *marucho*, or lad employed to round up the train ready for cargoeing, and to see that the animals did not lie down after they had their cargo on. Besides this, his only duty was to cook his father's (the *capataz's*) dinner, and help him eat it. His father must have been a good and somewhat clever man (not to be compared with the usual run of mule train-drivers), as from his earliest childhood he seems to have struggled to instil into his sons many good and useful lessons. Education he could give them none, but he taught them to love hard work, to be strictly honest, and intensely religious. All these qualities my poor old friend retained to the day of his death.

I first met him in Sandy Point, a few days after my arrival. He was then occupied as a *vaquero*: viz. he and others did nothing but hunt the wild cattle, at that time so plentiful in the woods round Punta Arenas. When I arrived in 1872, this business was in full swing, and the men did really well at it for some years: not only did they get 20 or 25 cents per pound for their meat, but they brought in all the young bulls and heifers alive; the former they turned into working bullocks, and the latter made splendid *milch cows*. For many years no animals were imported and, even at the present time, no breed is with reason so appreciated — both for milking and working purposes — as that coming from the good old wild stock.

These *vaqueros* supplied the entire Colony with meat. Where they could not get cattle they brought in guanacos or *deer*; in this business they were the mainstay of the Colony as — beyond about 80 sheep, and 100 or so tame cattle belonging to the Government or the Governor (which means the same thing) — there were no animals whatever in the Colony. The entire population was dependent upon the rations of *charqui* and dried fish, served out to each family by the Government, and the supplies of meat brought in regularly by the *vaqueros*.

And so, it was in the exercise of his calling that I first met my old friend Zamora, whilst travelling with an old friend of mine, Mr. John

---

[2] Zamora's place of birth — This remains unknown. His Chilean death certificate records him as Argentine. (Civil Registration, Chile, Deaths 1892, Book 1, N⁰. 70). However, the Argentine explorer Agustín del Castillo states clearly that Zamora was a patriotic Chilean. (Del Castillo 2007: 59–60).

Leesmith[3]. We had determined to cross the spur of *Cordillera* at the back of Sandy Point, and drop onto the shores of Otway Water, where we hoped to enjoy some wild cattle and *deer* hunting; and also, to do a little prospecting for gold.

The ascent was very easy: the trees had been much thinned out for some miles and, all the roads being formed by big trees without much undergrowth, afforded us an easy passage. From the top of the ridge we got a splendid view of the Straits of Magellan to the south, and Otway Water, FitzRoy's Channel and Skyring Water to the north[4]. We followed a little stream down the slope, which gradually widens into a fair-sized and rapid river; on its banks, about a mile from the coast, we tumbled across the *vaqueros'* camp where, with our leader Zamora, they were pursuing their usual avocation.

He was a man of medium height but magnificently framed. At that time he must have been about 65 years old, but his appearance did not demonstrate more than 50 years. His eye was piercing black, and his nose hooked like an eagle's beak; beard slightly grizzled, but hair coal-black. You had only to glance from him to his companions to note the marked difference between them. Every movement denoted activity and intelligence: he was never idle. While his companions (all of whom had the usual expression of apathy common to most of their class) loafed round smoking cigarettes or sucking *mate*, he was always doing something.

When we first saw him, he was busy plaiting a *lasso*; suspended from the tree above him was an enormous bull's head, evidently recently killed. The hide of the same animal —and a huge one it was — was

---

[3] John Leesmith — Greenwood adds: *"a gentleman who years ago was, I believe, well-known to 'The Standard' and contributed to its columns under the sobriquet of Holderness."*

[4] Compass bearings — Greenwood is inaccurate: From the back of Punta Arenas, the Magellan Strait lies to the E; the other points mentioned lie to the NW.

staked out in the middle of the encampment, whilst the quarters of beef (and splendid beef too, as fat as butter) were hanging from the trees, ready for transport to the Colony; and, tied up to various trees, were two or three young bulls or heifers, which were to be taken in alive.

Since our arrival, we had been looked upon by every resident in the Colony with much interest and curiosity. Tourists were unknown at that time, and we were considered "natural curiosities". These *vaqueros* had both seen and heard of us, and were glad to have such a good chance of finding out who we were, and what we wanted. Moreover, we carried grog, cigars and other luxuries with us, which alone would have ensured us a welcome. They soon put a splendid fat roast and some coffee before us — and finer beef it was impossible to desire. The coffee was made of toasted wheat, very indifferently ground, so we made some tea instead and had a most satisfactory meal; after this, we tried to find out all about the sport in the neighbourhood, but our new acquaintances did not appear inclined to give us much information, probably thinking we might interfere with their pursuits. This did not matter: we had now been in Patagonia some time, in Chubut and the north (where game was pretty scarce), and had no intention of starving in this land of abundance.

The *vaqueros* were returning to Punta Arenas the next day, but we resolved to remain and explore for a bit, prospecting for gold, etc. We were asked many questions by these men, which showed their utter ignorance of the outside world: for example, old Zamora asked me if Napoleon I[5] was still a prisoner in the island of St. Helena, and numerous other questions all relating to a long dead past. Of what was going on in Europe they knew nothing, but were thoroughly conversant with all that was happening in their own, and the other South American Republics.

This was the beginning of my acquaintance with the man and, from that time till his death, which took place some 3 or 4 years ago[6], I never lost sight of him. Of course, when I commenced sheep farming, he

[5] Napoleon I — Napoleon Bonaparte, first French emperor, had died about half a century earlier (1821).
[6] Zamora's date of death — The civil death register reads: "*November 29, 1892, Santiago Zamora, nationality Argentine, 86 years old, labourer, father José María Zamora, mother Merchora Peña, cause of death 'old age'.*" (Civil Registration, Chile, op. cit.). Since Zamora died in Punta Arenas in 1892, this article may have been written about 1896.

continued his old life; but, previously to that, we had travelled together for 7 years and shared many adventures, some of which I shall recount.

Soon after this, a new Governor[7] was appointed, a man about as tyrannical and grasping as his predecessor, Señor Oscar Viel, had been sympathetic, kind and generous. This Governor (who eventually left the Colony in ruin) came to the conclusion that the *vaqueros* could not be allowed to work unless half their entire gains were handed over to him; moreover, he ordained that all animals and produce brought in should pass through his hands — for what reason can well be imagined. The poor *vaqueros* tried to work on these terms; but, at the end of 2 or 3 trips, found they were getting hopelessly into debt, instead of making a more than comfortable living, as they had done before. This industry naturally came to a standstill, as the *vaqueros* either went to trade with the Indians, or took employment as carters or *peons* in the Colony. Old Zamora, however, never caved in, but continued to work on his own account.

It was soon after this that he joined me, and from the day we worked together we had an almost uninterrupted run of prosperity till we parted. I don't think, taking one year with another, we ever made less than $100 gold a month; but we stuck at nothing — hunting, wild horse catching, gold washing and Indian trading — it was all the same to us, so long as we made money. When the glorious rise in price of *ostrich* feathers took place, we were, of course, in our element.

The price of feathers had been so low for some years — falling even to 20 cents per lb. and no buyers — that we had not even attempted to sell those we had collected; but, luckily, had not left off taking care of them, as many other people did; neither did we neglect our *ostrich* dogs, but kept a good stock of the old Scotch cross-bred hounds. Therefore, when, all of a sudden, some new use was found for these feathers (in Germany I think), and they were rising in price like a skyrocket, we were ready to take advantage of the chance. I think this was in the year '81 or '82 when, from 20 or 30 cents, they actually rose to 2 and 2½ $ per pound; and kept at more or less the same rate for 3 or 4 years, when they fell to

---

[7] New Governor — Diego Dublé Almeida.

80 cents or a dollar per pound again; and retained that price more or less up to the date of my leaving Patagonia. This was a glorious chance for us — a regular gold mine — during the years the really high prices lasted. Moreover, the winters were in our favour: very severe, not much snow, but hard frost after hard frost.

There were very heavy rains at the beginning of one winter, and great portions of the *camps* were covered with two or three inches of water, which afterwards froze into a solid mass of ice, as slippery as glass. Now was our chance. We could not go on horseback, as no horse could travel over the ice, but we went on foot, each armed with a thick stick with a spike at the end to help us along. When we came across a flock of *ostriches,* we simply followed them; directly they tried to run, they went down on their breasts and could not get up again, so we walked up quietly and killed them. Dogs were of no use, as they were as much afraid of the ice as the *ostriches* — nor did we require them. In this way, during 3 months, we collected no less than 700 pounds of splendid, clean feathers; beside these, numerous puma, fox and skunk skins.

At the conclusion of the winter, which we passed in the two north branches of the Coy Inlet, we stowed away all our produce in a cave (which we blocked up with huge stones), and went across to the Santa Cruz to see how things looked there. No game whatever did we find, either on the road or in the valley of the Santa Cruz: only ducks and geese, on which we principally subsisted. But, on nearing the river, we were greeted with the most insufferable stench, apparently proceeding from hundreds of dead carcasses. This was exactly what was the case: every little bay on the river banks, more especially where there hap-pened to be a few bushes, was literally full of dead animals, *ostriches,* and guanacos etc. — some piled up 3 or 4 deep in numbers of 50 or 60; others singly, or scattered about in twos and threes. Here was another rich harvest for us, and on no account to be neglected.

It was impossible to camp near the river, as the smell was intolerable; and there was not a blade of grass anywhere, only sandbanks and thorny bushes. Instead, we picked out a very decent camping place on the side of the Lion Range (the long range of hills which runs right from the Atlantic coast to the *Cordillera,* forming the southern boundary of the bed of the Santa Cruz), and within easy reach of the river. On the next day, we started on our "agreeable" task. We found it quite impossible to take the smaller feathers, as they were dried right into the skin, and could not be plucked; but we cut off the wings of every bird we found, to the number of between 500 and 600, and conveyed them to our camp, where we spent the best part of a week dragging out the feathers: we filled five more big sacks weighing over 500 pounds. We now had just about as much cargo as we could manage, so we resolved to return to the south as soon as possible, sell what we had, and rig ourselves out for a new and longer expedition.

Well, to make a long story short, this prosperity went on with little change, except that Zamora and I, being now small capitalists, worked on a larger scale, and employed two men and two boys to help us. Moreover, we had more than seventy working horses and innumerable dogs.

The Baqueano's Final Years

Loss of left eye—Amputation of fingers of left hand—Remarkable recovery—Accomplished storyteller—Bad fall—Plays nurse to peon Torres—Greenwood has accident—Guide to Captain del Castillo—Death in Punta Arenas

We were really prosperous till poor old Zamora met with his first accident: viz. a kick from a favourite black mare of his, which extinguished his left eye, rendering him more or less useless, as his right eye had some defect and was of very little use.

However, the old man worked somehow or other, and — blind or not blind — was always doing something. He could not bear any reference to his bad sight, and continued to catch his own horse, and to go out hunting as usual. A few months afterwards, another (and even more serious) accident overtook him. What I am about to relate may seem incredible, but it is in all respects strictly true.

One bitterly cold winter's morning, the horses were drawn up as usual so that each man might catch his *camp* horse for the day. The old man, according to his usual custom, must needs go to catch his, disdaining as usual all offers of assistance. I soon caught my horse, and was only waiting till all had done the same to go and saddle up, when I heard an exclamation from old Zamora (who was next to me), and saw the poor old man staggering as if he had received some sudden shock; also, I saw a *bayo* (yellow) horse he had *lassoed* clearing out, with the *lasso* on his neck. What had happened was that the old man had *lassoed* this horse, which was always rather skittish, and, on feeling the *lasso*, it had made a bolt; by mere chance, a turn of the *lasso* had got round his left hand, and the flesh from all the fingers and thumb was literally dragged off, leaving just the bones. The flesh, including the nails quite entire, was lying on the snow, and this brave man was calmly picking it all up, and fitting it onto the bones. There was no sign of blood whatever: I suppose, from the hands being excessively cold.

I was simply thunderstruck, and stood staring; whereupon he turned and cursed me, and told me to get his bed made for him. This I did, after helping him to tie up his lacerated hand — on which he had fitted all the fingers, somehow or other — with all our available handkerchiefs. As soon as he was safely in bed, with the greatest *sangfroid*, he described to me several herbs he required to make a wash with. Two or three of these were very common enough, but the most important — a kind of houseleek — only grows amongst rocks. The nearest of these rocks to us were the caves of Car-Aiken (*vide* maps of Messrs. Moreno, Rogers and Castillo), about a *league* down the coast of the Lake; so I rode there at once, and brought back a large bag of roots and leaves.

On my return, I wanted to remove the temporary bandages we had put on, and wash and dress his mutilated hand; but, this he would by no means allow, as he swore the fingers were growing onto the bones again and must on no account be disturbed. All he would allow me to do was to remove all but the lower bandage, and then steep his entire hand in a strong solution made from the various herbs I had under his direction collected; and this I continued to do all that night, at intervals of an hour or so. Although the poor old chap must have been suffering terrible agony, he never complained: he ate his supper with good appetite; and, afterwards, he asked me to draw up a kind of will (or letter) containing his last wishes, in which he divided all his available property — principally consisting of horses and dogs — amongst his most intimate friends. After this, he seemed easier in his mind, and even slept for a little time.

In the evening I was perfectly certain (from the horrible atmosphere) that decomposition was commencing in the wounded limb, and begged him to allow me to remove the bandages, and thoroughly cleanse the wound; he resolutely refused, saying he was sure all was going on well. However, what I said must have made some impression on him for, on going to his tent some little time afterwards, I found he had removed all the bandages and was surveying his hand. On seeing me, he said coolly: "*I believe you are right, old friend, the whole d—d hand appears to be topsy-turvy! Look at this!*"; and he extended the wounded limb. In removing the bandages, all the fingers he had stuck on (with the exception of the thumb, which actually had a healthy look) had turned round, with the nails inside, and you could see fully half the hand was dead and mortifying.

Presently, the old man said very quietly: "*Pass me that piece of board, please,*" pointing to a small square bit of wood which we always carried with us, and used for cutting tobacco on, and also for fixing the horses' hoofs off, when they required it. I did so, without having the faintest idea of what he intended to do. He placed the block beside him on the ground, laid the wounded hand flat upon it and, catching up a short heavy *machete* (which he always carried with him), with one blow he deliberately cut off the four fingers close to the palm of the hand. Then, in the coolest possible manner, he requested me to cut him a large piece of raw meat, and just warm it over the fire to take the frost out. At the same time, said he: "*You may as well chuck those fingers of mine on the fire, I don't want the dogs to feed on my cast-off limbs.*" I obeyed him blindly; and when I had brought him the meat, I found him bathing the limb in the lotion I had made him. I then assisted him to wrap all the stumps in the meat (which I had cut long and thin, according to his instructions) and, after that, bandaged the whole thing up; he did not appear to suffer any particular pain, and neither hand nor arm appeared at all swollen.

Zamora directed me to put fresh meat on his wound every two hours; and said, if I could put it on just cut, warm from a recently killed animal, it would be better. Of course, we could not do this regularly, but there were thousands of guanacos, and we managed to kill several close to the tent; on each occasion, we applied the meat warm, affording him each time great relief. We also killed several *ostriches*, and utilised the herbs and pepsina taken from their stomachs as poultices. This cure is constantly used by the Indians for cuts and wounds: it is wonderful how it draws the inflammation and bad humour from them. I have constantly used it myself for small injuries and can answer for its beneficial effect.

At any rate, on the 3rd day from the accident, the old man was quite free from pain and his hand assumed a perfectly healthy appearance; but we kept on washing it well with our solution, and putting on fresh meat, to make sure. On the 4th day, he announced his intention of going out hunting with me; only, he said he should keep close to one of us, so that we could assist him in cutting up whatever his dogs killed. Nothing would stop him, so we had to let him go with us. The first day or two he behaved very cautiously: he stuck to one or other of us. On the 3rd day he got independent and missed us; he killed two *ostriches*, and then nearly killed himself in trying to cut them up and get off and on his horse without assistance.

His hand progressed in a most extraordinary manner and, although it took some months to heal up completely, yet in a very few weeks he was able to work almost as usual — I mean rough work. However, his favourite occupation of gear making and *lasso* plaiting came to a complete standstill. I pitied the poor old man, as it was not in his nature to be idle; I verily believed he grudged even the hours he spent in sleeping and eating. Now it was evident that his day was about done: he must have been at least 75 years old, and the two severe accidents, one after the other, had shaken him sorely.

He was very fond of storytelling, and had an unending fund of long, extraordinary fairy and ghost tales. He would spend hours recounting these to the boys at night by the campfire. I wish I could remember some of them as he told them — they would really amuse people. The beauty

of it was that he believed every word he recounted to be the truth; if he once got the idea into his head that you were laughing at him, he would go into a huff and tell no more stories for several days. To amuse him and the boys I commenced to take my part in the programme, and began translating Dickens'[8] works to them, one by one. Their delight ought to be seen to be imagined: "*Oliver Twist*" I must have repeated at least 3 or 4 times before the winter concluded. This was their favourite, but they also liked "*David Copperfield*" and "*The Old Curiosity Shop*," and roared over such parts of "*Pickwick*" as they could understand.

Before this, we had moved from our unfortunate camping place as far as the first woods: our long stay there had made game very scarce and wild in the vicinity, and a move was absolutely necessary. I shall never forget the trouble it took to pack up old Zamora's traps: he had a thousand and one odd articles, and everything had to go in its exact place. He was accustomed to do everything himself, and no doubt found it inexpressibly annoying to have to trust to others for the disposal of his treasures. However, we got off at last, and I was very glad to turn my back on the "*Alojamiento de la Mala Suerte*" ["*Ill-Luck Camp*"] as I baptised it. It really seems as if there were a fatality in some places, and nothing goes well with you when you stop at them: this may seem a superstition, but in my experience is nevertheless the fact. This was the case with this accursed camping place: 4 times did we stay there, and on each occasion did some serious disaster befall one of us; and after this (laugh if you will!), I always avoided this place.

The first accident was what happened to poor old Zamora. A second one would follow.

We had finished our work and had as much cargo as we could carry, and more too: so, about August, we determined to return to the Colony; but, we had no sooner got to our new camping ground in the woods, than this latest disaster happened.

The *roble* (or Antarctic bush) bears a kind of fruit, which the natives call *pinatre*: it is white, about the size of a large plum, and grows in big clusters, like grapes, from the lower branches. It is not particularly

---

[8]   Charles Dickens — Prominent English author of the 19th century.

palatable, but it is better than nothing where there is no other vegetable. There was a quantity of this fruit growing on the tree under which we camped, and the indefatigable old man with his one hand, must needs climb up to pick it. He had got about halfway up when a branch broke, and down he came with a tremendous thwack on the hard frozen ground. The fall dislocated his right shoulder, and broke two of his ribs; so, we had to help him to his tent, and start to patch him up again. We fixed his ribs and shoulder up as well as we could; but, I am afraid, *bad was the best*. This latest accident had completely incapacitated him, so I wanted to get him home whilst there was anything of him left.

Now there was nothing for it but to set out at once for the Colony. It was no use loafing around with a sick man, more especially as we had made a splendid trip: even the old man himself saw he was played out, and that this was the best plan. So we packed up and marched our first stage back to the *"Alojamiento de la Mala Suerte"*.

Here happened accidents 3 and 4, one after the other.

We had no meat when we arrived at our old camping ground, but there were herds of guanacos on all sides: so I gave the *peon* Torres a Remington sporting rifle I always carried, and asked him to go and shoot us a fat one. He was a good shot, and had used the rifle a hundred times before. (Dogs are useless as they always catch lean and scabby ones.) He was only a short time gone when I heard him fire; presently, I saw him come staggering towards me with no meat and minus the rifle. What had happened? Why, in crawling through the grass, he had unknowingly shoved the muzzle of the rifle in the ground and filled it with earth. He then fired and — it is not necessary to say — the rifle burst near the breech; it carried away part of the barrel and lock, and with them poor Torres' thumb and forefinger, besides inflicting injuries on the hand and wrist. Surely, the Devil was in the luck this trip ! ! !

Here was a nice kettle of fish: two men maimed for life, and 250 miles to cart 11 cargoes of valuable produce. The first thing to be done was to patch up poor Torres' hand, which was in a very bad way. I don't know how it was that lockjaw did not set in: not only was his thumb blown off, but the ball of the thumb was frightfully mutilated, as well as his wrist. We pursued exactly the same treatment as in the last case, only old Zamora constituted himself head-nurse and left me free. Torres was not by any means so patient as the old man had been under an almost similar injury. I think he suffered a good deal more, and certainly his wound was much longer healing up; this I thought strange, as he was a strong healthy man, not more than 25 years old.

Whilst waiting till Torres was able to march, I met with an accident myself, which did not improve matters.

I was cutting *incense wood* one day, and a large log fell on my leg, and drove one of the long poisonous thorns into my kneecap. I know nothing more venomous than these thorns, which are generally as sharp as needles and are sometimes 6 or even 8 inches long; the smallest prick from one of them very often occasions a bad swelling and subsequent sore. For myself, before I could get back to the tent, I could not put my foot to the ground; and, on arrival, my leg and foot were so swollen that I had to cut my trouser leg and boot off. After that, I poked about to get the thorn out, and each of the two one-handed men had a try — but all in vain. So, we had to go in for fomentation and herb poultices; and, at last, the wound festered and the thorn jumped out of itself: but, I was useless for 20 days.

I mention this little accident of mine as a warning to people travelling in Santa Cruz, and other parts where the *incense bush* is plentiful. This bush is excessively poisonous, and the smallest thorn you get into you will very often occasion a very painful sore. There is a remedy, however, which I did not know until recently. The *incense bush*, when old, yields a lot of yellow gum, like that you find on an old cherry or pear tree, only in much larger lumps. Melt this, and apply it to the wound, and it will cure you in no time.

At last (I think about the beginning of October) we managed to make a start. I forget if I mentioned that, some time before this, one of the men and one of the boys we had brought with us had got discontented, so we sent them back to the Colony. Now there only remained a little lad I had brought with me to put on all the cargoes and, in fact, do all the work. The other men were, of course, utterly useless, except to stand by and criticise my manipulation of the cargo, ropes, etc. This criticism did not tend to improve my temper; but, at the same time, it did me some good, as I began really to master the noble art of swearing. This was a great advantage to me afterwards, when I joined the noble army of Patagonia shepherds, and showed my companions my talents in this direction. None of them would believe I had not been working sheep for years, and even the sheep themselves were thoroughly deceived. Fame is easily gained, if you only know how to go about it.

To return to our trip to the Colony: we got over it better than could be expected, and I was right glad when I could hand my two friends over to Dr. Fenton. He was perfectly astounded at the way their wounds had healed up, and said he would not have believed it, had he not seen it. Having now deposited old Zamora in the Colony, I must bid him goodbye, as I gave up the free *camp* life and subsided into a *thorough-paced* Patagonian shepherd with — as was *meet* and right — no ambition, no thoughts, hopes or fears, joys or sorrows, except those connected with sheep.

After leaving me, the old man wandered about in a desultory manner, sometimes making a trip to the *camp* to hunt, sometimes stopping for weeks in the Colony with some of his old friends and *vaqueros*. On another occasion, he acted as guide to Captain del Castillo's expedition [1888]. But, he never did any hard work again; and, 3 or 4 years before

I left, died peacefully in his bed in our home at Sandy Point. I am sure
he was sincerely respected by all who knew him: his career in Patagonia
had been most useful and praiseworthy[9].

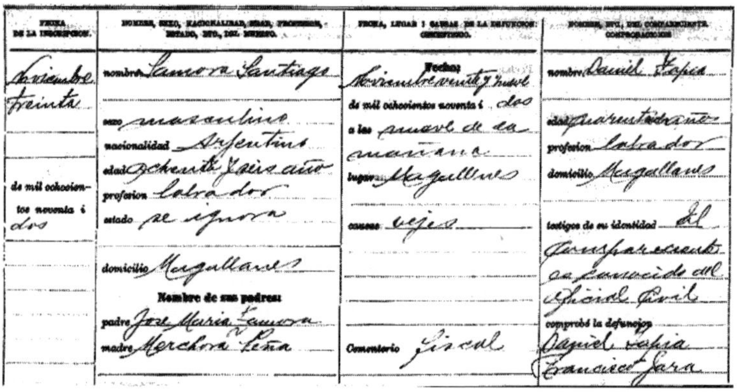

[Handwritten Spanish civil registry document]

70				

[9] Role of the *baqueano* in the region's development — See "Los baqueanos, adelantados
de la colonización y el progreso". (Martinic 1980: 9–17).

⚜ 6 ⚜

Indians

Encounters with the white man, customs and beliefs

Sheep-farming in Tierra del Fuego—Indians turn sheep-stealers—
Barbarities committed by settlers—Traditional coast access usurped—
Favourite food, the cururo—Hunger can drive anyone to steal for
food—Tehuelches have advantages over Fuegians—Expert horsemen—
Hard-working women—Love for children—Gualicho ritual at Cerro
Palique—Tehuelche Indian beliefs

Ten years ago (with the exception of the missionary settlement of
Ushuaia), Tierra del Fuego was a desert, given over to the savage
and the wild animals. Now it is full of prosperous settlers, each with
large numbers of sheep and many leagues of *camp* fenced in. In the island there are no *lions* — only a large red fox, called a *culpeo* (probably a
corruption of *vulpes canis*), which sometimes kills a few lambs and even
big sheep, but is nothing like so mischievous as the pumas. However,
the Indians[1] are, and have been, a terrible nuisance, sometimes driving
off an entire flock of sheep, cutting the wire fences, etc.

On one occasion, the Indians made a clean sweep of one poor man's
sheep, in the following clever manner. A few Indians came in, cut the
wires and drove off a small *point* of sheep (about two hundred); of
course, all the men on the *station* turned out to follow the invaders. No
sooner was the coast clear than in swept the main body of the Indians

---

[1] Indians of Tierra del Fuego — Selk'nam (formerly known as Ona).

and drove off the entire flock. When the men came back from their pursuit of the first Indians, the place was bare: that is to say, there were no sheep left. The men immediately started out again, but in vain: the Indians had too big a start of their pursuers and, moreover, knew the *camp* well, which the shepherds did not. When the savages could not get a sheep to travel, they cut its throat or speared it; and when they came to a river or bog, drove the sheep pell-mell into it, leaving dozens drowned or crushed. Only a few hundred straggling sheep were eventually recovered; and most of them had arrow or spear wounds in them. After this, it was war to the knife, and the poor Indians went to the wall.

I am sorry to say that great barbarities were committed by some of the men. Women and children, as well as men, were killed. I have been told on reliable authority that one firm paid to their men so much for every Indian they killed, it being only necessary to produce the ears of the Indian killed to receive the money. I hope this is exaggerated, but fear it is not.

For myself, I pity the poor Indians. It must indeed be hard upon these poor wretches to see the country they were born and bred in (which they naturally considered as entirely their own) drifting away from them, bit by bit. One of their principal resources, viz. the seashore, they are now completely debarred from. Previously, the coast was their great wintering place: there, there was no lack of food. If they could not hunt anything, at any rate, there were crabs, clams, *choros* and other shellfish in abundance, and also a certain kind of seaweed of which they are very fond. Besides this, they could very often kill a seal or two; and, not infrequently, a whale would wash ashore — in which case, any family of Indians, who happened to be within scent of the prize, was in its glory. In fact, there was a grand feast: not for Indians alone, but for every dog, fox, sea-fowl, hawk, etc. in the neighbourhood. It is extraordinary in how short a time the carcass of this whale, seal or whatever other prey was cast ashore, would be stripped to the bare bones; even the

small bones are not wasted, as they are in great requisition for making
lances, harpoons, etc.

Now that the sheep farmers have occupied land all along the coast,
of course, they cannot allow the Indians anywhere near them, and the
latter have had to retire to the inner *camps* and mountains at the back.
In summer they can manage to live, as there are quantities of wild fowl
of every description in all the lakes and rivers of the Interior; and also
a few guanacos, and plenty of their favourite food, the *cururo*, a kind
of guinea-pig or tailless rat, which is a great delicacy and much appreciated. I have often eaten them myself, and really they are very good
eating, and taste like a tender young rabbit.

Talking of these rats reminds me of an incident that does not redound
to the credit of the pioneers of civilisation, or hold out a lesson of charity
and mercy to the savage.

A party of white men pursued a band of Indians who had, as usual,
been robbing sheep. They came up with them and soon made short work
of the males. Those who were not killed cleared out; but some of the
squaws and children were left behind. One of these came crawling up to
the most notorious and successful "ear hunter" amongst the white men.
She held out to him as peace offering two of these little rats. In reply to
this the ruffian drew his knife, made a show of receiving her present,
and then deliberately stuck her! Never mind, this was nothing! — one
human being the less, perhaps a few sheep the more! What matters it
as long as the sheep were saved, and the fellow received the money for
his victim's ears? This incident was narrated to me as a fact by several
witnesses, and I have no doubt of its authenticity.

If any unfortunate white men should, by any chance, fall into the
hands of the Indians, how can they expect to receive the mercy which
they have not rendered?

Personally, I do not believe that these Indians are as bad as they are
painted. Look at Bishop Stirling's doings in Tierra del Fuego: he not only
founded a flourishing little colony of [Yahgan] Indians, with the assistance of the late Rev. Mr. Bridges, but went out personally amongst the
completely uncivilised tribes, mixed with them and talked to them in
their own language; and I never heard that he was in any way molested.

Of course, the Indians were a nuisance to the farmers — but, what did the Indians know about sheep? They probably rejoiced greatly when they saw what appeared as a provision of Providence placed right in their hands. If you or I were half-starved, I think we would jump at the chance, if a lot of fat mutton came in the way — I know I should. In fact, I have done so on two occasions, but on each occasion I had reason.

Once I was coming from the mountains of Upper Gallegos and was half-starved, as I had killed nothing but one skunk and a hawk in four days. My dogs were so weak from want of food that they could not catch even a fox or a guanaco, much less an *ostrich*. Wandering disconsolately about, looking for something to eat, I suddenly came upon a *point* of about twenty sheep, stragglers from a distant farm (this was in the time when the establishments on the Straits of Magellan were just starting, and I did not even know that the aforesaid farms had been started). In one moment, my hungry dogs were upon them and pulled down eight. The sheep had no ear-marks and had certainly been lost a long time, as they had a year and half's wool on them; but, still, I had no right to kill them. At the same time, I rejoiced greatly, and both dogs and master had a splendid feast for some days.

On another occasion, much the same thing happened to me under similar circumstances, only I killed two or three strayed mares I found. These were also unmarked and probably belonged to the Indians; certain it is that they belonged to somebody, and I had no right to kill them: but, when one is half-starved, he does not stick at a trifle. I may mention that I made enquiries about these animals I killed, with the intention of paying for them, but could never discover to whom they belonged.

With regard to the Patagonian or Tehuelche Indians, I think it is wonderful that they have not proved a greater nuisance than they have been. They also were much disgusted when they saw their *camps* and best hunting grounds being taken from them little by little; but, on the other hand, these Indians had been — for years — carrying on a regular trade with the Punta Arenas and Santa Cruz people: sugar, flour, tobacco, shirts, etc., etc. having thus become absolute necessities to them. Unlike the poor Fuegians, they had any amount of game (guanacos, *ostriches*, etc.) to subsist on and, moreover, a ready sale or exchange for their feathers and skins. I can speak well of these Indians as I have mixed with them a great deal; and, unless they were drunk, I found them a very harmless race. Like all Indians, they are frightfully lazy and dirty, but many of them are generous and, if they once like you, will prove true friends.

They were a fine race of men when I first knew them, excessively powerful, but no good on foot; but, give them a decent horse, *bolas* and *lasso*, and they would catch anything. Some of their *quillangos* (*rugs*), *jergas*, saddle gear and silver ornaments are really beautifully made. Of course, the *squaws* do all the hard work, such as removing the tents, loading the cargo horses, making the *quillangos*, etc., etc. The men only hunt, make their saddle gear, lances, *bolas*, etc. They have many great advantages over their Fuegian brothers, being on horseback and having comfortable *toldos*; and, as I said before, unlimited guanaco and *ostrich* to eat — besides this, they have every opportunity of trading their produce, which the Fuegian has not.

One very good trait in their nature is their extreme love for their children. If a child dies, the father mourns him or her most sincerely and will frequently change his name, kill his horses, burn his tent, arms and ornaments, and begin life quite anew. Moreover, the name of the defunct is never even mentioned, and the parents are very much annoyed if any reference is made to the calamity. I think they mourn most sincerely and would give a good lesson to many of us *Christians*.

I should like to say that it appears to me very strange that none of them seem to have any fixed ideas or belief in any kind of religion, except in the existence of *Gualicho* or some kind of evil spirit. No good spirit is mentioned and their superstitions are very few.

I am excessively sorry that I cannot respond as fully as I could wish to the questions asked: I do not think anyone can do so. The Indians are so particularly retentive and careful in all they say and do, that it is difficult to know what they really do believe. I can only describe a scene I have witnessed in the Indian Camp, and in which I took part. Please remember that every man's memory is liable to err and I only speak from recollections, which are very vague.

It was in the Cerro de Palique (he was formerly a great chief amongst the Indians) that I witnessed this ceremony: there were about 150 Indians present, besides myself and another Englishman. About dark, the performance commenced. First of all, a mare was brought in and strangled in the clear space in front of the tents. Then the High Priest Palique came out from his *toldo*, naked — except his waist belt — and painted all over his body in streaks of black, white and red. He went to the animal and, with one stroke of his knife, opened the entire stomach. He then inserted his hand into the intestines and drew out a handful of blood, which he sprinkled to the four quarters of Heaven. He then retired to his *toldo* again and there was a dead silence for a few minutes. Then there was a jingling of bells, and a tremendous yelling and howling inside his *toldo*; and then, a dead silence again. Meantime, all the Indians present had gone to the body of the mare, and each one dipped his fingers in the blood in imitation of the High Priest, going through exactly the same motions.

Presently, Palique came out again, and this time he had his *capa* on, and several silver ornaments, and a brand new handkerchief tied round his head. He then squatted on the ground, and all who wanted to ask him anything went to him one by one. I had just lost a *point* of mares, and was told by a Chilean trader that Palique could surely tell me where they were, after the ceremony. I accordingly went to him, in my turn, and asked him where they were. "¡Quién sabe! Pagando botella de wachakai, Gualicho sabrá." ["Who knows, paying with a bottle of wachakai, Gualicho will know."] I immediately purchased the desired bottle, out of which he took a long drink, and then remarked, "Gualicho dice, caballos por allá, lejos." ["Gualicho says, horses over there, far away."] There was not a great deal of divination necessary to determine this, as all my horses were southern horses, and would most assuredly strike in that direction; but, be that as it may, I found them in exactly the direction he pointed out.

I saw several similar ceremonies carried out in the same style. I really don't believe these Indians know what they do believe themselves. Certainly, it is not in any "good spirit": a demon of cruelty and wrath they do believe in.

Ostrich hunting, Tehuelche-style

How the Indians hunt ostriches—Native cuisine—Joy of eating—Firewater—Unscrupulous traders

Since I was a boy, I have been fond of all kinds of sport, and there is nothing I enjoy more than a really good *ostrich* hunt, with good dogs, *bolas* and horse. This is not only my opinion, but that of every tourist and naval officer whom I have ever taken out hunting (and they are many). So, before concluding this article, I will give a description of a regular Indian *camp*[2], as carried out in past years, when the principal occupation of nearly everyone was either trading with the Indians or hunting guanaco and *ostrich*. (There are very few of the old hands left — either natives or *Christians* — but I believe a few still remain.)

The Indians hunt *ostriches* in circles, which may be interesting to those who have never witnessed it. Personally, I prefer myself going out with my dogs and *bolas* alone: it gives the poor *ostriches* a fairer chance to pit their astuteness against that of a single man — rather than to be surrounded by a hundred yelling fiends in the shape of Indians and dogs, who spare nothing that comes in their way, either big or small.

On arriving at a new camping ground, great excitement prevails amongst the men, women and children, and solemn are the consultations as to where is the best place to shut in their prey. To close a circle it is necessary to have some obstacle which the poor animals cannot pass, but must either conceal themselves in the long grass or break back through the line of hunters and dogs. The shores of a deep river, a small bay on a sea-coast, or a range of perpendicular cliffs is generally selected. Except in the very shortest days, the Indians do not trouble their heads to start very early.

---

[2] Regular Indian *camp* — Traditional native organised hunt in which the participants form a circle.

Two of the best men are first chosen as *punteros*; these have to make a wide detour, lighting fires as they go on each side. These are followed at intervals by the other Indians, at distances of one or two hundred yards, according to the number of hunters — not too far from one another, but just so far that they can stop anything that tries to break out. As they near the point where the circle is to be finished, the *punteros* hurry up and take up their station on the most rising ground, each side of where the circle has to be concluded.

All those coming behind hurry up, and the unfortunate *ostriches* and guanacos find themselves shut in before they know where they are. As they near the closing point, the fun becomes fast and furious: *ostriches* get up from the long grass in every direction and rush about looking for an outlet of escape; troops of guanacos are either standing uncertain what to do, or making a bolt clean through their enemies. Many fall, but many escape. The whole is a scene of confusion and slaughter, which lasts till everything that can possibly be killed is killed.

This is when the *camp* has been well made: then very few animals escape. If, on the contrary, any man has been careless (as fortunately is generally the case) and left his post unguarded, you may be quite sure that the greater part of the game will have taken advantage of the opening to escape. Were it not for this, the game — which is now more plentiful in Patagonia than ever — would be very scarce, instead of being steadily on the increase. No sooner is the camp concluded, and the game collected, than fires are made in every direction, and feeding is the order of the day.

The *picana*, or rump, is the great *bonne bouche*. The bone is first removed, and the meat well *charqueado*. A kind of bag is then formed, full of the most luscious meat, and red hot stones are inserted in certain places. The bag is then sewn up with strips of skin (drawn from the foot down the whole length of the leg), in such a manner that not the smallest atom of steam can escape; it is then placed on the embers for a few minutes, turned round and round, and from side to side, till the outside is well roasted. The strings are then cut, and the stones removed, leaving a delicious bag of meat and soup. No one who has not tasted it can even imagine how good it is.

Perhaps there are twenty or thirty of these *picanas* roasted at the same time. Each party of Indians squat round their particular property and cut off chunks of meat, which they dip in the soup. When all the soup is finished, the remainder of the meat and fat is cut into as many long strips as there are people, and one given to each member of the party, and devoured with great *gusto*.

The idea may be a savage one; but, if anyone wishes to taste meat cooked to perfection, with a delicious gamey flavour, let them try an *ostrich picana* made in true Indian fashion. I would I had one here now; and I verily believe, if I ate about six pounds of it, the inflammation of the lungs (with which I have been stuck in bed for the last three weeks) would disappear like a flash of lightning.

Well, the day's work is done and, taking every bit of meat they can carry, the men return to their *toldos*, where the remainder of the night is passed happily in sucking *mate*, eating, smoking and recounting their adventures. That is, unless any of the harpy[3] traders (who are always hovering about, waiting till the Indians have made a successful *camp* to bring in their infernal *fire-water*) should arrive; in which case, the poor Indians' happiness is turned into drunkenness; they are soon stripped of all they have gained that day, and probably plunged into debt besides.

This is generally the ending of a successful Indian *camp*: the traders retire with their ill-gotten gains, leaving the poor Indian to collect more feathers and skins; when they will immediately swoop down upon their prey, and strip them as before.

---

[3] Harpy traders — Greenwood held a low opinion of certain unscrupulous itinerant salesmen who traded with the Tehuelche.

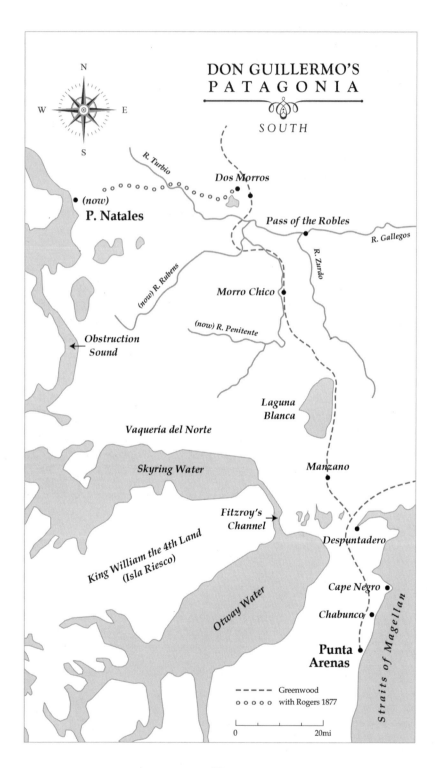

DON GUILLERMO'S
P A T A G O N I A

SOUTH

N
W E
S

R. Turbio

Dos Morros

(now)
P. Natales

Pass of the Robles

R. Gallegos

(now) R. Rubens

R. Zurdo

Morro Chico

(now) R. Penitente

Obstruction
Sound

Laguna
Blanca

Vaquería del Norte

Skyring Water

Manzano

Fitzroy's
Channel

Despuntadero

King William the 4th Land
(Isla Riesco)

Cape Negro

Otway Water

Chabunco

**Punta
Arenas**

Straits of Magellan

– – – – – Greenwood
o o o o o with Rogers 1877

0   20mi

7

Worst Winter of All

Journey to Punta Arenas

First snowfall of season—Log hut at Morro Chico—Greenwood departs alone for Sandy Point—Punta del Monte—Returns to collect companions—Unable to convince them to leave—Retraces route— More snow—Day after day of slow progress—Good hunting at Laguna Blanca—Two horses freeze to death—Crossing the frozen lake—Builds an "ice bridge"—Four more days to Manzano's house—Frostbite— Fortunate meeting on the road

I am giving my notes of this journey of mine in detail for two reasons. First, because they may be interesting to anyone who has been in the same straits. Secondly, because a stranger passing his first winter in these districts may perhaps encounter (as is generally the case) a fine season; and therefore imagine that he has nothing to fear from other succeeding winters; and neglect precautions which — if taken — might save him much trouble, anxiety, and money[1].

It was in the beginning of the winter of 1877 that I with two companions found ourselves in the woods, near the junction of the

---

[1] Severity of winters — Greenwood adds: *"I do not know what the season has been like this year; but last year, to judge by the quantity of water which rushed down from the hills and flooded the settlement of Santa Cruz and all the valleys in the vicinity, I should imagine that the fall of snow must have been almost unprecedented."* This event occurred in 1899.

three principal branches of the river Gallegos. One was an old man who had been my servant for many years; the other a young fellow not long in the country[2], who had joined us in a hunting expedition — much against our will because, although a very good fellow, he was quite unaccustomed to the *camp*, and therefore a great nuisance. The season had been a tolerably successful one: we had collected a large amount of skins and feathers; our horses and dogs were in fair condition and, hitherto, neither tobacco nor salt had run short.

Up to the 19th May the weather had been unusually mild, and we had every anticipation of a mild and pleasant winter. Unfortunately, my old servant James Kelly (may his bones obtain the rest they so well deserve) was — partly from rapidly advancing old age, and partly from the many knocks and bruises received during a long and adventurous career, both as a sailor and an explorer — in a very feeble state, and quite unfit to travel. So, on arrival at the Morro Chico, situated on the most southerly branch of the river, I knocked up some kind of a log hut and called a halt for a few days.

About the 20th May, we had the first snowfall of about three or four inches, if I remember rightly; but a quick thaw followed, and the *camps* were all full of water. A severe frost converted this into a mass of ice. This was succeeded by several successive snowfalls. By the 26th, the ground was covered by eight inches of snow, which — as it had a solid frozen surface to rest upon — appeared likely to last all the winter. All our provisions and tobacco being now quite exhausted, I determined to make a trip to the Colony of Sandy Point, to dispose of our produce and bring out the necessary stores — my companions remaining at the camping place, to take care of the horses and dogs, and to continue hunting. Before I left, we killed seven or eight guanacos and *ostriches*, and hung them on the trees as a supply, in case of bad weather preventing the hunting.

I left for Sandy Point on the 29th May early, taking with me two horses, a mare and two dogs — a bright cold day, with occasional snowstorms. I found the snow deeper than I anticipated, and at dark only arrived at the Punta del Monte, between the River Gallegos and Laguna Blanca. The long night shut in pitch dark, lowering and bitterly

---

[2] "young fellow not long in the country" — Charles Sterry, formerly a bookkeeper with the "British" steamship company. (Rogers 1878: 73).

cold; but I made a good fire, and fixed up a comfortable camp on the lee side of a big *roble* bush. About dark, it began to snow heavily; the horses, which I had left hobbled in a small clearing in the forest, came close to my bush to get shelter and warmth.

The snow continued to fall steadily, with an occasional violent gust of wind which drifted over us in a most unpleasant manner; by ten o'clock, it was getting so lively that I commenced building up a shelter with branches, covered by about a dozen large *deer* skins which I had brought as part of my cargo. This protected us in a great measure from the violence of the storm but, by the morning, the drifted snow was piled up at least six feet behind my shelter.

About ten o'clock the next morning it cleared up beautifully, and the sun shone out over a vast white plain below me. I determined to return to my companions, and try to persuade them to accompany me further to the south, as I saw there was every prospect of a most unusually severe winter.

The snow was so deep that it was unadvisable to attempt even this short journey on horses which had a long weary trip before them. So, I set off on foot, skirted the *point* of woods in which I was camped, and struck the river, which I followed up to the camping place where I had left my companions. Walking was very easy on the ice, as there was very little snow on it, and I arrived at the camp before dark. I found my two friends in excellent spirits, and with a roaring fire; moreover, they had secured more guanacos, and a *lion*. They did not for one moment share my apprehensions as to the prospects of a very severe winter, and the consequent migration of all the game in the vicinity.

The reader must understand that at this time, twenty-three years ago, the *ostrich* hunter depended entirely on what he could hunt and find for his own subsistence: the few provisions which he could afford to purchase — at exorbitant prices — in Santa Cruz or Sandy Point, were finished in the course of a few weeks; but, so long as he had good fat meat, salt and tobacco, he was happy enough. Once let the game supply cease, he was completely floored: for this reason, it was absolutely necessary to select a good and secure hunting ground for the winter, or he would starve.

On this occasion, my companions were obstinate, and firmly declined to budge an inch: they had a good fire, plenty of wood handy, and game in hand, besides their anticipations of killing more. They also said they were quite sure the snow would all clear away in a few weeks. Therefore, after a good feed and night's rest, I again started on foot, carrying a shovel with me to clear away the snow, in case I should get amongst the drifts.

It was a lovely day, and I arrived in good time at the spot where I had left my horses and dogs. That night it commenced to snow again, and by morning we were in a regular *corral* and it was still snowing. The snow lasted all this day till nightfall, and the night shut in clear and bright, with a bitter cold frost; however, I made an enormous fire, roasted some meat, had a smoke of *roble* bark, cut a lot of green branches for my bed, and turned in with my dogs. The horses amused themselves by gnawing all the branches they could reach (grass, of course, there was none); they also gnawed the bark off all the trees they could get at. We were warm enough, as the snow was piled up all round us, and no wind could penetrate.

Early in the morning, I got up and breakfasted on a fat skunk I had caught on the road back to my camp. By the way, there are many worse things than a fat skunk, if you know how to cook him.

Then I commenced clearing a track out of our snow *corral*, as I saw it was a question of moving on at once, or leaving our bones there. That day I managed to get out of the camping place, and get as far as another *point* of *monte*, about half a mile distant, where I camped for the night. From this point I could distinguish Chorillo del Finado Zurdo, on the eastern side of which I could see, by the numerous dark patches on the snow, that I should probably find a better track than hitherto. I went to bed happy in the anticipation of finding myself well on the road the next night. Fool that I was, I forgot that I had still to get down to the stream: my troubles were only just commencing, and were to last four or five months more.

The next morning (I think the 1st June), I finished the road, saddled up and packed all my skins, etc. — except the *deer* skins I had used as a barricade (which were frozen and stiff) — and marched to the ridge I mentioned, where the wind had taken away most of the snow. Looking down to the valley of Finado Zurdo, I saw at once, by the peculiar blue tinge of the snow on the slopes (which deep snow invariably has), that to get down to the stream that way was quite impossible. Therefore, I followed along the ridge above the valley with little or no trouble. Arriving at the last *point* of *monte*, I made a splendid camp under an old hollow tree which took in about half my body (with a dog on each side), and passed a comfortable night — no snow, only some frost.

The following day, I remained in the same place and went out hunting. I found a puma eating a *deer*; I could not kill him, as he travelled over the snow much faster than either I, or the dogs, could. We took the best of the meat he had abandoned, and went home rejoicing. The next morning, we marched down to the plain of Finado Zurdo, in the confident anticipation of arriving at Laguna Blanca. I knew from experience I could find any quantity of game, as (at that time) it was a favourite wintering place both for guanacos and *ostriches*. My anticipations were not, however, to be realised, for the plain was simply one mass of deep snow, varying from 1 to 3ft. in depth, according to the lay of the ground. I may mention that this plain is about 2 miles wide, skirts the woods and hills, and opens into the lake of Finado Zurdo. We struggled on for about half a mile; and then, from sheer exhaustion, camped in the middle of the snow — without fire — and supped on raw meat.

To make a long story short, it took me just 3 days to cross that plain, which at another time would occupy about an hour. When, on the 3rd night, we arrived at the ridge above Laguna Blanca[3], I don't know which was in the worst condition: myself, horses or dogs. We had little trouble in crossing this little range, as the wind had swept away the snow in many places, and the *camp* was perfectly bare in parts.

Up to this time, we had not seen a living thing except the hawks and eagles, which constantly wheeled over our heads. I had managed to shoot two of the small brown hawks, which are very fine eating, and this was all we had for nearly two days: of course, we ate them raw. When I say "*we*," I refer to the dogs and myself for, in a case like this, dogs are almost like yourself, and we shared and shared alike. I could very well have eaten everything myself (bones and all), and 10 times as much. Mind you, there was selfishness in this, as my object was to keep up the dogs' strength, to catch me meat on my arrival at Laguna Blanca. On arriving at the one solitary *roble* tree, which stands (or stood) on the ridge above the northeast corner of the Lake, we stopped for the night.

---

[3] Laguna Blanca — Greenwood adds: "*… where at the present time several prosperous farms are established.*"

Looking down to the Lake, I was delighted to see there was little or no snow[4], and the whole country was literally covered with thousands of guanacos and numerous *ostriches*. I let all the horses loose, and went down to hunt towards the Lake — not much trouble about that. We were soon in the middle of the game: the *ostriches* cleared out fast enough. As for the poor guanacos, only those which were in fair condition made any attempt to get away; the weak and scabby ones either lay down to it, or tumbled head over heels in their efforts to escape. All of them were terribly thin, but that did not matter: the heads are always good, and so are the hearts, livers, etc. So I took as many as I could possibly carry, and went back to camp perfectly happy, after eating as much raw kidney and liver and wild celery (which abounds here) as I could possibly hold.

As for the dogs, they were helpless, and appeared to swell out to about three times their usual size. They absolutely refused to follow me back, and I can quite imagine them saying to themselves: "*This d–d fool has got us into this mess, and can now shift for himself until we pick up a bit.*" Of course, directly the poor beasts began to get cold, they followed me, and got under the blankets as usual.

My joy, however, was short-lived; for, on arriving at the camping place, I found that the horses had got into trouble — with the exception of the *baguala* mare, which was feeding peacefully by a little stream, or *manantial*. The two horses had struck a boggy place and were lying down in a helpless state, and half bogged. This bog would be nothing at any other time, but they were so terribly weak and emaciated that they had strength for nothing. I dragged them out somehow or other onto a dry patch of *murtilla*[5] close handy, but no efforts of mine could get them on their legs.

The night was falling fast — a dead calm with bitter frost. It had, of course, been freezing all day, but this night was terrible. The horses'

---

[4] Little or no snow — Greenwood adds: "*To account for there being little or no snow on this side of the lake, is easy. Snow does not lie near where there is salt water or salt currents of air from the sea, and at this point the air from Skyring Water appears to strike in full force. I can account for it in no other way.*"

[5] Murtilla — Greenwood adds: "*Much of the camp is covered with this creeper for many thousands of yards and it is a great detriment, as little or no grass grows near or amongst it. It grows perfectly flat on the ground, and in certain seasons is literally covered with a small round red fruit something like a cranberry, and which I consider delicious eating. Very good wine and jam can be made of it. The sheep are fond of the fruit; and ostriches, wild geese and ducks will eat nothing else if they can find murtilla berries.*"

legs, where they had been submerged, appeared to be frozen quite stiff. I covered them with all the clothes, skins, etc. I had; heated some water and poured it down their throats; and, with what wood I could collect, made fires round them. But it was all to no good, as they were past cure; and by the middle of the night were both dead; and in the morning were frozen stiff — a cheerful prospect. However, I made the best of it and ate their tongues.

The question was: what to do now? Of course, the main thing was to get around or across the Lake to the woods on the top of the hills on the other side. To go round was impossible, as I could see that all the slopes on both sides of the Lake were one mass of unbroken snow. These slopes are, or were, partly covered with *calafate* and *romerillo* bushes, but I could only distinguish a few black specks in the distance (probably the tops of the highest bushes), showing that the snow must be extraordinarily deep. So, I determined to try and cross the Lake from one side to the other on the ice, a distance of about 15 miles[6]. This may appear an impossibility, but I can easily explain how I did it: any *camp* man will understand the circumstances.

Snow does not lie upon ice as a rule, but melts as fast as it falls or, at the most, only 2 or 3 inches of snow remain; the surface is always rough, and any horse can travel over it. I have crossed many lakes under similar circumstances, and experienced no difficulty; but I did not know this at the time, as I had never been under the necessity of doing so before this, and I confess I was in a mortal funk. However, "*needs must be when the d—v—l drives.*" So I saddled up the unfortunate mare, and piled all my most valuable cargo on her, leaving the rest of my gear stuck up in the *roble* tree (out of reach of the foxes), and started to the Lake, leading the mare. The descent was not very easy as, though there was little snow, there was a good deal of ice and several bogs to pass; but, once arriving at the Lake, it was easy enough, and you could have raced on the surface if you had liked.

I did not know one thing, however: that was, that about halfway across, there was a crack or fissure of about three feet wide, with a strong

---

[6] Width of lake — This would be from N to S.

rapid stream of water rushing through it. On arriving at this obstacle, I felt myself completely floored. It was nearly nightfall, so I resolved to stop there for the night and think about it. I was certainly more than halfway across — and perhaps two-thirds — and my unfortunate mare was getting frightfully weak. I was, of course, well off, as I had brought plenty of meat with me, and the mare had had a good feed the night before; so we were all right in that respect and, bar the cold night for her, there was nothing to fear.

"Necessity is the mother of invention." So, after due consideration, I wetted a blanket (of which, fortunately, I had plenty), and stretched it across the crack — not tightly, but letting the middle sink several inches — making a kind of hollow or lath. The blanket was frozen onto the ice on each side, as hard as a dead board, in a very few minutes. I verily believe it would have borne my weight as it was; but, as for the mare, that was a very different question. Luckily, small pieces of ice kept floating down this crack and got jammed against the blanket; and I threw a quantity of pieces into the well formed by the blanket; and before morning, all was frozen into a solid mass. I was afraid the water might flow over it, and flood me out; but, fortunately, it did not do so, but passed over or below

it. In any case, in the morning, it would have borne far more than the weight of the mare, and we passed over without any difficulty whatever.

Arriving at the foot of the ridge, I felt quite happy and proud of having overcome what I considered the main obstacle, viz. passing the Lake: but I was very much mistaken.

The circuit from the Lake to the plain above is a matter of about twenty yards, a gentle slope, but it was now a perpendicular wall of drifted snow. The only thing was to clear a road, which I at once started to do. Luckily, the snow was loose and soft, and was not so difficult as I anticipated. Still, it took me till nightfall before I could get myself, horse and cargo onto the plain above. Once there, we camped in a little *manantial* under some big *calafate* bushes, with plenty of dry wood. As luck would have it, just as it was getting dark, two *ostriches* passed close by us, and the dogs caught both of them within thirty yards of the camp in a snow drift; they were both very fat, and we had a regal feast.

Early next morning we started up the ascent to the first range of hills, along the foot of which I intended to follow, till I reached the house of a friend of mine, *Don* José Manzano, who was just starting a farm in the first *point* of woods, about two *leagues* beyond the Laguna Blanca. It took us just three days to do this hour's ride; and when we got there ... I remember nothing more, till I found myself in a warm bed with someone rubbing my feet, which were frostbitten; however all appeared to be right, now.

Don José was in a terrible state. All round his house was a mass of snow; his horses and cows were dying daily; the only things which appeared to thrive were the dogs, pigs and fowls, which fed on the dead carcasses. He had, however, plenty of guanaco meat and provisions for about one day, which he very generously shared with myself and another poor devil who had arrived the day before. This man was in a worse condition than myself, as all his horses had died in the snow: he had had to leave everything behind, with the exception of the little he could carry. He had come from a different quarter, and he had also good long boots, so his toes were not frostbitten, as mine were.

I fully anticipated getting horses from here to take me to the Colony; and my old friend, *Don* José, would have been only too delighted to lend them to me, but he had none to lend: all were so terribly emaciated that none would be able to pass the two or three *leagues* of snow which lay between us and the coast. Although I was most welcome to what there was, to remain there would not have been right: so, I only remained a few days — till my feet were a little better and my poor mare had picked up a bit — and then, taking a supply of guanaco meat, set off on my road again.

From that time I had more luck: the first day I killed two more fat *ostriches* in a snowdrift, and remained in the woods for two days, feasting. After this, every yard I travelled there was less snow. At the conclusion of the third day's march, I found myself at the Despuntadero Bay, Straits of Magellan, where I struck the main road to the Colony, and found there was no snow at all.

I had barely reached the road — as luck would have it — when along came a big party of Indian traders, all of whom were friends of mine: it is not necessary to say they supplied me with everything I wanted, including horses. Next day we marched to Cape Negro and from thence to the Colony. My friends informed me that, although the snowfalls on the coast had been unusually heavy, the snow had not lasted more than twenty-four hours each time it fell; there had been nothing on the coast to stop traffic and trading. (Of course, it is a well-known fact the snow never lasts long near large bodies of salt water.)

Return to Morro Chico from the Colony

Sells goods at Sandy Point—Buys supplies and fresh horses—Begins return journey—Conditions no better than before—Enforced wait at Manzano's house—First horse drowned—Second horse drowned—Remaining horse recalcitrant—First attack by horse—Horse blinded in second attack—Journey completed alone, on foot

On arriving at Punta Arenas, I received a hearty welcome from all my old friends, and soon found myself clothed, and in my right mind.

The streets were a mass of ice and, as there were no proper roads at that time, it was rather difficult to climb about from one place to another; all the men used to make bets as to whether they could travel from the beach to the so-called town without a fall. The place being built on a slope, which was all frozen over, rendered this feat rather difficult.

I soon disposed of my small cargo, and purchased three more horses (the best I could get, which is not saying much). In about a week's time I started on my return journey, taking with me all the provisions I could cram onto the horses, and a lot of other necessaries, including a large packet of vegetable seeds of every description. These were of the greatest service to me afterwards: wherever I stopped, I sowed small quantities and, years later, when visiting my old camping grounds, I found self-sown plants all around: turnip, carrot, parsnip, cabbage and radishes. I daresay they exist to this day.

The road, as far as Despuntadero, was now full of water and mud, with only snowdrifts at intervals: it was frightfully boggy, but we got along all right as far as Laguna de Los Palos (a large lake situated about five miles from the main road). From here you could distinguish the ranges of hills round Laguna Blanca, which I was sorry to see were still completely covered with snow, as it was now late in the month of August. I hoped to find the bulk of the snow disappearing, as is generally the case at this time; but this was an exceptional year, and at the end of September the snow still lay deep upon the ground.

After resting the horses for one day, we started on again, and got as far as the Cañadón Malo, about halfway between Despuntadero and Laguna Blanca. There I drove a lot of *ostriches* into the stream, and fished out two of the biggest and fattest, which could not get out — no fear of hunger yet awhile, thank heaven.

The next day I arrived at the woods near *Don* José Manzano's house, and camped in the same place where I had stopped the night I left his house, when going into the Colony. There I found *Don* José with all his remaining stock (except the chickens and pigs); he told me the snow was worse than ever, and strongly advised me to turn back with him and wait. I wish I could have done so — and, as things turned out, it would have been by far the wisest course — but, of course, I had to think of the two men I had left behind, and who I knew must be in sore straits, as it was now many weeks since I had left them. The next morning, I left my friend to pursue his journey south, and went on my way north.

On arriving at *Don* José's *station*, I thought it better to stop and go forward and reconnoitre, which I did. I was both sorry and surprised to find that affairs were not at all improved; on the contrary, there appeared to be about double as much snow as when I passed before: to proceed, for at least some days to come, would be quite impracticable. So, I resolved to remain in the house for a week or two, till the snow began to melt, and then try and go ahead. This was a great mistake: there was, of course, little or no grass round the place, and the horses were losing strength every day; I had far better have tried to force my way on at once, whilst they had some strength left.

I think I waited a fortnight before I made a start. I could find but little meat, and that was very thin, so I consumed a large portion of my provisions. When, at last, black patches began to appear on the surrounding hills, I thought I could venture to try it. Accordingly, one fine morning I started, and from that moment commenced a succession of disasters, which lasted for many months.

I don't think I mentioned that there are a quantity of small streams running into Laguna Blanca. They appear nothing at all, but are indescribably dangerous[7], very often very deep; and, although only about a foot or two wide at the top, they get wide at the bottom, and very often run some distance underground on each side. If once a horse gets in, it is excessively difficult to get him out, except with a decent cinch horse.

One of these little streams ran down a little valley about two hundred yards from the house. It was only about two feet wide, but heaven only knows how deep. I got my saddle horse and one of the cargo horses across in safety, but the other brute declined to jump; after pulling, dragging, and driving him, and using all necessary expletives to convince him, he finally plumped in and disappeared bodily, the cargo and top of his head being alone visible. I worked like a *nigger* to get that beast out (of course, I had to cut off his cargo and *montura* — there was no other way to get at it), but could not move him an inch. The ground was so hard that I could not widen the stream, as I should have done at any other time. So there the poor animal had to remain till he died — not very long, I am glad to say, as it was bitterly cold. There is a small bunch of

---

[7] Dangerous streams — Rogers' expedition experienced similar problems in this area two months later, although without fatal consequences. (Ibar Sierra 1879: 19).

robles a little farther on, so I put the cargo on my riding horse and led the two animals to it. This was not a cheering commencement of a long journey over the snow — although I had a splendid fire and plenty to eat, I did not feel particularly cheerful.

I marched the next morning, and as there were now many patches of *camp* clear of snow, I reached the Lake in the evening; but some of the drifts were tremendously deep, and it took me all my time to cross them. We camped in the same springs as I did before, when I left the Lake leading my unfortunate cargo mare. Here the dogs again caught a fat *ostrich*, and I should have felt more cheerful; but I could see the range of Finado Zurdo looming dead white in the distance, and knew (more or less) what that meant. However, my evil star was still in the ascendant and, during the night, the best of my two horses tumbled into a spring nearby — which I did not know was in existence — and, in the morning, I found him frozen to death.

There now remained only one horse, a great *raw-boned* brute, which I had bought for twenty-five dollars. I never could understand why his owner sold him so cheaply … but I soon found out. Next morning, I crammed every mortal thing I possibly could on his back, leaving what I considered the less necessary articles on the top of one of the bushes, meaning to come back and fetch them when I reached my companions, and could get fresh horses. I did not know all that was going to happen to me, or I should not have built such castles in the air.

Of course, I could not cross the Lake this time — not only was there no snow on the surface of the ice, but it had melted all round the edges, and I could not get onto it — so, I had to go all round and travel about three times the distance I had traversed in coming. However, by great good luck, soon after I started, I struck a fine wide guanaco track, which I followed, leading my cargo horse, who did not believe in being led. And so, I put him on the track and tried to drive him along; but that did not pay, as the more I whacked him the less he would travel; and, besides this, he was constantly running backwards and kicking at me. So, I resorted to leading him again and, by dint of putting a *twitch* on his nose and tying down his ears with some hairs of his tail, I managed to get him to the other end of the Lake, where I first went onto the ice when I was marching for the Colony.

This was the best day's march I had made. I camped down, feeling tolerably contented; more especially as in the bushes where I camped I killed a fine fat *lion*, which was a great treat. The main difficulty still remained: to try to cross the two ranges of hills and the intermediate plain, which had given me so much trouble while going in to the Colony.

A few words about my sole remaining horse, "*Chaleco*": he was a big *raking overo*, with a white breast, blind with one eye — his other eye was that of a demon, not of a horse. So far from straying far away when I let him loose, he used to stop close to the bushes where I was camped; every now and then, he would bring his one eye to bear on me and you could see a thought come into it, which appeared to say: "*Wait a minute, my boy, I am going to find some means of paying you out for all the trouble and suffering you have caused me.*"

The next morning I saddled him up, and left him standing by the bush, while I had my breakfast, preparatory to putting his cargo on.

I had just comfortably commenced my breakfast, when he suddenly made a dash at me with his mouth wide open. I rolled into the bush to get out of his way; and when he found he could not bite me, he began kicking at the bush, the breakfast things, and everything round. Fortunately, however, he did not touch me, and when he calmed down, I managed to get hold of his rope; he then stood as quiet as a lamb, and you would think he had never been able to say "Boo" to a goose. I put his cargo on and started.

We made a capital march that day, got across the first little range of hills and the Finado Zurdo plain (which had taken me three days to pass when I was going in), and camped at the foot of the range of hills between there and the Gallegos. The snow appeared awfully deep on all these hills, and even the smaller bushes were completely covered; but they had to be crossed, somehow or other.

The next morning I was more careful whilst saddling up my friend "*Chaleco*", and took care not to let go of his rope for a moment; he behaved with the utmost discretion. On commencing to ascend the hills, I was delighted to find that the snow was frozen into a hard mass, forming a splendid road. We got on famously and passed all the hills on the other side, from whence you could see the entire plain of Gallegos, stretching far away in the distance right up to the Dos Morros. I was glad to see that the plain appeared more or less free from snow, and confidently anticipated joining my friends on the morrow, if they were alive — which I very much doubted.

Next morning, Mr. "*Chaleco*" started on his pranks again, as I had been fool enough to leave him loose whilst I had my breakfast. I was, however, ready for him this time and had my *boleadoras* close handy: I caught him a tremendous whack over the head, which stopped him at once; but, as evil fortune would have it, I struck him in the sound eye and extinguished it, and he was now stone blind. However, I put the cargo on him and tried to march, but no power on earth would make the poor devil move. So, I selected all the most necessary articles and, leaving the old horse and everything else behind, marched on foot to where I had left my companions.

Living without Horses

Friends found alive—Horses eaten—Dogs eaten—Young man leaves alone for Sandy Point—Kelly stays with Greenwood—"Pluto" returns—Departure for Dos Morros—Much melt-water—"Pluto" catches ostriches—Kelly swims three ice-cold rivers—His old blunderbuss—He does things his own way— Greeted at hut by "Salteador"—Rebuild food supplies—Unable to trade without horses—Successful search for baguales

I was glad to see smoke curling above the trees where I had left my friends — a sign that at least they were alive. I could see no horse, and no cheerful barking from the dogs greeted me. I gave a shout, and two wretched, half-naked scarecrows came out to meet me.

I did not ask them any question until I had given them some coffee and biscuits, which they did not eat, but devoured like wolves. There was a small pot on the fire, containing a most extraordinary composition: I could not make out what it was. Afterwards I found that it was horsehide, cut into small pieces, which they boiled down till it became a kind of glue, and ate when cold in slices.

After they had eaten I gave them a smoke, and then commenced asking questions: *"And the horses?"* *"That is all that remains of them,"* said one, pointing to a bit of lean, greenish-looking meat, hanging from a branch. *"The dogs?"* *"Oh! We ate them first, all except old 'Pluto', who was condemned to death a day or two ago; but, in the morning he cleared out, and we have not seen him since."* I was very glad of this, as he was my very favourite old dog, fast, strong, and as sensible as a *Christian*. I asked them why they had made no attempt to get out, as I had done. They said they had done so many times, but the snow had been so deep on the flat in front of the camp that they even could not get across that, let along the hills on the other side. I could quite believe this, having reason to do so from my own experiences.

The younger man announced his intention of going straight to the Colony, and getting out of the confounded country as soon as he possibly could. My old friend Kelly said he would stick by me, as I had resolved not to go back until I made a strike of some sort or other.

Of course, the first thing to do was to go and bring up the provisions, etc. which I had left behind the day before. Those that I had left at Laguna Blanca, I had resolved to abandon, as it was too far for us (in our weak state) to undertake such a journey on foot, let alone having to carry such a heavy load back. As for the old blind horse, I never expected to find him alive; nor did I, as we found him lying stark and still, close to where I had left him. After giving the young man, who was leaving us, sufficient food to take him to where I had left the other things stowed away, the old man and I packed all the remaining gear on our backs, and returned to the wintering place; the other man went away south.

Arriving at the camp, my old black dog bounded out to meet me in perfect delirium of joy. How on earth he knew I had come back, I cannot tell you: he must have been prowling about the place somewhere near; but, having a rooted objection to being eaten, had kept himself quiet — he was as fat as a pig, and so full he could hardly walk.

As we were getting very short of meat, we thought we would try and find out what he had been doing. I could see by his tracks on the ice that he had come across the river. Picking up the tracks on the other side, which was very easy as there was still plenty of snow, we followed them to a bunch of woods about 400 yards distant, where we found two *deer* almost close together, which the dog had recently killed — both of them were partially eaten. We took all the meat we could carry and went back, and there remained about a week, feasting and enjoying ourselves — a most stupid thing to do, as we wasted a large portion of our small supply of stores.

Before starting for the south, I had built a small log house in the woods, on the borders of the Laguna Dos Morros. Here I had left a small quantity of stores and ammunition, besides all my books and numerous articles. The main point was to reach this shanty as, not only had we stores there, but it was a breeding lake for every kind of wild fowl. If we could not get anything else, we could for the time being get any quantity of eggs, besides catching fish, of which the lake was full.

The worst of it was, we had to pass the three branches of the Gallegos[8], all of which were flooded. It did not matter for me (who was young), but I feared for the old man who, although he could swim like a fish, was very weak and thin — the water was, of course, icy cold. We packed up the most necessary articles and resolved to make a start the next morning. The greater portion of our gear we, of course, stored away out of reach of the foxes.

The entire plain was covered with water, and some of the gulches which traversed it were very deep; but, by nightfall, we managed to reach a small hill covered with woods — a favourite camping place of mine — and completely sheltered from all the prevailing winds. You may be sure we were very glad to get there after our long wading (for you can call it nothing else). We rejoiced still more, when up got a big *ostrich* from a nest, which old "*Pluto*" promptly drove into the water and killed. So we were not going to starve yet, more especially as the nest contained 32 beautiful, fresh eggs. Now we both knew perfectly well that in the morning early the females would probably return to lay; so, we concealed ourselves as much as possible, and went to sleep very comfortably. Of course, we left the nest intact, with the exception of 3 or 4 eggs, which we took to eat that night. In the morning, sure enough, they arrived about an hour after dawn — 9 or 10 of them — and, before they knew where they were, I had shot one and the old dog had killed another. We were now rich; and, had it not been for those three confounded, flooded rivers, which we had to pass before we could arrive at our hut, we should have been happy. For the present, as we were well supplied with everything necessary, we determined to stop for a few days to see if the water went down a little.

At the end of a week the plain was comparatively free of water, but the river was still overflowing its banks and large masses of ice were floating down it. I asked the old man if he did not think that it would be better to go to the main branch of the Gallegos, and to cross there and make one business of it, instead of crossing the three branches — these, of course, although much narrower, were at the present season quite wide and bad enough.

<hr />

[8] Three branches of the Gallegos — The modern names are (E to W) Río Penitente, Río Rubens and Río Turbio.

There was a good deal of selfishness in this, because, after helping the old man cross, I should have to carry all the gear on my back — a matter of three or four journeys, backwards and forwards. However, he said he did not feel strong enough to cross the big river, but thought he could manage the others with my assistance. I had to humour him for, as previously he had been the most amenable and amiable of men, he was now so cranky and irritable as to be almost unbearable.

I said to him: "*Look here Kelly, we have got into a scrape, and we must get out of it; look upon it as a paseo; we shall laugh over it afterwards, no doubt,*" and he replied: "*D— such paseo, and the country and everyone in it; when once we get out of this, I shall very soon be on board ship again.*" However, it was no good quarrelling over it, so we made all our gear into different bundles convenient for carrying across, and carried them down to the bank of the river, the poor old man cursing and blaspheming the whole way.

Now I must tell you, there was one thing the old chap possessed which he valued far more than his own soul: to wit, an old Spanish musket. Into it he used to cram about half an ounce of powder, half a newspaper, and as many square chunks of lead as he could get hold of. I believe he used to pass about half his time in cutting up a large piece of sheet lead, which he invariably carried with him. When that failed, he used to look for small round stones, and shove in a fistful of those. We would wait for hours alongside a lake or stream till he got a quantity of geese or ducks together in a lump, within reasonable range, and then let fly into the middle of them; and you would hear a report like the crack of doom, and see the old man sprawling on his back with his legs in the air. He used to put a thick towel under his old *monkey jacket*, where the stock of his old fossil rested, to prevent the concussion breaking his old bones. He would pick himself up, and look into the lake to see what mischief he had done, and then proceed to take off his clothes to pick up his dead and wounded. He rarely killed less than ten or twelve at a shot, and on one occasion I saw him pick up no less than 29 after one of his discharges. I was absolutely debarred from any participation in the manoeuvres and, if he even thought I had been watching him, he would be cranky for the rest of the day.

Well, having got all our things down to the edge of the river, and chosen what I considered the deepest spot, where I could see no sign of any rocks, I packed all our blankets and my own gun on my back, and took them across to the other side with no difficulty whatsoever.

I begged old Kelly to let me carry his old blunderbuss across for him, but he absolutely refused to let it go out of his hands, and said he would carry it across himself or die in the attempt — so there was no help for it. After he had spent that half an hour in wrapping up his murderous weapon in old scraps of oil cloth, and lashing it on his shoulders, we made a start; and, as he had been a bold swimmer in his day, and did not want for pluck, we got across safely enough.

I only carried all our clothes this time, as I had to take care of the old man, and could not manage a heavy load. I told Kelly to dress himself as quickly as possible, so as not to catch cold. He only gave a grunt, and said I had better go back and fetch tobacco, matches, powder and shot, and then we should be all right; so, I obeyed orders, swam across and brought all he required. When I came back with my load, I found he had not attempted to dress himself, and was sitting on the ground in a state of nature, polishing his cursed old gun. I suggested the advisability of making a fire, as all the river was fringed with thick wood, and there was a splendid camping place close by. I think he was getting cold by this time; and, as he was quite happy now he had got his tobacco, powder and shot, he (for a wonder) obeyed with alacrity, put on his clothes, and commenced collecting a huge pile of wood, of which there were tons lying all round.

In the meantime, I crossed over and brought back our small supply of provisions, cooking utensils, and an axe, without which the old fellow (as an old backwoodsman) would not be happy. I determined to leave the rest of the things until the morning, as we had all we required for the night. On my return, there were no signs of any fire, and the old man was sitting on a log, smoking. I was chilled to the bone, and remarked: *"Hang it all man, you might have made a fire."* He did not deign to reply, but got up to see what I had brought with me; and, on seeing the axe, gave a chuckle of satisfaction and grunted out: *"How the _____ do you suppose I can make a fire without a green log at the back. Now I can get on."* He proceeded to cut down the biggest tree he could find (luckily, not very big), and in a few minutes he had fashioned a log to his liking; after which he proceeded to cut a small log from the same trunk for the front of the fire, and stacked up the dry wood between the logs in true Nova Scotian fashion[9].

---

[9] "Nova Scotian fashion" — This reference to Canada is not elaborated further.

He had been too long with me for me to attempt to interfere in the proceedings. I knew him too well: if you wanted to turn him into a raving lunatic, you had only to offer a suggestion or assistance. In any case, he thoroughly understood the business, and in a very short time there was fire enough to roast an ox. In the morning, whilst Kelly went out shooting, I crossed the river again and brought back all our remaining gear, tools, books, clothes, etc. in two trips; so then, we had got over one difficulty. Kelly had not returned yet, but presently I heard his cannon boom in the distance and judged we should not run short of wild fowl that night. The old fellow never fired more than one shot a day, for economy's sake, but that shot was a sure one. Presently, he came

back in triumph with 5 Brant geese[10], deliciously fat: this was cheering, for in my opinion there is no bird such splendid eating to be found in any country I have ever been in. We passed a lovely evening; even the old dog, whom I have forgotten to mention for the moment, managed to kill a half-starved guanaco which came near the camp, and had a good feed.

The following day, we marched to the second (or central) branch of the river, which I believe takes its rise in the Sierras of Diana, and camped on the banks, preparatory to passing in the morning. This river is deep, sluggish and narrow, with few rocks; and, to anyone who can swim, is a very small obstacle. Whilst eating our dinner, a large puma came down to the other side of the river, stood looking at us for a minute or so, and then retired; it was no use shooting the brute, as we already had more than we could carry. We passed safely the next morning, early; in such good time, in fact, that we were enabled to march the same day as far as the third and last branch, called the Rio Turbio, and camped on the banks of the river, exactly in front of the *point* of *monte* where I had my little log hut.

---

[10] Brant/Brent geese — This species is found only in the Northern hemisphere; Greenwood probably refers to the Upland goose.

This stream I particularly detest, being very deep and very boggy. It carries a very large body of water and, though apparently very insignificant, has its headwaters close to the well-known Sierra Paine[11] (the highest and most peculiar formed mountain in that part of Patagonia); and travels, in its course, far more *leagues* than either of the other branches. Mr. Kelly — now being exceedingly bumptious, and there being no current to speak of — refused any assistance, and swam the river by himself, carrying his beloved gun; and, not only that, but came back again and carried over his own blankets, clothes, and other odd gear. We were very soon on the other side, with all our traps; and, by midday, arrived at the log hut, which I found in much the same state as I had left it (except that the roof was broken in several places by the weight of the snow, which had evidently drifted over the whole affair during the winter).

On going to the opening, where the door ought to have been — but which had never existed — we heard a thumping sound inside. Looking in, we saw, lying on one of the old beds, a very favourite dog of mine called "*Salteador*" ["*Highwayman*"], whom I had lost about eight months previously in the *camp*, wagging his tail with all his might. He did not testify the smallest surprise, or trouble himself to get up to receive us: in fact, I do not think he could get up without great exertion — he was simply like a ball of fat. On his neck he had a curious, silver-mounted collar, evidently of Indian workmanship: no doubt, he had for some time been living with the Indians. Be that as it may, I was delighted to have him on any terms, as my poor old dog "*Pluto*" was quite fagged out and lame from working so much alone. Whilst I commenced repairing the roof, Mr. Kelly loaded his blunderbuss and repaired to a large swan rookery, to collect eggs and slaughter swans.

Before dark, old Kelly came plodding wearily home, with an immense load on his back, his gun in one hand, and 3 or 4 swans in the other. He appeared, by the grim smile[12] on his face, to be in a particularly good temper, which increased when he saw the house more or less fixed up,

[11] Headwaters of Río Turbio — These lie to the SE of the Paine district.
[12] Grim smile — Greenwood is being ironic.

and the dinner cooked or cooking on the fire. He unstrapped his burden and deposited it on the ground; he had made his coat into a kind of bag, into which he had crammed as many eggs as he could manage, a quantity of wild celery, and a few ducks — so he had not done so badly. After criticising the arrangements I had made, and pointing out how much better they could have been managed had he been present, he sat down to supper; and, after a splendid meal, had a smoke and turned in.

The next day we dedicated entirely to collecting eggs and salt: we got together about 300 goose, swan, and duck eggs, and also found 2 *ostrich* nests close to the house, each of which contained more than 40 eggs. The dogs also were well provided for, as they killed one of the *ostriches* belonging to the nests — very thin, of course — but, in any case, they thoroughly appreciated it. The bulk of the *ostrich* eggs we buried, as they will keep good for 2 or 3 months in that way. The smaller eggs we placed in two barrels, and we covered them with salt; there was no fear of this supply failing for some time, and we could always get enough in a few minutes to last us a week.

The old man expressed his intention of going fishing, and produced what he called a ditty bag, which article he invariably carried slung round his neck. I believed this bag contained every mortal thing, from a brush and a comb to a brass button; amongst other things in it were several fishing lines, and hooks of all sizes, from which he selected what he considered necessary. By my advice, he waded out to a small island right in front of the house, which I knew had good deep water on the other side. I continued patching up the roof, and then took my rifle and went out for a stroll into the woods; the snow was still tolerably deep all around and inside them, but I was glad to see numerous tracks of *deer* in every direction, and some of them quite fresh; also, several puma tracks, wandering about on all sides.

I followed the *deer* tracks, and soon came upon a small *point* of them, feeding in a little sheltered glade. These animals are so perfectly tame, or were at that time, when they had rarely or ever seen a human being, that they never thought of clearing out: they would come straight to you, staring at you with all their might with their beautiful, large brown eyes. It seemed cruelty to kill them, but there was no remedy — *"necessity has no law"* and we absolutely required their skins for our beds. It is impossible to imagine what splendid beds these skins make, or how good they are for a man suffering from rheumatism. I shot three without the least trouble, and carried the skins back to the hut, leaving the best of the meat hung in a tree, ready to transport on the morrow.

The old man had arrived before me, and lit a fire (for a wonder); he had brought with him 12 or 14 lake trout, varying from 1½ pounds to 8 ounces — so, he had made a splendid day's work of it. We staked out the *deer* skins in front of the house, had supper and turned in; and I think we slept the sleep of the just. Being now well supplied with provisions for the time being, we broke up our bit of garden ground (which I had fenced in some years before) and planted the few potatoes we had, besides sowing every kind of seed; we were glad to find of the latter there were plenty, so we enlarged the garden and, by nightfall, had everything snug and all the seeds sown.

The next day being Sunday, we did nothing at all: I remained at home reading and making notes all day; the old man went out for a long ramble with his blunderbuss and the dogs. This was really the first peaceful day I had passed since the commencement of my journey, and I think we had every reason to be thankful that we were, at last, able to come to a standstill.

The old man returned in the evening with an unusually large quantity of wild fowl. I told him it was utterly useless killing any more, as we already had far more than we could eat while they were good; and, moreover, the quantity of powder and shot was beginning to look small. For once in his life, the old man was pleased with the remark, and *"was glad to see I had some sense."*

After dinner we had a long consultation as, although our circumstances were very much improved, they were not at all satisfactory. Moreover, we were on foot: not a desirable state for, how on earth to carry all our skins, feathers, etc. into the Colony for sale went clean ahead of me. I proposed to make a short trip of a day or so into the Interior, where I knew there were many small *points* of *baguales* (wild horses); if we could find no means of catching them, we could at least kill 2 or 3 and get their skins, meat, hoofs and *grease*, which would be invaluable under the circumstances. Moreover, I had lost several horses in the same place, and thought, if they had not joined the wild horses, I might find some traces of them.

So, we started very early next morning, and marched straight for the Interior. The *camp* was frightfully boggy, so we resolved not to remain out for the night, but just to go to the top of a high hill, from whence we could see all the surrounding country, and then return. By the way, we found 2 large *ostrich* nests on the road containing many eggs, which we took and buried under some bushes for a future occasion. When we reached the top of the hill, we were glad to see several small troops of animals feeding in various parts of the plain. This was all I wanted to know: from this resource there was always a supply of food, as long as we had powder and lead; and perhaps, by strategy, we might manage to catch some of the stray, tame horses, which were doubtless mixed up with them.

We returned home early, each carrying a few eggs, very well satisfied with our day's work. We had our fried fish for supper that night; it never does to cook these fish quite fresh but — after keeping them a day — very slightly salted and fried in *ostrich grease*, they are delicious.

We had every reason to be thankful for our good fortune, as far as it had gone. Many men have been in a worse case; and we were, for the time being, free from absolute want: but, this was in the present. How would it be when the breeding season was over, when our powder and shot were finished, and the winter commencing again?

※ ※ ※

$\stackrel{\text{\tiny ❀}}{}$ 8 $\stackrel{\text{\tiny ❀}}{}$

Guide to Captain Rogers

*Arrival of Chilean expedition—Greenwood invited as guide—Head for
Obstruction Sound—Underbrush and mosquitoes—Abandoned camp
of the Canoe Indians—Expedition continues northward—Unexpected
recall—Gift of a horse*

I think it was around the 13th of November [1877], the date of the
Colony mutiny; but, of this, of course, we knew nothing. About this
date, Fortune seemed to take a turn in our favour. The weather was
oppressively hot, so much so that it was impossible for the dogs to hunt
in the daytime — only in the very early morning or in the evening —
so, I used to get up before daybreak, and go out to look for game while
it was cool.

$\stackrel{\text{\tiny ❀}}{}$

One morning[1] I had gone out as usual with this intention, and was rounding some woods on the eastern shores of the lake, when I suddenly perceived the Chilean flag flying from the top of a high tree, and numerous tents, and animals picketed around. This turned out to be the expedition organised by the Chilean Government for the exploration of the *canals* and fresh water lakes, which intersect the *Cordillera*, north and south. There appeared to be no one stirring in the camp, but the *campañistas* were evidently out looking for horses, as sunrise does not find this class of men sleeping. Presently I saw three men driving in the troops, and was delighted to recognise amongst them a very old friend of mine, Santiago Zamora, the very man who was with me when we discovered the wild horses. He was very sorry to see me in such poor case, but delighted to find me, as they had come that way expressly to look for me and to get me, if possible, to act as a guide to the expedition.

Commander Rogers (chief of the expedition) and two junior officers had by this time turned out, and I need not say I was only too glad to fall in with their views. They offered me liberal pay; that, I did not require; what I did want was a good, serviceable, strong horse (with which to catch others), and a supply of provisions for the present. These they were very ready to give me, if I would take them to the shores of Obstruction Sound[2], and afterwards help them to pass the spur of the *Cordillera* which runs between there and the northern lakes. As is usual in all these expeditions, they had brought with them far more provisions, etc. than they required.

We then made arrangements to start the next morning, as early as possible; meantime, they gave me a horse and a saddle, and as much ammunition and provisions as I could conveniently carry. I went back to inform my old friend of our good fortune, promising to return that evening, so as to be ready for the start next morning. I need not say how glad the old man was to hear we should not be entirely on foot any more, and more glad was he to see the supply of provisions and ammunition.

I returned in time to dine with my new friends, and, oh, how I did enjoy that dinner — not to mention cigars and wine, which accompanied

[1] Meeting with Chilean expedition — November 29, 1877 (Rogers 1878: 75).
[2] Obstruction Sound — A more accurate modern reference would be the Golfo Almirante Montt. The map provided by Rogers in his official report shows that the group travelled further to the N of Obstruction Sound, coming close to the S entrance of Canal Señoret (slightly S of present-day Puerto Natales).

it. I conversed with the officers until sundown, and found Commander Rogers a most intelligent and agreeable person; his subalterns were also most pleasant, well-informed, young men. One of them was a naturalist[3] attached to Commander Rogers' ship.

We had a glorious morning for our start, and by 8 o'clock were fairly on the way to the Interior; and by the night-fall arrived at the dense forest tract bordering Obstruction Sound, extending from the beach — in an apparently impassable line — about 10 miles inland. To pass this, however, was provided for: two years previously I had cut a road straight down through the wood to the shore, and passed some time on the seashore looking for gold and sea otter. This road would no doubt be covered by undergrowth by this time, but I had no doubt of being able to find it; more especially, as I made the entrance close to a huge stone which towered high above the undergrowth around, on which I had carved an inscription with dates, etc.

That night we camped on the edge of the *monte*, killed a couple of *deer*, and made ourselves generally comfortable (or should have been so, but for the clouds of mosquitoes, which tormented us day and night). We started very early the next morning, following my old track to the beach; this was not so easy as I expected, as a dense undergrowth of *michay, leñadura, calafate* and blackcurrant[4] bushes covered the track to a height of three or four feet — this was so plaited and intermingled that we had to force our way through, inch by inch. Soon enough, poor Commander Rogers' trousers, which were of cloth (and also his under-clothing) were torn off him; only the posteriors remained, and a pair of knee-boots — a most propitious circumstance for the mosquitoes, who took a mean advantage of the occasion to settle on whatever bare spot they could find. As for Zamora and I, we both wore the cow-skin leggings commonly used in Chile, so it did not matter to us.

At last we reached a small round hill, about halfway to the shore, ascending which we distinguished the whole line of coast and numerous wooded islands, of which Obstruction Sound is full. Captain Rogers said from here he could take the necessary observations without going down to the shore; so, we unsaddled for an hour or two, to rest our

[3] Naturalist — Enrique Ibar Sierra. His account of the difficulties crossing the dense forest tallies with Greenwood's own (Ibar Sierra 1879: 26).
[4] Blackcurrant bush — *Ribes magellanicum,* a native wild currant known locally as "parra", "parrilla" or "zarzaparrilla".

horses. I say *"rest,"* but this was a matter of impossibility, as the mosquitoes were literally in clouds; the horses lay down in the long grass as is
their custom; we covered ourselves as best we could with our blankets
and tried to take a *siesta*, but in vain. First of all, we had to improvise
some kind of trousers for poor Captain Rogers: he, poor fellow, was in
a very bad way, his face, hands and legs being one mass of bites and terribly swollen. We managed to rig him up some kind of a *chiripá* with a
blue blanket and, finding it impossible to get any rest, started to follow
our tracks back to the camp. Captain Rogers took one or two compass
bearings, and made a few notes; beyond this, we could do nothing.

It was easier getting back than coming down, as the bushes were
more or less trodden down. I forgot to mention that at the foot of the
little hillock, where we had stopped, was a very large Indian camping
ground with about 10 bark huts still standing. The Indians had probably
wintered there and only recently left, as the place was full of bones of
every description — whale, seal, *deer*, guanaco, and even wild cattle —
a proof that they had not starved during the winter. There were also 2
or 3 half-starved, wolfish-looking dogs, who promptly retired on our
approach. Of the Indians we saw nothing, though they were doubtless
quite close to us. It is extraordinary how the Canoe Indians can conceal
themselves at a moment's notice: you may just by chance catch a glimpse
of one of them, wriggling through the undergrowth like an eel; but, in
a moment he has disappeared, goodness knows where.

I afterwards mixed with this race of Indians, perhaps the lowest
human race in existence — utterly savage, with no cares beyond those
of the moment, to obtain food and shelter. Still, in my opinion, they are
a harmless, kind-hearted race: nothing can be done by severity; but,
treated kindly, they can be turned more or less into useful members
of society (as Bishop Stirling has proved by his work at the missionary
settlement at Ushuaia)[5].

We arrived at the edge of the wood in safety, minus poor Capt. Rogers'
improvised *chiripá* which, being loose and flapping, had been torn into
shreds long ago. However, we were now clear of the woods, and soon
got to our camping ground and spent a comfortable evening, in spite
of bites and scratches.

---

[5] Canoe people — In reality, Greenwood is talking about two different native
groups. Those at Ushuaia (Tierra del Fuego) were Yámana, whereas the natives that
Greenwood mentions here in Última Esperanza were Kawéskar.

The following morning Capt. Rogers, although terribly bruised and sore from the mosquito bites, was resolved to continue his march to the north. I was glad of this as, once concluding my duty as guide, I should have a good horse with which I could kill many guanacos, the calving season being on the point of commencing. We started in good time, and by 1 o'clock I had them on the top of the range, from whence I indicated to them exactly the route they had to take. This route, I may mention, they followed according to my directions, and in four days after leaving me arrived safely on the shores of the Lake Santa Cruz.

When I said good-bye to them, Rogers' officers were most generous and kind: not only giving me my horse, but also providing me with all the ammunition, provisions and tobacco they could spare. It being still early, I determined to join my old companion that same day, and arrived at the log hut before dark. I found Mr. Kelly having his supper, which consisted of fried fish, biscuits and coffee, which I willingly shared with him. We were now more or less on our legs again, but had to think of the future. After due consideration, I determined to leave the old man where he was (as he had all he required and could get on by himself), and go down to the River Gallegos to kill a few young guanacos, to keep the pot boiling.

A few words will conclude the history of this expedition. The morning after their arrival at the Lake, two *chasques* arrived from the Colony, sent out by the commander of the "*Magallanes*"[6], to announce the mutiny in the Colony, and ordering the officers to return immediately — which order, of course, they obeyed. They left behind them two lame horses, and many stores, etc., all of which came in remarkably handy to me when I went to the Lake to winter, a year after.

---

[6] "two *chasques* arrived from the Colony" — The mounted messengers González and Muñoz reached Rogers' group at their camp on the S shore of Lago Argentino on December 15, 1877. (Ibar Sierra op. cit: 37; Rogers, op. cit., 89).

Captain Rogers, who was a most enthusiastic explorer, was much disappointed at being called back in the midst of his exploration, but he afterwards headed an eminently successful expedition[7].

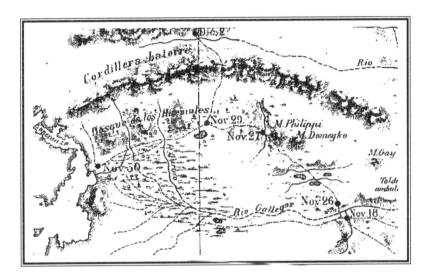

---

[7] Rogers' second expedition — Departed Punta Arenas 4 January 1879.

9

Sandy Point Mutiny

*Bad events are good publicity—Governor Dublé's harsh regime—
Excessive punishments—Mutineers' plans carefully prepared—Imperfect
execution—Governor's escape—Arson and rampage—Scheme to capture
a steamer—Thwarted by British worthies—Mutineers flee towards
Argentina—Captured rebels executed in Chile—Will it happen again?*

I will fully describe this mutiny[1], as the occurrences in it were most interesting and well worth a chapter to themselves. I doubt not "*The Standard*" had many accounts of it at the time; but doubt if the really true details came to hand, as affairs were kept very dark. In any case, it took place so long ago that I am sure it will be interesting to again recount the circumstances.

We may call this Mutiny, Revolution, or whatever it may be termed, the turning point of our career as, since then, everything has gone on prosperously and well. Before the mutiny, the country had been grievously neglected and both Argentines and Chileans evidently considered that Patagonia was a bad speculation, and really not worth the trouble of looking after. Certainly, it required a fillip to remind people that such a country existed; and, in fact, this circumstance acted as a very good advertisement. Be that as it may, it is certain that everyone's attention was drawn to the place: it was no longer a myth, but a country, worthy of even a mutiny and massacre. From the date of this occurrence, you can commence a record of undisturbed prosperity, which has existed with few interruptions till this date.

---

[1] Date of mutiny — Night of the 11th–12th November, 1877.

124

⁎⁎⁎

I mention in another article[2] that our Governor, Sr. Viel, was super-seded by a Chilean officer named Dublé. I do not think he was a bad man, but he was certainly more injudicious, and the greatest tyrant I have ever met. I remember that a favourite expression of his was: *"I came here to arrange the affairs of this neglected colony, and mean to do so."* To do him justice, he kept his word and did arrange it in a most satisfac-tory manner: inasmuch as, when he left, half the place was reduced to a pile of ashes, the soldiers and convicts had cleared out *en masse*, and a hundred or more of the inhabitants were massacred in a most barbarous manner[3].

Everyone knew that the tyrannies exercised by the Governor and his myrmidons must eventually lead to some climax or other; but, when the event eventually took place, it came like a thunderclap and took everyone by surprise. The leaders of the mutiny, viz. Sergeants Riquelme and Estuardo, had arranged for the affair to take place on the National Feast Day, 18th of September, and everything was most correctly fixed off for that date.

It was not the idea of the mutineers to destroy the Colony, or in any way to injure the colonists; all they wanted was vengeance on the Governor, the Captain of the troops, and other tyrannical officers. I do not blame them in the least: the soldiers were good men and the regiment quartered in Sandy Point was an exceptionally good and well-disciplined one, and a credit to any country. Notwithstanding this, the officers treated them with the utmost severity, discipline was never relaxed and punishment — principally by flogging — took place every day. For the smallest offence a man received 100, 200, or even 300 blows with a *leñadura* stick; if he could not stand it all the first day, he received the balance as soon as his lacerated back was able to bear it. Once sentenced, the poor wretch was never forgiven; the chiefs took the greatest delight in witnessing the punishment, and were very angry if the blows were not inflicted in really good form. As for the unfortunate convicts, it can be easily imagined how they fared — constantly in

---

[2] "another article" — See 5, HOMAGE TO SANTIAGO ZAMORA.
[3] Number of dead — The exact number of casualties was 52 dead and 16 wounded. (Martinic 1988: 193)

chains, in solitary confinement, or receiving corporal punishment. Who can wonder that they were driven to absolute desperation?

Well, on the 18th Sept., it poured with rain all day. The soldiers, being wet and uncomfortable — and on this day at least having every comfort provided for them, and also most unusual license for general amusement — proceeded to get hopelessly drunk, and remained so till long after the hour named for the general *rendezvous*. Moreover, they were in a good temper, as men will be when they find themselves well-treated and generally happy. So, the rising did not come off.

However, the fire was only smouldering, and required but a very slight effort to fan it into a blaze. This happened on the following morning: for the officers, after the dissipations of the 18th Sept., had all sore heads and were (if possible) more vicious and inclined for cruelty than before. A lot of innocent men were flogged, and all suffered more or less abuse. This was the last straw, and the mutiny was arranged for a few weeks later (some time early in November — I forget the exact date).

Everything was arranged in a most methodical manner at first; and, had the orders of the chiefs been obeyed when carried out, nothing could have saved the destined victims from complete annihilation. Unfortunately, it was not so. I use the word *"unfortunately"* deliberately for, in my opinion, the doomed men well deserved the fate intended for them.

First of all, the guns belonging to the Regiment were dragged out from the *Cuartel* and made all ready for action, exactly in front of the Government House. Sentinels were placed at both front and back doors, both of the Governor's residence, and those of the various officers. The intention was to call them up one by one and then kill them — and this would most certainly have been done — but, some enthusiastic mutineer, who was in charge of one of the guns, lost patience and discharged it full at the Governor's residence.

The ball passed clear through the place, and even pierced the wall over the bed where His Majesty was sleeping. He immediately sprang out of bed with a revolver in each hand and, rushing to the front door, found a sentinel stationed there. Unfortunately, the man was young and had lately joined the regiment: so, when the Governor appeared

in sleeping guise and presented two revolvers at him, he judiciously lowered his arms and let his superior pass. The Governor, of course, immediately saw that what he must have been expecting had come to pass; and — without taking thought for wife or children — made tracks for the beach, which was the only place of refuge (all the outlets from the colony being guarded).

The Commander of the troops did not escape so easily. Rushing to his door, on hearing the report of the cannon, he was confronted by the sentinel — an old soldier, whom he had flogged a few days previously without rhyme or reason. This man did not let his enemy pass, but shot him dead on the spot. Several soldiers, on hearing the report, came to the spot, amongst them Sergeant Riquelme. They mutilated the dead body in a barbarous manner, but did no injury to the dead man's wife, family or servants; only, they told them to leave the house at once, which they were of course — only too glad to do.

The mutineers then set fire to the house, and went to the Governor's house, to see what was going on. On finding the sentinel at the door, Riquelme asked him where the Governor was. The man answered: "*Salió, Señor.*" ["*He went out, Sir.*"]. Hearing this, Riquelme shot the man dead, and afterwards proceeded to ransack the house where, of course, he only found Mrs Dublé and her children. At first, the infuriated men seemed inclined to wreak their vengeance on them; but, restrained by their leader, they allowed them to pass, and contented themselves with ransacking the house from top to bottom. All the other officers' houses were visited; but all, with the exception of the commander of the troops, had cleared out to the woods.

Up to this time, there had been a certain amount of discipline amongst the mutineers; but, finding that their principal objects of hatred had escaped them, they were literally mad with rage, and commenced pillaging and burning in every direction. I must, however, do them the justice to say that, up to this time, they respected the women and children; and even went so far as to give Mrs Fenton, the wife of the English Doctor, and her family, and other ladies, an escort, to see them safe out of the place. The late Doctor Fenton was so much beloved by everyone that, although he was a Chilean officer, no one attempted to injure him; but, they kept him a prisoner to tend the wounded, who by this time were numerous, as the mutineers had not only quarrelled among themselves but were firing promiscuous shots in every direction. Another great mistake they made was to break open the *Cuartel* and set free all the convicts, to whom they supplied arms; after this, there was nothing but confusion, bloodshed and rapine. More than half the mischief was done by the convicts who, when once they found themselves free, started on plundering the stores, killing all who resisted and committing every atrocity they could think of.

The plan, which had been arranged between the leaders of the insurrection, was to board the first ocean steamer which happened to pass, seize her and clear out for some other country[4]. With this object, they had made prisoners of the Captain of the Port, and all the sailors who were not mixed up in the conspiracy. Their intention was to board the vessel they intended to seize — in exactly the same manner as that officer and his crew would have done in the ordinary course — and then take possession of her. This plan was, of course, frustrated by the mere fact of all the men getting drunk and disclosing their intentions to everyone.

Amongst the first to hear this were the two principal English residents, viz. Mr J. Dunsmure, the British Vice-Consul and his partner and friend Mr H. L. Reynard. Some of the mutineers paid these gentlemen a visit at their little *quinta*, about three miles distant from the Colony; but, beyond a little promiscuous plundering and drinking, did not molest them; however, their intentions leaked out, and Messrs. Dunsmure

[4] Plan of escape — The strategy of commandeering a passing ship is reminiscent of the previous Punta Arenas mutiny (1851) whose leader, Cambiaso, fled in the captured US vessel "*Florida*". (Brown, 1854).

and Reynard determined to frustrate them. Therefore, when they first saw the smoke of the Kosmos steamer[5] coming from the south, they embarked in a little boat they had, and set off to intercept her. The mutineers, who were occupied in drinking and plundering, did not see them till too late; they fired several shots after them (luckily without effect). The Englishmen managed, therefore, to cross the steamer's path and stop her. Had it not been for this, it is impossible to say what end the affair would have had: I think it more than probable that the vessel would have been taken, and all these ruffians would have got clear away. I, in common with everyone else, considered that great praise was due to both the English gentlemen mentioned, for the energy they displayed in this matter.

Of course, forewarned is forearmed, and, on hearing the news, the Captain of the vessel armed all his men; and, being a plucky fellow, determined to distinguish himself. Arriving at Sandy Point, the vessel anchored on the usual place and lowered her side ladder. The Captain placed a line of men on each side of the gangway, all ready to arrest the expected enemies. The boat duly came alongside and the crew came quietly up the ladder, having the Captain of the Port (whom they had brought with them in full uniform) before them, to make it look as if it was only the ordinary visit. I imagine their surprise when, as each man came aboard, he was quietly arrested and his arms taken from him — nothing could be neater. The vessel then steamed off, without

---

[5] Kosmos steamer — Ship "*Memphis*", belonging to the German line "Kosmos".

further intercourse with the shore people. On arrival at Montevideo, the prisoners were sent back by another vessel, which deposited them on board the Chilean man-of-war[6] which had been for some time stationed at Sandy Point, but happened, by ill-luck, to be absent on a surveying expedition at the time of the mutiny.

These men were eventually shot at Punta Arenas — a fate they well merited — although they were not the ringleaders in the affair. In fact, Sergeant Pozo, one of them, had been strongly against it from the very first; but, having many friends amongst the men, he could not avoid being drawn into it. He was, I considered, a highly respectable man, and worthy of a better fate; but it was impossible, in a case like this, to exonerate him. He was certainly taken in company with the other offenders, and had had ample opportunities of warning the authorities of the disaster that was impending.

To return to the unfortunate Governor Dublé: he arrived safely on the beach, and then followed along the coast, always under the shelter of the cliffs, till he came to Cape Negro, where he fetched up at a farm-house occupied by one of his friends[7]. They did not at first recognise him, as he was very lightly clad in his night gear, had no hat, and held a loaded revolver in each hand. However, he soon made himself known, and demanded the loan of horses and a man as guide to take him to Skyring Water, where the man-of-war was surveying. As was natural, he was in a terrible state of alarm or excitement, and was trembling all over — whether from fear or cold, he knows best: to judge by the way he abandoned his family, I should say it was the former. In any case, he had reason to tremble, for if the mutineers had caught him, it is no common death he would have experienced.

After refreshing and clothing him, he was given good horses and a competent guide and set off for Skyring Water, to warn the man-of-war of what was happening. He reached there safely, got on board and arrived at Sandy Point just in time to find all the mutineers had cleared out for the north, taking with them every horse they could find, and all the valuables they could carry.

---

[6] Chilean warship — The "*Magallanes*".
[7] Governor Dublé's friend — Guillermo Dacquet (or Darquié) (Dublé Almeida 1938).

It will not take long to follow the fortunes of this party (of about two hundred persons, including a few women and children) to the end. The men were constantly quarrelling on the road, and the two leaders were both killed. One of the women was barbarous enough to abandon her two little children a few *leagues* from Punta Arenas, and the poor little wretches starved under a bush, close to the roadside. They could not possibly carry half the booty they had brought with them, as the horses they had were quite insufficient for the work, being very poor after a terribly bad winter.

By the time they arrived at Santa Cruz, a great many had strayed away and got lost, and not a few were killed in quarrels, which occurred on the road. I think about 100 passed the river, calling on the road at Pavón Island, where they exchanged some of their stolen goods for provisions, and proceeded up the coast with the intention of reaching the Argentine territories[8].

Fortunately for them, they met a man-of-war surveying the coast, which took them on board and conveyed them to Buenos Aires; I believe they were put in prison for a short time, and afterwards liberated. I saw one of them not very long ago, serving in the Argentine troop of soldiers in Santa Cruz. I held a long conversation with him: he considered the whole affair a capital joke, and recounted with much *gusto* the history of his adventures whilst engaged on the Sandy Point Mutiny. The details he gave me were too revolting for me to mention them here. He told me that some of his companions were doing very well in Argentina, and that one was an officer in the army. Whether he was speaking truth or not, I can't say.

The few mutineers who were captured in the Colony of Punta Arenas were shot there, after a long and impartial trial. They all died game to the backbone: each one declared in his dying speech that — far from being sorry for what they had done — their only regret was that they had not carried out the main object they had in revolting, viz. to kill the Governor and a large portion of the officers, by whom they had been constantly ill-treated and abused. They, one and all, declared that it had not been their intention to destroy the Colony or maltreat the

---

[8] Argentine territories — At the time of these events, the boundaries between Chile and Argentina were still not fully agreed.

inhabitants. I fully believe this, and consider that the most horrible things were committed by the convicts they so foolishly let loose.

This is the history of the great Sandy Point tragedy, so far as I know it. I do not wish to be a bird of ill omen; but still, I must say that I do not think it will be the "last" thing of the sort that will occur — unless times are very much changed since I left.

✿ 10 ✿

Festivities, Visitors and Trade

Christians and Pagans

Bountiful guanaco hunt—Horse stolen by Indian boys—News of the mutiny at Sandy Point—Horse safely recovered—Christmas feast with Kelly—Savage banquet at Dos Morros—Injury and self-pity—Pedro Major—No horses to spare, and few to be found—Pedro's generosity—Good journey to Sandy Point—Evidence of the mutiny—Doctor Fenton's account—Successful trade—At last, more horses!

The season was just commencing; I knew that, treating my horse carefully, I should very soon get enough guanacos to make ten or fifteen *rugs* — a regular fortune to me at that time. I am quite sure that old Kelly was quite delighted at my departure, as he could then do exactly as he pleased.

Arriving at the main branch of the river, I found, as I expected, the breeding season in full swing. On my way down to the Pass of the Robles, where I intended to camp a few days — as I knew it was a favourite breeding place of the guanaco — I managed to get enough skins to make a *rug* and a half. At the end of thirteen days, I had skins enough for thirteen *rugs*: that is to say, about 170 skins, all dried, packed and ready for sale. I may mention that, at this time, the skins realised from $7 to $7.50 Chilean per each 13 skins — the number necessary for a *rug*.

Xmas Day was now fast approaching. My horse was losing condition, and the young guanaco were getting very wild and big; so, I determined to return to my old man to pass Xmas, and afterwards make a trip to the Colony, to see if I could raise another horse or two. *"Man proposes but God disposes."*

I had my horse tethered about two hundred yards from the camp, and whilst I was occupied packing my skins, two Indian boys passed by and quietly carried him off. I had no idea there were any Indians in the neighbourhood or I should have been more careful; although, to do them justice, I must say I had very rarely seen them steal a horse in this manner — but  they were only boys. The ground was so hard that I could find no tracks whatever, except where the horse had been tied, where I could plainly see marks of several horses standing together.

Of course, I knew my poor horse had been carried off, but I could not understand it at all, as I had seen no signs of Indians and no smoke whatever — the most extraordinary thing where Indians are about, as they generally set fire to anything that will burn, either grass or woods (anything to do mischief). In fact, there were many things I could not understand in this business; but, in the afternoon, there arrived a large party of Indian traders from the Colony, who gave me the history of the mutiny in Sandy Point. They said everything was in great confusion, the Colony half-destroyed, and everyone did as they liked. So, they had come out to trade with the Indians, who were camped about two *leagues* distant, in a place called the Punta del Monte. These Indians were hiding themselves for fear of meeting the mutineers, who had escaped from the Colony, and were supposed to be looking for them, to steal their horses. Of course, I could now understand the disappearance of my horse, and why the Indians had made no fire, according to custom.

One of the traders, an old friend of mine, kindly volunteered to go to the Indian camp that night and bring back my horse; and also see, in his own interest, how the Indians were off for trade. This he did, and by 9 o'clock returned with my horse, and a message from the chief, Pedro Major, saying how sorry he was his boys had taken him. This Indian was a particular friend of mine, and certainly the bravest and most honest I ever met amongst them. Some years previously, he was attacked with virulent smallpox whilst in Sandy Point; some of us Englishmen, finding him lying in the street raving, had him taken to a little room and looked after; this he never forgot, and proved it to me afterwards by many little kindnesses.

I sold a few skins for tobacco, biscuits, and a bottle of grog for Xmas. Next morning, after wishing every good luck to my friends, I packed myself and skins on my old horse and went back to Mr. Kelly, whom I found safe, well and fat, and occupied making preparations for Xmas Day. He had several fat geese hung up, some fresh eggs and a pile of fruit — *calafate, murtilla, manzanilla*[1] — all of which were now in their prime, and abounded in the vicinity. I think this was about the 23rd of December. We passed the next day in preparations for a grand feast; after which dissipation I had made up my mind to go into the Colony and buy another horse (or two, if possible), and bring out stores for the coming winter.

We passed a most satisfactory Xmas, and thoroughly enjoyed ourselves. The pudding made of biscuit crumbs, *ostrich grease* and *murtilla* was a grand success, as also the roast geese stuffed with wild fruit.

In a day or two I was ready to start to the Colony — and should have done so — but suddenly a party of Indians came upon us unexpectedly and frustrated my intentions. They were looking for wild horses, and asked me for all the information I could give them, promising me a share in what they caught. I was too glad of the chance: it only meant postponing my journey to the Colony a few days more; and, moreover, there was a chance I might pick up one or more of my own strayed horses. Next morning, therefore, we started to look for wild horses, the Indians kindly lending me a tame horse for the occasion. We searched all day, in every place I could think of, but could find nothing but tracks till the evening, when we suddenly came upon four *baguala* mares and their foals. Our horses were nearly played out, and consequently we only succeeded in catching two of them with their foals; the others disappeared in the woods.

The Indians, however, appeared quite satisfied and pleased. They were literally enchanted with the idea of a good feed, so we returned to the log hut with our prizes: I verily believe, in less than ten minutes

---

[1] Manzanilla — In fact, this is the Spanish name for the chamomile herb and its flower; it is not a fruit.

after our arrival, one of those mares was killed, skinned and the ribs and titbits roasting on the fire. It was a savage banquet: all were ravenously hungry and ate till they could eat no more. I never saw men eat like those Indians: I don't think they could have eaten less than fifteen or twenty pounds of meat each[2]. When they were surfeited, they took an enormous drink of water, just rolled themselves in their *capas*, and went to sleep in the long grass. I confess I enjoyed the meal immensely, but old Kelly disdained to eat with the Indians, and made a roast on his own account.

In the morning, the Indians appeared rather sulky than otherwise (as they generally do after one of their enormous feeds): they ate no breakfast, but took only some *native tea*. As they offered to lend me a horse or two, I thought I would go back with them, and see if they would keep their word (not that for one moment I anticipated them doing so); but, I wanted to meet my old friend, Pedro Major, who I knew would help me, were it in his power.

The Indians left as much meat as we required, and wanted me to take the foal whose mother they had killed; but, it was no good to me, as I had no tame mare with which to suckle it. I told them they had better take it along; they therefore collared the two foals together, and led the wild mare to save trouble. Whilst collaring the foals, one of the lads approached too near their heels, and one of them promptly knocked him back by a severe kick in the face, drove some of his teeth down his throat, and cut his face and nose in a terrible manner. His companions were not in the least affected by this, but laughed heartily and, as far as I could make out, chaffed him for being such a fool as to get in the way. Old Kelly, who was tender-hearted enough in his way, washed the lad's face, and plastered him up with some concoction of his own. The boy looked grateful, but said nothing.

An extraordinary thing among these Indians is that most of them appear to have no feeling for others in pain; whilst, if they have a small hurt themselves, they make more fuss about it than a white man would if he were at death's door. I remember seeing one of the chiefs called

---

[2] Meat consumed by Indians at meal — The quantity is apparently exaggerated.

Pedro Platero have a rough and tumble with his fists; the man got a little bit bruised and a black eye (nothing but what an English schoolboy would have laughed at); but he sat down and cried like a child, surveying himself from time to time in a three-cornered broken piece of looking glass; and this performance he kept up the whole day and night, without eating or drinking. An Indian cannot bear the sight of his own blood: it seems to upset him completely.

It was rather late when we started for the Indian camp, but the days were long, and we very soon crossed the three branches of the Gallegos, which now carried very little water. On arriving at the wooded hillock where we had camped on our way up, we found a solitary Indian *toldo* pitched there, which I recognised as that of my old friend Pedro Major. None of the men were at home, only two of Pedro's wives and some children. It is rather strange to see an Indian living all alone in this manner; but, as far as I could make out from some scraps of conversation between the Indians, there had been a fight amongst the main body of them; Pedro, after having killed his men as usual[3], had cleared out with his family to avoid the vengeance of the other Indians. I was sorry not to meet him, but determined to stop and see him on my return.

We continued our journey, and an hour or two before nightfall arrived at the Morro Chico, where poor old Kelly had passed the winter. Arriving there, one of the Indians suddenly turned to me, and asked what I had come with them for. I naturally replied. *"To fetch the horse you promised to lend me,"* to which they answered: *"We have no horse to lend."* I saw they had been only fooling me; and so, after consigning them in my choicest English, Spanish and Indian to a particularly warm place, turned round and rode back towards Pedro Major's camp. I reached there very late and — knowing by experience how much an Indian objects to being disturbed when he has once turned in with his family — I unsaddled about 300 yards from the *toldo*, had my supper, cold meat and biscuit I had brought with me, and was soon snugly asleep in the long grass by the river.

---

[3] "Pedro ... having killed his men as usual" — Greenwood's meaning is unclear: he may be referring to the frequency of conflict within the native group, or to Pedro Major's great strength.

At early dawn I was awakened by a laugh close beside me and, looking up, saw the splendid form of Pedro Major, standing watching me with much amusement. When I say *"the splendid form,"* I speak deliberately. I never saw a finer specimen of a man: he was about 6 feet 6 inches, or 6 feet 7 inches in height, but perfectly proportioned, so did not appear so tall. After shaking hands, he asked what I was doing there all alone, and why I had not come and stopped the night with him. I told him because I did not like to disturb him so late, and I could see he appreciated my thoughtfulness. *"Well,"* he said: *"You had better come now and have some breakfast, at any rate."* So I left my things there, and accompanied him to his tent, where all his people were up and taking *mate*, in which performance I assisted.

I saw very few horses about the camp. Pedro told me more than two thirds of his mob had cleared out, owing to the mosquitoes, and he could not find them anywhere. I told him I was sure they were not where I was camped, or in the Interior, as I was just come from there. He agreed with me: they must have gone against the wind towards the sea. This was a death-blow to my hopes of getting horses, as I saw the poor man had barely enough to remove his family, tents, gear, etc. He said: *"The best thing you can do is to wait here today, whilst I and my lads go out and look for them, and if we can find them I can help you."* So they started away, while I remained in the *toldo*, and amused myself by cleaning up all Pedro's arms, rifles, guns, revolvers, etc., of which he had a miscellaneous assortment — good, bad and indifferent. After that, I got some powder and shot from the *squaws* and, taking an old gun (which had formerly belonged to me, and which I could trust), went out to look for some Brant geese, which appeared to abound in the neighbourhood. I soon returned with half a dozen, as fat as butter, much to the delight of the *squaws*, who fully appreciate this delicious bird when they can get it.

About nightfall, Pedro and the boys came back from the *camp*, bringing with them only a mare and two or three old horses: they appeared gloomy and dissatisfied, as they had reason to be. *"Well,"* he said at last: *"All I can do for you amigo is to lend you an old* mancarrón *to put your cargo on: riding horses I have barely enough for my own family, as you see."* He then divided with me the little ammunition he had, and also insisted on my taking a portion of his biscuit, sugar and *harina*. I did not wish to take these things, but he said he was going to join his tribe immediately, and could then get all he wanted. The women asked me to bring out a few things for themselves and the children from the Colony, which I only too gladly promised to do.

I arranged to meet Pedro at the lake of Finado Zurdo in about three weeks' time, when I would deliver him up his horse and the things he wanted from the Colony. Now you see what a "good" Indian is. Of all the *Christians* I had met in the Pass of the Robles, not one had offered to assist me with either a horse or provisions: all I got from them, I paid full value for. This poor Indian, on the contrary, gave me a share of all he had — both willingly and cheerfully — and would have given me more, had he had it. I don't say, mind you, that a great portion of the Indians are not selfish, mean and cruel in the extreme; but if you make a friend of a good Indian, who really likes you, there is nothing he will not do for you.

After a good night's rest (I need not say, not inside the *toldo*, as there was too much livestock running about to make it pleasant there), I saddled up and returned to old Kelly, very well satisfied with the results of my expedition. He was glad to find me arrive with another horse and more supplies. Things were looking up again, and we felt generally cheerful.

It was now time to think of going into the Colony, so we started fixing up all the cargo neatly for the trip. I had no fear about leaving old Kelly alone, as he had a plentiful supply of salted meat and eggs, besides the fish and game he could catch; also, the wild fruits were in their prime, and the garden was coming along finely. Therefore, I started directly I was ready, without any misgivings on his account, promising to return in about 14 days if all went well.

I arrived at Despuntadero without any trouble in 4 or 5 days and, on striking the road, soon found evidences of the mutineers having passed that way: clothes, bottles, and odds and ends of every description strewed the track, and now and then I came across a dead horse. All I picked up, that was of any use to me, were two tins of sardines and a half-pound tin of Navy Cut tobacco, which were stowed under a bush. Also, in a little well just where the Colony road turns away from the bay, I found a bottle of champagne and a bottle of brandy sunk; this was a piece of good luck and I resolved to camp there for the night and enjoy myself, which I did; and, the next morning early, marched for the Colony.

I shall never forget what a desolate looking place it was: the Government house, church, barracks, and most of the principal stores a heap of blackened ruins. I did not know where to go, but presently I tumbled across my oldest and dearest friend, Doctor Thomas Fenton, walking with the Chief of Police. I need not say how glad we were to see each other, and I was soon down at his house — a little miserable two-roomed shanty, down by the beach — his own beautiful house, furniture, plate, clothes, and everything else having been burnt and utterly destroyed. All he managed to save were a few silver spoons and forks, and some of Mrs. Fenton's jewellery, which he managed to cram into his long riding boots at the first alarm. He had moved into this new house and had his house-warming, only the night before the mutiny took place. From him I heard the whole description of it, and found that report had not exaggerated the atrocities committed at that time. The only thing that was not true was that the sick in the hospital had been burnt alive: all the beds were carried out into the plaza before the fire had even reached the building; the bodies found burnt there were those of some convicts who went into one of the rooms to have a drinking bout.

I had no difficulty in disposing of my cargo at a fair rate, but money there was none, and I had to take a portion out in flour, sugar, tobacco, etc.; for the balance, the storekeeper gave me an old *moro* horse, which served very well for a *carguero*, if for nothing else. Dr. Fenton very kindly made me a present of one of his horses, and the Governor, Col. Wood, lent me another, and also confirmed the gift of a black horse, which Capt. Rogers had left me in payment for my services as guide. At the end of 3 days I was completely fitted out and rested, and on the fourth day started on my return journey.

❧

Prosperous Times

*Speedy return to Pedro Major's camp—Kelly in good form—A lucky find,
thanks to the mutineers—Another room for the cabin—Horse-hides for
roofing—Californian gold prospectors—Limited success—Death in Tierra
del Fuego—349 swans—Ready to trade again*

As the reader can readily understand, it is a very different thing to
start on a long march with 4 fair horses, well clad, and with everything one requires in the way of clothing and provisions, to marching
along on foot, with only a few possessions on your back — and so I felt
it. The first thing to be done, of course, was to meet my friend Pedro
Major, to return him the horse he kindly lent me. The *camps* were now
in splendid condition, so that in two and a half days I reached the Indian
camp, in Finado Zurdo, where the greater portion of all the Indians in
the vicinity were holding their annual big meeting, and kind of general
council. Pedro was delighted to see me, and much pleased with the
things I had brought him. He had recovered all his strong horses, and
utterly declined to take back the one he had lent me: "*Four horses were
none too many*," he said, and I could repay him when I was better off. I
only stopped a short time there, as there were lots of traders selling grog,
etc. (and the Indians were all more or less drunk), but marched straight
on towards the Dos Morros, where I arrived late the following night.

I found old Kelly in a high state of preservation, and delighted to see
me back again, more especially with horses. The garden was looking
very nice, and he had dug up a large piece of ground, and transplanted
cabbages, cauliflowers, lettuces, etc., which were thriving wonderfully
on the virgin soil. In fact, everything looked as bright before us as things
had been dark and gloomy two or three months previously. The first
thing to do was to arrange some plan for making a livelihood; nothing
could be done now in the way of hunting, as all birds and animals were
shedding, and we had two months before us ere either feathers or skins
would be good for anything.

I forgot to mention one thing, which happened to me on my trip
out. On arriving at Despuntadero, I stopped under a big bush (where

the mutineers seemed to have camped on their way out) to have a smoke and a drink. On looking into the bush, I saw something shining, which on examination proved to be a Winchester repeating carbine, one of the arms used by the artillerymen in the Chilean service. There was also a pair of long military gauntlet gloves, crammed full of Winchester cartridges — at least five or six hundred of them — and a silver mounted duelling pistol, which was of great service to me for many years. This was a find and no mistake and, occurring in my first camping place on my journey out, seemed to augur well for the success of my trip.

I thought that, as we had really nothing to do beyond hunting for our living, we might occupy the time in enlarging the house, as it was not very comfortable living in one room — more especially as we had now a lot of gear of one kind or another. Therefore we built a good, large, big room, a continuation of the other, about 12 feet by 12, and finished it — all but the roof, for which I required either horse or cow skins. In the corner, we also put a large chimney of clay and stones; and put up two standing bed places, which we lined with guanaco skins, of which we had several. After that, we took our horses and rifles and left the house to its own devices, whilst we looked for skins for roofing.

By great good fortune, we came upon a large mob of wild horses (at least 50 of them); amongst them I recognised two I had lost some time before, and several other horses, which had evidently been tame and escaped. I would far rather have found the wild horses alone, not mixed up with escaped tame animals: there would then have been a chance of corralling the whole lot, in the same manner as we did the *baguales* when we first discovered them; but the 5 or 6 escaped animals were, as is always the case, ten times worse than the wild ones, who knew nothing about a man. I saw we could do nothing at all without killing the *quondam* tame animals, which only made the others wild. Therefore we waited till we discovered their favourite watering place, where we lay in wait for them; and when they came down to water, managed to pick off no less than 4 of them, including my own two strayed animals, which were the worst and wildest of the lot. With these four skins we returned home, taking also with us all the *grease* and primest portions of the meat, tongues, *tapapechos*, etc., etc. The four skins, when well stretched, made a capital roof for the new room, and when we moved into it we felt very comfortable.

Just as we were settled, two old California miners prospecting for gold arrived and, having nothing to do for some weeks, I accepted their invitation to accompany them on a short tour, to see if we could make a strike. We remained away about six weeks, prospecting every small stream which looked promising; we got the colour everywhere, but found nothing that would pay, except a tiny stream with a *tosca* bed which was honey-combed everywhere. This we turned and washed all the little pockets, taking from them no less than 480 grammes of gold, then worth about 1.10 per gramme. After this, strangely enough, all signs of gold disappeared; and although we turned the course of the stream in several places, both above and below where we had been successful, found nothing worth the trouble of washing. Gold is a strange thing, and one never knows where you may find it. How many times have I made what I thought was a really good discovery, and yet, after working many weeks, turning stream etc., etc., have made next to nothing.

My two Californian acquaintances soon came to the conclusion that the ground round there was not worth working: gold there was, and is, everywhere; but it is so fine and so scattered that it would never pay the trouble of working, unless on a very large scale, and with large capital. We therefore returned to the house, and they determined to go down south to the Straits of Magellan, and from there to cross to Tierra del Fuego or King William the 4th Land, where they had heard rumours that rich alluvial strata had been discovered. This intention they carried out: one of them was very successful, the other was killed by the Fuegian Indians, or supposed to be. I was told that his boots were found with the legs in them (cut off close to the top); also, some of his clothes and tools: he himself was never seen or heard of again. This man had a blind confidence in the good qualities of the noble savage. He said he had mixed with every kind of Indian in all parts of North America, from the Digger Indian of the Rocky Mountains[4], to the Apache and Sioux of the Plains, and they had never done him any harm: he said it all depended how you treated them. He was repeatedly warned not to trust himself with the Fuegian Indians, as they are most cunning and treacherous; but he would not take advice, and the result was what I have stated above.

Meantime the old man and I had commenced our hunting and were very successful, game being very plentiful all around our lake. My great wish was to get enough money together to buy a really good, fast horse, with which I could catch any wild or tame ones I came across.

About the beginning of May, the lakes began to freeze and all the wild fowl to migrate. In a very few days there was nothing left but a few hundred swans: these, either because they had not finished shedding, or were too weak or thin to fly. They all kept bunched together in the middle of the lake, in a large round hole about 50 yards in circumference, which the warmth of their bodies, or perhaps some warm spring running into the lake from underground, kept entirely free from ice. There they swam round and round, unable to get out. They could not

---

[4] Digger Indians — In fact, an indigenous people of Northern California.

fly, even if they had strength, as there was not sufficient space to enable them to rise from the water: a swan requires a distance of about 8 or 10 yards to flutter along the surface of the water, before he can get on the wing.

This was a splendid stroke of good fortune for us. When we were quite sure the ice would bear our weight, we armed ourselves with the old blunderbuss, long sticks and ropes, and started for the slaughter. The old man would lie down on the ice and fire at the long line of black necks — killing 15 or 20 sometimes at one shot — whilst I knocked down any that ventured near the edge, with a long stick. In fact, by nightfall, we had killed the whole lot, amounting in all to 349; we very easily dragged them across to the hut, where we piled them up, ready for skinning the next day. This was a glorious haul, and gave little or no trouble. Swan-skins at that time were worth from 1.50 to 2 dollars Chilean each. We passed the next two days in skinning them, and putting them two and two together, with salt between to keep them good.

I now determined to take all the produce we had into the Colony, buy a few more stores, and a really good horse. I had plenty of time to return before the winter regularly set in; and indeed, up to the present, there was every indication that this winter would be as mild as the previous one had been severe.

⁂ 11 ⁂

Destination Lake Santa Cruz

Preparations for the Expedition

Comparative riches—Greenwood buys horses, provisions and a pedigree hound—Enough supplies for a two-year expedition—Safe return as winter begins—Profitable hunting—Ready to start—Kelly dies

This time I went to the Colony under very different circumstances: two good strong horses, 100 grammes of gold in my pocket, and a valuable cargo of skins and furs. My intention was to spend every cent of the money I took in, in buying a really good horse and every kind of necessary; then, to change my hunting ground for one further north, and remain outside perhaps two or three years, till I was fairly on my legs. If I could not manage on the capital I had, I was quite sure that now I was getting on so well I could get credit anywhere.

I had a very pleasant march: the weather was lovely — frosty days with no rain or snow — and I arrived at the Colony in less than the usual time. I had no difficulty in disposing of my swan-skins: I sold them to a German for a Chilean dollar apiece more than I expected to get. The same man also bought my feathers at 2 Chilean dollars per pound; and both swan-skins and feathers were on their way to Germany within 13 hours of my arrival. I forget exactly what I got for my gold, but I think it was a dollar a gramme; the odds and ends of skins, etc. I sold advantageously.

I was now possessed of a capital of between 7 and 8 hundred dollars, which appeared to me a regular fortune; this I disposed of, as follows. First of all, I bought a beautiful *moro* horse (which I had coveted for a long time) for 50 Chilean dollars; and a tame mare, for a *madrina*, with two fine colts following at her heels for 90 dollars; also a half-bred greyhound, a grandson of "*Brenda*"[1], a Crystal Palace prize-dog, which an Englishman had brought from England some years previously as a speculation (for this I paid 50 dollars). The balance of the money I expended on every class of provisions, tobacco, a bolt of strong canvas, clothes, ammunition, etc. — enough to last me 2 years, with care. I could have taken many more things, but had not the means of carrying them. There was a little money left and, as the annual Government horse sales were going on, I bought six wild mares which I delivered to a friend of mine in Cape Negro who had an *hacienda*, and promised to look after them until my return, for one third of the increase. In fact, after a stay of only two days, I had every reason to be satisfied with what I had done, and felt if I did not get on well now it would be my own fault.

Though now well advanced in June, there were no signs of any snow, and it was impossible for the dogs to run without cutting their feet to pieces; but, at Laguna Blanca we drove a *point* of guanacos and *ostriches* on to the ice, when they began slipping and tumbling down; and we could have had meat enough for 100 men, had we wanted it. However, we took only the *ostrich* skins and meat enough to carry us on, and proceeded on our journey.

We had some difficulty in crossing the rivers on the ice, but managed it by throwing down wet sand from one side to the other, which soon froze and made an excellent road. Arriving at "our" lake, we met the old man wending his way home with the best part of two fat *ostriches* on his back, which he had killed on the ice.

Everything had been going on satisfactorily, but the two horses I had left were rather thin with being constantly tied up; I could, however, let them now go with confidence, as the horses I had brought with me were quite accustomed to the bell-mare and followed her everywhere. We determined to wait a few weeks, till the days were longer, and then start away for the north; we could do no hunting, as the ground was too

---

[1] Deerhound "*Brenda*" — Second prize-winner at the National Dog Show, held at the Crystal Palace, South London, June 1875. Her owner was James Dunsmure.

hard for the dogs to run. A friend of mine in the Colony had offered to make a contract with me for puma and big red fox skins — the former at 5 dollars a head, the latter $3 — so we filled up our time with tracking these animals. My old dog "*Pluto*" had a capital nose, and rarely missed finding what he followed. By the beginning of August we had a fine collection of skins of various kinds, which we dried carefully, sewed up in canvas, and hid in the woods until our return.

With the bolt of canvas I had brought, the old man (who, as an old sailor, thoroughly understood the use of *palm and needle*) made a splendid big tent, capable of holding ourselves, dogs and gear, and twice as much if we had it. With the scraps he made a suit of overalls for each of us, which were eminently useful during the wet season that followed: in fact, we had everything we desired for our long trip, which I anticipated would last 2 years. It was, however, exactly 5 years and 4 months, from the time I left the Colony till I returned and slept under a civilised roof; but ... I was in a new country, very interesting, abounding in fish and game, and a thousand things of interest. These 5 years were the happiest of my life, although the greater portion of them was passed entirely alone as, after we started, the old man got hurt by a *lion*, and had to go to the Colony for repairs, from whence he never returned.

I think it was about the middle of August when we eventually made a start, and about the end of the month when poor old Kelly met with his accident. I wish I had taken him to the Colony at once, instead of letting him follow on, as he did for some months, and then his life might have been saved; but he was as obstinate as a mule, and nothing would induce him to go back till he really could not knock about any more. I describe his death and funeral in another article[2]. It seemed hard, after following my evil fortunes so long, that he was not spared to share my better luck.

----

[2] Kelly's death and funeral — See 17, SOUTH AMERICAN LIONS (PUMAS) for an alternate version of this story.

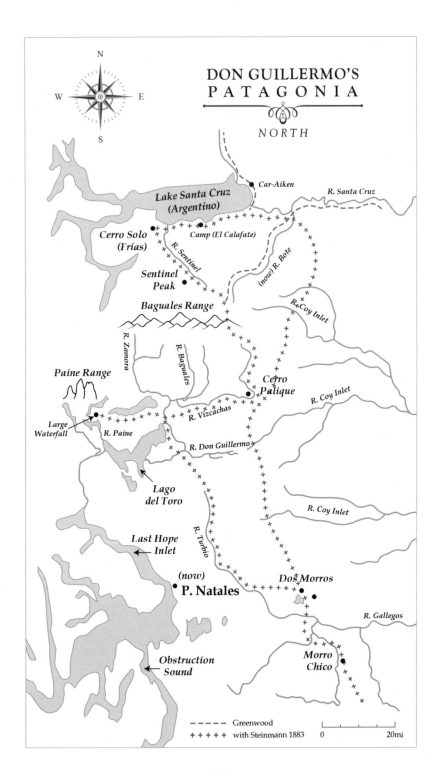

DON GUILLERMO'S
PATAGONIA

NORTH

N
W E
S

Car-Aiken

R. Santa Cruz

Lake Santa Cruz
(Argentino)

Cerro Solo
(Frías)

Camp (El Calafate)

R. Sentinel

(now) R. Bote

Sentinel
Peak

Baguales Range

R. Coy Inlet

R. Zamora

R. Baguales

Paine Range

Cerro
Palique

R. Coy Inlet

Large
Waterfall

R. Vizcachas

R. Paine

R. Don Guillermo

Lago
del Toro

R. Coy Inlet

Last Hope
Inlet

R. Turbio

(now)
P. Natales

Dos Morros

R. Gallegos

Obstruction
Sound

Morro
Chico

– – – – Greenwood
+ + + + + with Steinmann 1883   0   20mi

150

Enchanting new surroundings

Grandeur of Santa Cruz valley—Perfect paradise—Good fishing—Glaciers and icebergs—Beautiful lake—Evidence of volcanic activity—Traces of former human presence—Structure reminiscent of Stonehenge—Water-birds and lizards—Ideal camping ground

I think, owing to Kelly's untoward accident, which threw me back in my trip many months, that it was not until the end of August 1880 I found myself, horses and dogs on the top of the *Cordillera* looking down upon the splendid valley of Santa Cruz, with a magnificent panorama of mountain, glacier and lake spread out far to the north and west. No one can imagine the beauty of this scene, and it is well worth a journey to see this alone. Far away to the north on a clear day you can distinguish the peak of the celebrated Cerro Chaltén, the highest mountain in that part of the Andes, exactly behind which is situated the Volcán de los Gigantes, which occasionally sends up a cloud of smoke, accompanied by rumblings and reports like cannon. I was in the north when the great eruption took place, which covered the entire country with ashes from north to south, and even reached to the Falkland Islands. I describe this eruption elsewhere[3] — it is well worth an article to itself.

I shall never forget the delight to me of exploring this unknown country. I marched down the slopes of the hills and arrived at a little river, a tributary of the River Santa Cruz, and camped in a sheltered nook on its banks. Everything seemed different and full of interest — birds, insects, bushes, stones and everything else — even the fish, which were jumping in the stream in every direction, were quite unknown to me. The *camp* was, however, terribly dry, utterly devoid of grass except close to the river. All the plains were covered with a kind of black creeper, mixed with *mata negra*. Huge *incense bushes* dotted the plain in every direction and also a few *calafate* bushes, but grass there was none — sometimes, long stretches of pure white clay, with no sign of any verdure whatever. However, I knew I should find plenty of grass and everything I wanted when I reached the Lake, which had been described to me by Captain Rogers and others as a perfect paradise.

---

[3] Eruption of Volcán de los Gigantes — Greenwood refers to his experience in 1883. See 13, VOLCANO OF THE GIANTS IN ERUPTION.

So I determined to remain here only one day. I fished that evening in a deep pool close to the tent, and caught three different kinds of fish: one was something like a carp with big gold scales; another, a long blue-ish fish with very sharp teeth, something like a hake; the other was the ordinary trout, found all over the country; but the former proved delicious eating. After that, as it was still daylight, I took my gun and strolled down to inspect the River Santa Cruz for the first time.

I could see at once that it was excessively low, as masses of rocks far higher than a man on horseback towered above the water, and I could see by their well-worn appearance that they must be covered by water a great portion of the year. This I found to be the case, after some years' experience: both the River and Lake Santa Cruz fall tremendously from the month of August till the end of October and, at that time, appear to contain only half their usual amount of water. Directly the sun begins to get power, it melts the glaciers and ice fields in the valleys and on the mountain sides, and huge pieces of ice are constantly falling from the mountains and glaciers into the numerous branches of the Lake. The noise occasioned by this is almost deafening and, when once the thaw commences, you can see fleets and fleets of icebergs sailing out from the interior of the *Cordillera* — all shapes and sizes; some coal-black, being covered with mud; others shining in the sun, showing in some cases all the colours of the rainbow. The deep blue of the Lake (when the sun is shining on it), the clouds, and the green woods reflected from the mountainside, form a beautiful picture. I will mention, however, that the water of the Lake is really a particularly dirty, clayey white — but beautifully sweet, and good for cooking and drinking.

I could not leave this dear little river without remaining a day or so to explore: all the country round seemed so interesting. The bed and banks of the stream were covered with beautiful pumice stone, probably discharged from an almost perpendicular mountain, far above the head of the little valley. You could see at a glance, by its formation, that it was one of the extinct volcanoes which abound in that district. There must have been lively times when all these were in a state of activity — that is to say, if their performance was in any way equal to the Volcán de los Gigantes.

I followed the little stream up that morning, every moment finding something new to interest me, including hundreds of huge scorpions concealed under the loose stones. On the western bank I came upon some large caves in the *barranca*; the walls were blackened with smoke, and there was every indication of their having been occupied at some unknown period by an unknown race. I after found these and the many other caves in the vicinity very useful for living in, and storing gear, etc. The higher I ascended, the more the canyon opened out and, on arriving at the first plateau, it was no longer a valley but a plain, well grassed and wooded, dotted with little herds of guanacos and *ostriches*.

I ascended one of the nearest mountain peaks to try and get a better view of the surrounding country, and a splendid panorama there was from there. It was evidently an extinct volcano, as there was a hole in the centre, apparently of profound depth, which had doubtless been the crater; this was nothing extraordinary, as this formation is so very common in all this district. What was very curious and interesting was a number of huge stones, exactly in the form of a heart, built precisely the same way as those druidical remains so well known at Stonehenge[4] — only, of course, much smaller — viz., two perpendicular stones and one on the top. The entrance to this *corral* or "sacrificial temple" was at the base of the heart, the apex pointing due east. I afterwards took tools up there and dug all over the place, but found nothing except 2 or 3 of the arrows and lance-heads so commonly found in this country. All this was, of course, a mystery to me, although probably a man of science would understand it at a glance. I returned home, much pleased with all I had seen; the only thing I saw of interest on my way back was a beautiful vein of blue and white marble, precisely the same as that used for mantelpieces; it was, of course, useless for working on account of its distance from civilisation and the difficulty of transport.

I saw several beautiful, blue kingfishers in the river, and also a specimen of a lovely white grebe with the scarlet head[5]. I have only seen 3 specimens of this lovely bird, and all were on this little river; on neither of the occasions had I a gun with me, so I was unable to procure one. I could have killed any quantity of *ostriches*, had I wanted any; and, as

[4] Huge stones reminiscent of Stonehenge — Greenwood alludes to the famous prehistoric megalith in Southern England.
[5] White grebe with scarlet head — Probably the Hooded grebe (in Spanish, "macá tobiano"). The river on which it was observed would be the modern Río Bote.

for eggs, I could have loaded a couple of horses with them (they were so plentiful), but I only took a few for myself and dogs. One thing I noticed, which I had not seen in the south, viz. the enormous quantity of lizards, some of them of the most brilliant colours, which darted across my path in every direction. Everything was a change from the dead sameness of the south and, as you will see, the nearer I got to the mountains, the more I found to interest me.

I was sorry to see that, even at this early part of the season, the mosquitoes were very troublesome, and the poor horses were wandering up and down in a frantic manner. This made me anxious to get on as soon as possible, as I knew that further in the Interior there were plenty of woods and long grass to protect them. So the next morning found me early on my way, and in a very short time I arrived at the junction of the River with the Lake. There was no grass whatever there, nothing but sand and thorny bushes, so I followed on for 2 or 3 hours more, till I reached a river which I afterwards baptised "*Río de la Mala Suerte*" ["*Ill-Luck River*"][6], on account of constant misfortunes which always happened to me whenever I was camped there.

Here, there is a beautiful breeding lake, connected with Lake Santa Cruz by a narrow entrance, but profoundly deep[7]. I never saw a lovelier spot to camp in: the breeding lake was literally covered with wild fowl of every description, swimming about amongst little green islands and patches of bulrushes. I determined to make this lovely spot my headquarters for some time, making expeditions from time to time to explore the Interior. If it had not been for the mosquitoes, no camping

---

[6] Ill-Luck River — The "misfortunes" mentioned by Greenwood are narrated in 5, HOMAGE TO SANTIAGO ZAMORA.
[7] Breeding lake — Modern Laguna Nímez, lying close to El Calafate.

ground could have been more perfect; but, as these are found every-where for at least 4 months in the year, it was only what I anticipated. Now was the time when I should have liked to have a boat, to have gone sailing about, exploring the numerous recesses of these lakes, which as far as one could see intersected the *Cordillera* in every direction.

Potential for Farming and Tourism

Two pioneer stock-farmers—Captain Prichard's river navigation—Fine-looking land for farming—Two stray horses—Greenwood turns veterinary—Pestered by flies—Plentiful food supply—Splendid viewpoint—Brilliant rock crystals—Downhill chase

Some English farmers, named Game and Cattle, are now [1900] set-tled on Lake Santa Cruz; and, as they were both old naval officers, they have doubtless done something before now. They started badly, however, as when they went up to commence farming, they took up a powerful steam-launch with which to tow their wool down; unfortu-nately, she never arrived there, as they ran her on a sharp-pointed rock in the river and knocked her to pieces, only just managing to save their cargo. This was a pity, as it made others unwilling to repeat the experi-ment, although it is well known to be quite practicable: the Government sent up a launch under the charge of a certain Captain Prichard in 1875 or 1876, which arrived safely at the Lake, and returned in safety, but did nothing else. It was a pity, when they had got up there and conquered the main difficulty, that they did not continue to explore the *canals* and the interior of the *Cordillera*; but I believe, as usual in these expeditions, they ran short of stores, and returned in consequence. I remember Capt. Prichard told me it took him 5 weeks to get up to the Lake against the current, but only 37 hours to return with the current.

I started next morning for the woods at the other or western end of the Lake. The *camp* between the first range of mountains and the shore widened out gradually, till it became a huge, well-watered plain, extending almost to the foot of the *Cordilleras*. The entire plain was sur-rounded with hills, woods and *canals*; from the centre rises a beautiful wooded hill or mountain, down the side of which you could distinguish numerous little rivulets running down into the plain. I never saw a bet-ter place for establishing a farm: a few miles of fencing would shut in a tract of at least from 30 to 40 *leagues*, almost entirely fenced by Nature. If Messrs. Game and Cattle have not done well there, it certainly is to be wondered at, as the only difficulty they had to encounter was taking all their produce down to Port Santa Cruz for shipment. The rafts would cost them nothing, as they have heavy timber close to the shore of the Lake; and only the trouble of forming the rafts for the transport of their wool, etc. remained: a very simple business.

When I arrived at Lake Santa Cruz, I was camped in the breeding lake, about half a day's march from the Cerro Solo. I think I have said that when Capt. Rogers had abandoned his expedition to return to Punta Arenas two years previously, he left behind him two horses: one, because it was lame and was shedding a hoof; the other, which was brought by the people who came to fetch him back to the Colony after the mutiny, because it had a bullet in his flank — probably fired at him in sheer wantonness by some drunken mutineer — and was too weak to travel.

The morning after my arrival at the breeding lake, there was a great squealing and general commotion amongst my *tropilla*; on turning out, I saw these two animals mixed up with mine who, as usual, objected to strangers and any infringement on their feeding ground. This was good luck, as they would be very useful to me in the present, and I knew the Governor would pay me well for taking them in — most probably give me one of them (which turned out to be the case). One of these animals appeared in first-rate condition; the other (with the bullet in him) was very thin and lame, and you could see that his flank was much swollen. I found no difficulty whatever in catching the two strangers; I tied up my bell-mare and drove the whole lot of horses to her as usual, and the others followed. On examining the wound of the poor lame horse, I found the bullet had passed through both hind legs, and was now sticking just under the skin of the off one, which was terribly swollen. I could feel the bullet distinctly, and made an incision right over it; it did not want any extracting for, no sooner was the cut made, than it literally jumped out by itself; and, of course, was followed by a great discharge from the wound. In a month's time the poor animal was sound and fat, and was of the greatest service to me.

The flies and mosquitoes now became almost unbearable, especially in the evening. Much as I liked my present quarters, where I had everything I wanted, I resolved to march to the woods, where the horses could have more protection by getting into the thick woods. Where I was now camped, I generally had to spend half the day looking for them: they would climb to the top of the highest hills to get a breath of wind, or else look out for a place where there was very long grass and lie down in it till the wind sprang up; as long as it was calm, they would not move nor attempt to feed.

I was very glad, therefore, when we arrived at the Cerro Solo and camped by a little stream at the foot of it (on the same spot where we afterwards built our boat for the Steinmann expedition[8]). Of course, the first thing was to sow every seed I had, and this I soon did, in the rich black soil that covered all the hillside; next to no cultivation was necessary, and by cutting little trenches from the stream I could run the water wherever I pleased, without the slightest trouble. As for meat, I saw *deer* every day and some of them would sometimes feed quite close to the camping ground; so much so that I had to keep my dogs constantly tied up to avoid them chasing them away. The venison was thin and not of much account at this season; and the shedding time was just commencing, so that the skins were no good. I only shot one every three or four days to keep the dogs in meat and supply myself titbits, heart, liver, kidneys etc.

There was no lack of other food for me: eggs of every kind, parrots in huge flocks, and the Río Centinela (which passed through the plain below the woods) abounded in ducks, geese and fish. What more could one want? Of wild fruits I was glad to see there was every prospect of a good crop; at present there were only the strawberries, which abound on all the slopes of the mountains in the early summer months. Besides these, there were mushrooms everywhere. If the reader is fond of them, I can recommend him to South Patagonia in the early spring months; there he will find various kinds in absolute perfection. I give all these details to show, if a man suffers hunger in Santa Cruz at this season of the year, he deserves to suffer. The great drawback was the quantity of sandflies and mosquitoes, which unless there was a breeze, never left off worrying one from daylight to dark.

---

[8] Steinmann Expedition — See 12, ADVENTURES WITH PROFESSOR STEINMANN.

I determined to at once climb to the top of the mountain from which I had been told there was a splendid view. This appeared easy enough, but turned out a longer business than I anticipated. It was all right as long as we were in the woods; but, once clear of them, there was a dense growth of bushes — principally thorny ones, about 3 feet high — all matted together and most difficult to pass. However, we got through them somehow or other, but it was nearly nightfall before we got to the top; this was perfectly flat, and not more than a few hundred yards in circumference. In the centre there was the usual deep cut or indentation showing that this, in common with nearly all these solitary peaks, was an extinct volcano. The soil at the top appeared to be pure gravel and I saw no signs of any lava at all. What there was, however (which I had never seen before in this part of Patagonia) was rock crystal in quantities strewn all over the little plain; the fragments were not large, but singularly regular in form and brilliant in colour — a perfectly clear crystal; to see them shining in the sun, one would almost imagine he had discovered an El Dorado of magnificent brilliants[9].

The view was simply magnificent: to the westward, snow-clad peaks, glaciers and lakes appeared endless; due south rose the peaks of our old acquaintance, Sierra Paine, towering above all his brethren; whilst to the north, the point of Mount Chaltén was plainly visible, evidently the highest mountain anywhere in this part of the world. The Lake appeared from this altitude a beautiful blue, full of shining icebergs floating about in every direction. It was a beautiful scene and one well worth making the ascent to see. Time pressed, however, and I had to make a start home again. This time I went a different way, and found a very much better road, only a few hundred yards of low bushes before I arrived at the big timber, after which all was plain sailing.

The dogs had got on the track of a herd of *deer*, and I could not hold them in. I could hear them baying all down the mountainside; they were apparently on a hot scent and running in, it seemed to me, straight for our camp. Of course, there was no chance of their catching anything till they got their quarry into the plains, as a *deer* can travel twenty yards to a dog's one on a mountainside and going downhill. They don't run, but take the descent in a series of huge jumps, clearing large masses of

---

[9] Clear crystals — Greenwood's description matches modern-day Cerro Cristal, so-named for its abundance of quartz.

fallen timber of 7 or 8 feet high with the greatest ease, whilst the dogs have to scramble over or under as best they can. I was soon down at the camp, and found that the dogs had killed two *deer*, a buck and a doe, within a hundred yards of the tent. The *deer* had evidently struck this and, frightened by the white canvas, had turned back right into the dogs' teeth.

The horses in the woods were safe: there was no fear of their leaving there so long as there were so many mosquitoes about. Moreover, there was any quantity of *leñadura* trees mixed up with the *robles*, and as everyone knows both horses and cattle prefer the green shoots and leaves of this tree to any kind of grass that ever grew.

I was not sorry to turn in after my long climb, but it is well worth the trouble to anyone who is fond of beautiful scenery; and, as you see, the whole thing can easily be managed in one day.

❧ 12 ❧

Adventures with Professor Steinmann

Into the Interior

German scientists in Punta Arenas to observe Transit of Venus—Greenwood hired as guide for Professor Steinmann—Character of the Professor—Purchases an unsuitable horse—Members of the group—Many observations mean slow progress—Heavy collection of rocks and fossils—Morro Chico—Official lantern-bearer—Mysteries of skat—Astronomical observations—Giant ammonite—Sierra Paine—The Professor sets fire to the woodland—Imminent threat to life—Unexpected refuge

The observation of the Transit of Venus[1] was an important event in the annals of Astronomy. Of course, everyone knows that expeditions were sent to different parts of the world by all the most important Universities and Academies in Europe. Amongst others was that from Strasbourg Academy, under the surveillance of Professors and Doctors Auwers and Gustav Steinmann[2].

This latter gentleman, of whom I am going to write, combined his extraordinary gifts of astronomy with even greater ones as a geologist. After his astronomical work was concluded, I had the pleasure of accompanying him on a geological expedition to the Andes, which

---

[1] Transit of Venus — This occurs when the planet Venus, observed from Earth, passes across the face of the Sun. Such events, which occur roughly twice per century, are of great interest to astronomers since they permit reliable estimates of the size of the Solar System. Greenwood refers to the transit of December 1882.

[2] Strasbourg Academy — Strictly speaking, only Steinmann was from Strasbourg; Arthur Auwers, head of the German commission in Punta Arenas, was from the Berlin Academy of Sciences.

extended over a period of more than 5 months[3]. Now I am going to chaff the Doctor most unmercifully, and send him two or three copies of this paper, with which I know he will be delighted. The Doctor was a tall, thin man, ornamented with the usual stoop and blue goggles, which seem part and parcel of a German Professor. He was, however, such an excellent man, so generous, and willing to suffer in the cause of science, that it was impossible not to love and respect him, even when you had only known him a few days.

Of course, he had never been in the *camp* in his life and, being a very clever man, considered that he would easily learn all that was necessary … in about 5 minutes.

The first step was to insist on purchasing a horse himself, instead of allowing me to do it. Of course, instead of choosing a good steady horse for mountain climbing, he picked out a nice-looking bright bay, very slim and gentlemanly like, but utterly useless for the work he had to undertake. For this horse, he (who had probably never owned a horse before) speedily entertained the most profound respect, admiration and love, deliberately declaring that he believed there was no horse in Patagonia to equal him; and, when he returned to his own country, actually took the brute with him — much to my disappointment, as I had been hoping he would have been left behind with me, so that I might have had the pleasure of eating him as soon as I had fattened him up.

I should not advise anyone who wishes to take a pleasure trip in Patagonia to do it in company with a German Professor and a cartload of astronomical instruments, let alone two or three cargoes of articles which are no earthly use to a *camp* man. The cargo of instruments was my special aversion, as it could not be let loose with the other *cargueros*, and I had to lead the brute the whole road. However, we had undertaken the trip, and there was no getting out of it; moreover, the Doctor was such a splendid fellow, that no decent man would think twice about going to a little trouble on his account.

---

[3] Steinmann's geological expedition — January–May, 1883: a summary of findings was published the same year. (Steinmann 1883).

I may mention that our staff was formed of eight persons. First and foremost, the Doctor; a young Swiss[4], who came with us as a guest, more with a view of seeing the country and passing his time than anything else — he was a very clever, well-read man, and a capital sportsman, so we were glad to have him; then came old Santiago Zamora, my old friend, and myself; two good Chilean *peons*, a French carpenter, and a boy of all work.[5]

The first two or three marches, although the quantity of cargo we carried was enormous, passed off very satisfactorily. The greatest drawback to the rapidity of our marches was a little eccentricity on the part of Doctor Steinmann: whenever he saw a likely point or high hill from which he could take an observation, he made a regular duty of ascending the same, and remaining there sometimes until he had concluded his work.

After that, he would gallop off to overtake our party, without having the faintest idea which direction he had taken, and it very often took some time to pick him up again; on these occasions he was invariably bad-tempered, and swore he was following right in our tracks. This happened two or three times in the first day or two, though, after that, we never let him go without one of us accompanying him.

In any case, we arrived safely at the Morro Chico, the curious formation of which much interested the Doctor. He wished to stop there a day or two, which suited us very well, as our horses — just arrived from the Colony, where there is little or no grass — needed a rest. Moreover, both cargo and packs were in a great muddle (which is always the case when starting on a long expedition), and wanted thorough overhauling. This we attended to, besides catching meat to keep our large party going.

The Doctor found much to interest him in this basaltic hill, and collected a pile of specimens, which he unwillingly consented to leave behind, on our giving our word we would call for them on our return. We thought to ourselves that, if the Doctor was going to collect a similar quantity at every place we stopped, by the time we had finished the journey we should require a traction engine and a few trucks to get them into the Colony. However, he went on with his researches in the calmest

---

[4] "young Swiss" — Identified subsequently as Emilio (Bays).
[5] Members of expedition — Steinmann's biographer says "*three hunters … six persons, 40 horses and 60 dogs.*" (Wilckens 1930: 391).

possible manner: we never left a camping ground without leaving a ton of stone behind us to pick up on our return.

By this time, I had the honour of being appointed lantern-bearer to the Professor, for he not only worked as a geologist during the greater part of the day, but pursued his avocations as astronomer at night. To do this he had to choose some high point in the vicinity, to which his first care was to convey his telescope, aneroid (barometer), and other instruments. After dinner, about dark, he would ascend a hill, and I had to accompany him to hold the lantern, whilst he was fixing up his false horizons, etc., etc. At this early part of the night he did not work much (perhaps half an hour or so), just to get ready for his principal observations at midnight: so, we used to return to the tents to pass the evening.

The Doctor used then to remark: "*Now gentlemen, we will have von leetle game of* skat, *and just a little* kimmel, *and den we will work*." This was the moment I dreaded. It was all very well for the Doctor and our Swiss acquaintance, who had every intricate German game at their fingers' ends; but, as I could never even play a decent game of whist, it was not very likely I was going to pick up this infernally difficult game in under half a lifetime. However, they insisted on my playing with them every evening, and I cannot tell how I used to dread the time. For the first two or three nights, the Doctor treated me with exemplary patience, but on the fourth evening I was told I should now have to shift for myself.

I am sure I forget all about the game now, but I know I used generally to find myself (as evil fortune would have it) playing in partnership with the Doctor. No sooner were the cards dealt than the Doctor would have his hand fixed up in the twinkling of an eye — long before I had even picked mine up from the *rug* we were playing on. He would sit watching my operations through his enormous goggle glasses, get up, light a cigar, drink a glass of *kümmel*, and ask in a long-suffering voice if I was ready. Far from being so, I had generally by this time got into an inextricable muddle: the only thing I really had learnt being that the 4 knaves[6] were the most valuable cards in this game; so, if I happened to have one or

---

[6] Knave — Jack in a deck of traditional English playing cards.

two of them, I used to jam them in a corner by themselves, in company with what I considered the best cards I had in my hand.

On telling him I was ready, I was ordered to proceed. Somehow or other it always seemed I had the lead, and it took me some little time to consider what was best to play; but, eventually I would throw down what appeared to me the most advisable card. The Doctor, by this time, either by some infernal power — or by sly glances at the other men's cards — knew exactly where every card lay; and, on seeing my lead, would dash his cap on the ground one side of him, and his cards on the other, get up, pace up and down the tent, exclaiming at the top of his voice: "*I knew it! I knew it! You are without exception the d—dest, stupidest dunderhead of an Englishman I ever met.*" Having thus relieved his feelings he would sit down and play his cards, with the resigned air of a martyr. So the game would go on the whole evening; at the conclusion of which I had generally been bullied and laughed at to such an extent that I could not tell the ace of hearts from the knave of clubs.

Then all was forgotten, we had supper, and climbed up the hill to take observations. I did not mind this, as I was not expected to know anything, but only to hold the lantern, an operation which even I could attain to. This part of the business was pleasant enough unless, as happened on one or two occasions, I fell asleep and dropped the lantern — generally, of course, just as the Doctor was in the midst of his most abstruse calculations. When this did happen, I used to turn and flee for my life and take refuge in my tent, pursued by a whirlwind of German imprecations. However, they were happy times, and I certainly learnt more whilst assisting the Doctor for these few short months than I ever did before or since.

We were taking a very long time over our journey to Lake Santa Cruz, owing to the continual excursions we had to make into every *rincón* we could get into, to look for geological specimens. The Professor was a wonderful man; he would find things of great value where no one else would dream of looking for them.

I remember once we came upon a large blue granite-like rock, in which I saw nothing very particular (as was the case with Mark Twain's frog, when his visitor observed: "*… that he did not see nothing particular* *about that there frog more than any other frog*")[7]. The Doctor, however, was of different opinion. Scrambling down from his horse as fast as the half hundredweight of stones — which he invariably accumulated on his person during the day— would allow, he informed me that he was going to blast that rock, as he was certain there were several curious things inside it; he told me to fetch along the dynamite, cartridges, drills and sledgehammer, which we carried with us for this purpose. The rock had to be perforated in many places, and it took some time before we were ready; however, we finished at last and, lighting the fuses, cleared out as fast as possible.

After the explosion, we found the rock split into pieces, and the

Doctor began speedily to unearth his treasures. The first of these was a very large ammonite (I think he called it so), about 2 feet in diameter, and weighing perhaps a hundred pounds or more. He also picked out many smaller fossils of various classes. Of course, it was utterly impossible to convey these things along on our saddle horses, as the whole collection weighed at least 200 pounds. The Doctor was very wroth at this, but I pacified him by promising to come the next day and fetch them to the camp.

---

7 Mark Twain's frog — Reference taken from the short story "*The celebrated jumping frog of Calaveras County*," published in 1865; Greenwood's wording differs slightly from the original.

We were then camped just in front of the Sierra Paine, the highest peak of the Andes in this district. The Doctor announced his intention of ascending it, and taking observations from the highest point he could reach: so, we resolved to make the attempt on the morrow. The Swiss, the Doctor and myself therefore started off at daylight, and got well on to the foot of the mountain, through the dense woods which covered the plain, when — somehow or other — the Doctor missed us, having probably stopped to examine some rotten old stone or other. He soon rejoined us, as we fired a pistol shot to recall him.

Suddenly, I smelt a strong smell of smoke and, looking back, saw a column of smoke and flame, which the wind was spreading in every direction. We looked reproachfully at the Professor. We had warned him at least 100 times never to attempt to light the pipe or cigar — one of which was invariably between his lips — without being very careful that the match he had used was extinguished. To do him justice, he looked ashamed of himself.

We pushed our way through the dense wood, somehow or other: I am sure we could never have done it but for the fright we were in. The flames gained on us rapidly but, by great good luck, we struck a small clearing in the forest, about 200 yards in circumference, in the midst of which Providence had placed a small lake, with green grass round the edges. We hurried to this unexpected haven and, dismounting, led the horses to the deepest part, placing them with their tails to the coming foe. Then we lay down in front of them, holding their bridles, having tied up the head of each in our *ponchos*, which had a stupefying effect on them.

In an incredibly short time, the fire reached to the glade, licked up the grass on either side of the little lake, and swept through the woods, cutting them down like corn before the scythe. In less than five minutes all had passed by us, and we could only see the flame and hear the fire cracking and roaring in the distance. The trees increasing in size and height as we got nearer to the mountain, the flames ran up them and licked them all over, and then rushed on, leaving only the bare, blackened skeletons behind them.

We resolved to camp there that night, as it was not safe to pass the forest over the numerous smouldering logs and roots. There was no wind, so we lay down beside the lake, where there was a little green grass, making our supper of the cold rations we had brought with us. The Doctor sat sulkily by himself, without making any remarks nor, although he had his cards in his pocket, did he offer to engage us in a game of *skat*, much to my delight; moreover, there was no lantern to hold.

Paine and beyond

"Barking" ducks—A great waterfall—Impossible to cross river—Drowned deer—Forced change of plans—The Professor visits Indian tents— Unintended consequences—Crossing the mountain pass—Grand panorama —Descent to the Valley of the Sentinel

A lovely morning followed the conflagration. I awoke very early and my companions, dogs, and horses were all sleeping profoundly.

On the little lake, by which we had passed the night, were floating a quantity of the large barking ducks, so common in all the lakes and rivers of the *Cordilleras*, but never encountered away from the mountains. We call them "barking ducks"[8], because when they are in flight, they make a peculiar snapping sound, for all the world like the yapping of a terrier after a rabbit. They are beautiful birds, quite as large as the Picazo duck[9]. These birds are of a very uncommon class: they love the cold and ice and snow, and the colder the weather is, in the better condition they will be found. They are of a lovely brown colour on the back; the wings are variegated gold, green and white, which — when the sun shines on them — makes them resemble burnished gold; the heads are dark grey, crested with 3 long plumes, standing from the basis of the beak to the back of the head; a broad white stripe crosses the head on both sides.

They are splendid eating, so I clawed hold of my gun, which was beside me, waited until they got into a bunch, and let fly into the middle of them, killing 5 of them. My companions, horses and dogs all started up at once; I believe they thought the end of the world had come, but soon saw the ducks floating on the surface. The Doctor, who appeared to have quite recovered his usual good temper, dragged his lean person to the edge of the water and fished them out. We soon had breakfast under way, and I was very glad to get some meat, as biscuit and tea become monotonous.

---

[8] Barking duck — Greenwood refers to the Crested duck.
[9] Picazo duck — Measures 16 inches.

The fire was still raging to the northward and southward far away. Between us and the mountain everything was clear; only a few little spiral columns of smoke were curling up from some still smouldering logs or roots. The Doctor now, with great self-complacency, pointed out how very fortunate it was he had set fire to the *camp*; it might, he said, have taken us a week to get through all those woods; whereas, now, we had such a clear course. I replied: "*Yes, Doctor but if we had not happened to tumble across this little lake, we should most assuredly have all of us been turned into a lot of cinders; and then it would not much have mattered whether there was a road or not.*" There was no reply to this: what could the man say? I only wish the experience had made him more careful for the future.

⁂

The ducks were delicious; we were soon trotting merrily through the burnt forest, anxious to commence the ascent of the mountain that day. We had been sensible of a kind of roaring sound, which increased in volume as we neared the first slope; we could also observe in front of us a cloud of white spray or mist, rising high above the treetops. We soon found out what this was for, in a quarter of an hour, our progress was completely barred by one of the most extraordinary mountain torrents I ever saw. It was simply a succession of waterfalls and rapids, huge masses of rock towered up in every direction, and the noise of the water thundering against them was absolutely deafening. "*Here*," thought I, "*is the end of our expedition.*"

In the first instance, no horse could stand the current, even if he had a good sound gravelly bottom to stand upon, and give him foothold; whereas the entire bed of this river was formed of black slate: of course, as slippery as ice. I said to my friends: "*Well, gentlemen, I think our expedition is at an end: no horse can possibly swim that river and, as for a man trying to do so, he would be knocked to pieces before he even reached the first rock.*" The Doctor — who was now quite in his usual form — said he was going to get across somehow or other.

We proceeded down the river towards the mouth, which was not very far distant, as we could see the lake, into which it evidently ran, through the trees. At this moment, the dogs found a solitary *deer* close to the river; we were on the outside of him and, seeing no escape, the poor devil took a leap into the torrent, and boldly breasted the stream.

The dogs followed, but returned almost immediately; the *deer* meanwhile got about 30 yards from the shore, and then began to go round and round in a circle, and very soon disappeared altogether. Where should we have been had we attempted the pass?

We soon arrived where the river fell into the *canal*[10], which surrounds Sierra Paine on three sides. We saw at once the pass was impossible: masses of driftwood were piled up against the rocks, and the current was enormously rapid, as it neared the waterfall[11] where the river fell into the lake. One stroke of luck we had here, and that was to see the carcass of our drowned *deer* stuck against some logs close to the shore; we soon had him out, and cut him up. We then unsaddled our horses, and strolled down to look at the waterfall, which was not so large as we had expected to find it. Really it was more of a rapid. First of all, there would be a waterfall of about thirty feet, then a rapid many yards wide, and then another waterfall, which evidently fell over some sheer declivity, as the water struck the lake many yards from the ridge of rocks at the mouth of the river.

Anyway, our project of ascending the mountain was nipped in the bud, as there was no earthly means of getting across. I proposed starting on our return journey, but the Doctor said he should like to take a few observations from one of the surrounding hills, and make some sketches of as much as he could see of the interior; so we fixed our camp there for the night.

The Doctor went away all the afternoon by himself, and the Swiss and I had a real good rest and sleep, which we much required. In the evening after dinner we played *skat*, drank *kümmel*, and enjoyed ourselves. The Doctor started with his usual severe criticisms on my general imbecility — but I did not care a bit now, as I had him by the heels — and whenever he started his old game, I made some reference to the clever manner in which he had endeavoured to roast us alive the night previously. In the morning we started to return home, and, thanks to the Doctor's fire, were soon on the outskirts of the wood, and not far from home.

---

[10] River and canal — The river falls into a freshwater lake: the modern names are Río Paine and Lago Pehoé.
[11] Large waterfall — Known nowadays as the Salto Grande.

On the same river on which we were camped, we suddenly came upon three Indian *toldos*, occupied by the most disreputable lot of Indians in the country. Doctor Steinmann was delighted. "*Now,*" he said: "*I shall have an opportunity of studying the habits of the noble savage in his native plains.*" I assured him the best thing he could do was to ride by and take no notice of them, as they were the dirtiest, filthiest lot of scoundrels in the country; but I would take him to see some decent Indians on the way back. Oh, no: nothing would do; and in three minutes, I saw him dismounting in front of one of their tents; and afterwards, absolutely sitting down on a pile of dirty skins inside, surrounded by a crowd of gaping Indians, with whom he was evidently trying to converse.

He must soon, however, have found his efforts quite futile, for he came out, mounted his horse and came back to us, and said he was sorry he had wasted his time on a stupid lot of animals. "*Yes,*" I said: "*You will be far more sorry tomorrow, and perhaps some of us will also.*" At that moment, I noticed he had not got his whip with him, also that his silver-mounted knife was missing from his boot; and one of his silver spurs had evidently been cut off, as I could see the mark of the knife on his boot. Pointing out these little losses he had sustained from his new friends, I never saw a man get in such a frightful rage: he swore he would fetch his boy down from the camp, and they would go together well-armed, and search every inch of the tent until he found his goods. We laughed him to scorn, and told him he had got off very cheaply: his things he would never find, as they were long ere buried or sunk in the stream, till such time as all enquiry should be over. He did not say any more but, when we got home, unsaddled his horse, and turned into his tent, and no one saw more of him that night.

In the morning I went to the door of his tent, which was closely shut, untied the top string, and asked how he was getting along, and whether I could bring him anything. He said: "*Yes, come in, you can do something for me*"; this I declined to do for reasons best known to myself, and told him to tell me at once what was the matter, to see if I could do any good. "*Well,*" he said, in his broken English: "*Don Guillermo, I got little dears.*" After considering a moment, I knew what he meant: to put it plainly, he was lousy. "*Of course you are, I told you so yesterday when you came from the Indian tent,*" I said. "*However, just wait a minute, and I will cure you, if you trust me. Meanwhile, take off all your clothes, and chuck them out of the tent, as far as you can throw them; also the blanket you are sleeping on, and the upper one next to you."* This he promptly did, and we immediately put every available pot and kettle on the fire to heat water, and extemporised a bath by digging a hole in the ground, and then lining it with one of the canvas tents doubled, which we filled with water. Giving the Doctor some Condy's Fluid[12] and soap, we told him to scrub himself all over. We then removed all his things from where he had been sleeping, struck his tent, pitched it in another place, and burnt the grass where it had before stood. By this time, the Doctor was clothed in his right mind, and felt quite comfortable; he was very humble, and appeared to be learning that he did not know quite so much as he thought.

The boys meantime amused themselves by making a bonfire of the Doctor's clothes. The blankets we rolled up and put in a bush till we came back: by that time the hard frost would have killed anything that might be left in them. Seeing the Doctor very *triste*, I saddled up and went to fetch up his ammonite and fossils, which I knew would console him. He was much pleased at this, and passed the rest of the day very happily, assorting, examining and classifying. There was no mention of cards or observations that night.

It was now getting late in the season, being the beginning of April: so, we determined to push on early next morning, pass Sierra Cagual, and drop down to the lakes as soon as possible. By following the valley of the Vizcachas in which we were camped, right up to the head, we should find a pass over this little spur of *Cordillera*, which would take us to the head of Lake Santa Cruz in less than two days. Both the Swiss and I had passed there on two occasions before, and anticipated no difficulty, unless there had been a landslip or something of the sort to block up the road.

Time was getting on, and if we went round this spur of *Cordillera* it meant a delay of at least 10 days; and not only that, but we should strike the Lake far to the eastward, and have 2 or 3 days to march westward till we reached the glaciers and mountains, which it was our main object to explore. I persuaded the Doctor to leave his entire lot of fossils behind,

---

[12] Condy's Fluid — English brand of liquid disinfectant.

and also many other useless articles he carried. We had to pass the same place on our return, so it would be easy to pick them up. He had become, since the affair of the fire, much more amenable than before.

Therefore, on the following morning we marched up the valley; the cargoes were lightened, the animals rested, and everyone appeared good-tempered and anxious to get on. In 4 or 5 hours we were at the head of the valley, and camped at the foot of the pass, in some large caves in the rocks. Of course, at this altitude, there is not a stick of wood to be found; but we had brought a little wood with us to boil our big pot, and had besides 2 spirit lamps to make coffee with — so we were all right.

As there were still some hours of daylight before us, the Doctor went out fossilising and the Swiss (who for the future I will call Emilio) and I took our guns and went out to shoot rock marten (vizcacha) and rock grouse[13]. We soon killed plenty of grouse — fine big birds, dark grey with reddish breasts and legs feathered right down to the top of their feet. It was nearly dark before the martens made their appearance; but then, as if by word of command, all the rocks round were alive with them, gambolling about and making enormous jumps from crag to crag. They appeared so happy that we really did not care to disturb them, so we only killed two as specimens to take home with us; and these we killed with stones, so as not to disturb the others.

All retired to bed very early, as we had to be astir long before dawn if we wished to arrive where there was wood and shelter in one day. Everyone was so anxious to get on that there was no need to call anyone, and we had everything packed and were ready to start just before sunrise. I went ahead, leading the bell-mare, then two cargo horses driven by another man, then two more cargoes, etc., and the loose horses and mares came last, driven by the remainder of the party.

We went single file, and followed a zigzag course along a little guanaco track, about a foot and a half wide. The animals appeared as anxious as we were to get away from the rocks, snow and short grass to the luxurious pasturage of the lakes and, once started, followed like dogs. The ascent did not occupy more than an hour and a half, and we then found ourselves at a height of about 3,000 or 4,000 feet, surveying the magnificent plains and woods surrounding Lake Santa Cruz. Far away to the northward, we could just distinguish some parts of Lake Viedma;

[13] Rock grouse — Greenwood's own term; probably the Ashy-headed goose.

and, beyond that, Chaltén rose towering above all other points; and, behind him, rose a small spiral column of dense black smoke showing that the Volcano of the Giants was still in an angry mood, and ready to give us a specimen of what he would do (if he liked). On our left in solitary grandeur towered the great Sentinel Peak, looking from this aspect something like an old bearded man with a cloak over his head, stooping forward with his elbows on his knees, surveying the plains below. Years ago we had baptised the valley we were going to descend "Valley of the Sentinel," and it really is a very appropriate name.

One would suppose, and with reason, that — as is almost invariably the case — we should experience more difficulty in the descent than the ascent. Far from being so, we had only to lead our horses from the little plateau, where we were all grouped together, over a little step about 1½ foot high, into a tiny little green canyon, which we could see went winding gradually, but without a break, to the plains, fully 2,000 feet below.

Very soon we were on the plains themselves, and marching gaily towards the headwaters of the Río Centinela, where we intended to camp that night. By 5 o'clock we were camped alongside the river, in the circle of huge thick bushes, which effectively protected us from both wind and weather without pitching tents. We had no meat, so everyone went out to forage. The Doctor shot wild pigeons, which abounded in the valley; Emilio fished, and I went to get meat for the dogs, who were now rather hungry. All of us were more or less successful, and after a delicious supper of fish, pigeons and wild fruits, we turned in with the satisfaction of knowing we had thoroughly broken the neck of our journey.

Lake Santa Cruz

Nearing Lake Santa Cruz—Setting fire—Abundant flowers—Woodpeckers and parrots—Building a boat—Hill-top observatory—Scientific assistant—Hunter instincts prevail—Loss of saddlebags and instruments—Puppies to the rescue—Forgiveness—Boat launched—Time running out

We sent the men and cargoes on alone in the morning. It was only a short 3 hours' travel to the Lake, and old Zamora knew exactly where we had intended to camp: in fact, you could distinguish the *point* of woods at the foot of the Cerro Solo from where we were then camped.

The Doctor and I followed the windings of the river down inch by inch, as he was much interested in the formation, which he said was most curious. I did not see anything particular but, as long as he was happy, it was all right. The bushes were very thick on both sides of the stream, so much so that we made the greater part of the journey down in the bed of the stream, landing from time to time when we saw a clear space on one side or the other. There must have been an enormous quantity of pumas in the thick bushes, as the dogs found at least 5 or 6, but, owing to the density of the cover, only brought 1 to bay, which we shot.

These bushes appeared to spoil everything, and were only a refuge for *lions*, foxes and reptiles, so I determined to give the Doctor a treat and burn them. The fire could not reach the plains below, as the river had formed a huge shingly bed where it opened out into the plains, extending many hundred yards. Steinmann was delighted, and promptly dropped 4 or 5 matches amongst the undergrowth. The fire did not last long, but ran along the ground up and down by the river, right as far as where we had struck it, licking up all the resinous bushes and every blade of grass in an incredibly short time. After this we delayed no longer, but followed our party to the camping ground at the Cerro Solo. They were only there a few minutes before us, and had not yet pitched tents.

It was a great treat to be in the green woods again, after all the beastly, rocky, bare *camps* we had passed. The woods at this point are inexpressibly lovely, and the ground is literally covered with flowers: jonquils, daffodils, convolvuli and numerous species of calceolaria. At the foot of the mountains the woods are not thick, but dotted about in bunches like an English park. The only birds seen are 2 or 3 species of woodpecker, which keep up an incessant tapping, and two classes of green parrots, which dart about in large flocks in every direction, making row enough to wake the dead.

Whilst the men were fixing the tents, cooking the dinner, etc., Emilio and the French carpenter went out to cut straight spurs and ribs for the manufacture of our boat; we intended to make a clipper, as we hoped to do a lot of exploring in her. I knew from experience that the sea rises very high in these lakes; also, there are what we called "whirleys" — sudden gusts of wind, which rush down from the glaciers and mountain tops without warning, and churn the water into foam in one moment. We were therefore anxious that our boat should be good and strong, more especially as the season was drawing near when these sudden puffs of wind are most prevalent.

Doctor Steinmann wished to fix up some kind of observatory on top of a little round hill about 100 feet high, which rose from the plain just below where we were camped. As there were plenty of straight saplings about 6 inches in diameter, and 12 or 14 feet long, this was a very easy task. We managed to finish it that same evening and, when it was done, it looked just like an exaggerated Punch and Judy show[14]. We roofed it with old canvas and floored the small observing room with short round sticks — so straight that, when cut in proper lengths, they fitted in almost like a puzzle. Of course, we left canvas flaps, which we could lift or let fall at our discretion. Anyway, it was better than taking observations outside on cold nights, and it really was a success. The Doctor soon carried all his treasures thither and was perfectly happy.

The next day, everyone settled down to his particular avocation. Old Zamora and one of his men undertook the hunting and looking after the horses; Emilio, the carpenter, and one or two of the others devoted themselves exclusively to the boatbuilding department; and I, who knew less about carpentering than an Eskimo, was deputed *aide-de-camp*, lantern-holder and general bottle-washer to Doctor Steinmann. This suited me down to the ground so long as I could keep out of hot water. I felt I was the holder of a most important post, and resolved not to disgrace the position.

---

[14] Punch and Judy — Traditional English mobile puppet show performed in a tall booth, with an upper opening on one side.

I had now been 2 months more or less under the Professor's tuition and had even learned, and was trusted, to take simple observations entirely by myself. This first morning I was entrusted with the most serious work I had yet undertaken alone. Very early the Doctor called me, and giving me one of his aneroids and some other instruments, despatched me to the top of a high hill close to the glaciers at the S.W. point of the Lake, with instructions to make and carefully note down certain observations. He, for his part, ascended another hill to the N.W., from whence he was to take precisely similar observations, and we were afterwards to meet at the camping place to compare notes.

Please remember, I have not the faintest notion why he did this and, so long as I could please him, I had nothing else to trouble about. Well, my observations came off finely and, as at 12 o'clock precisely I, according to orders, concluded my work, I felt I was indeed a man of science. My heart burned with enthusiasm. I loathed the thought that I had for years wasted my undoubted talents as a scientist, and devoted myself to collecting greasy skins and feathers; but it was not too late, and from that day I resolved to abjure whisky, tobacco, hunting, novel reading, and all that made my life pleasant. In pursuance of this virtuous resolve, I caught hold of the saddlebags full of delicious instruments, and chucked them across my saddle with a violence which I should think must have put them out of gear for about six months, and pounded on my way home, mapping out for myself a better and worthier life. Of course, owing to this fit of high and noble feelings, I quite forgot to lash on the saddlebags; I simply sat on them, not meaning to gallop, but to go slowly, thinking good and worthy thoughts. The Devil is, however, always constantly on the watch.

On arriving at the foot of the hill, up got a magnificent cock *ostrich* from the long grass. In a moment, all my good resolutions vanished; and I, the dogs and Doctor Steinmann's instruments were in full chase. The *camp* was rough and the chase long and very zigzag, as the bird kept dodging the stony spots of ground; but he eventually gave in. Waiting a few minutes to breathe my horse and dogs, I chanced to glance at my saddle — Good Heavens!! The saddlebags were not there!! — I must have dropped them somewhere during my run. I did not even know what course I had taken, as the bird had kept turning and turning; but I did know exactly where I started, and where I finished, which was something.

I went back slowly and dejectedly to the foot of the hill I had started from, and commenced a careful search, but in vain. I remained till very late and then returned slowly home, meaning to come again next morning at dawn. The Doctor had returned long before, and was in his observatory. He asked where on earth I had been to, but, seeing the *ostrich* I carried, he imagined I had been hunting after I had finished my work. He promptly demanded my notes, and told me to let him be quiet whilst he worked out the day's observations. This I need not say I was only too delighted to do, so I went to take *mate*, free for the time being. I had hardly begun when he yelled out to me to bring the aneroid he had lent me, as he wished to compare the two. Verily the sword had fallen, and I felt my life was not worth a moment's purchase. However, I had to make the best of it, and told him I was very sorry but I had left the saddlebags in the *camp*. "*Why, what in the name of the Devil did you do that for? I suppose even a stupid lunatic like you must have known I should want to compare and regulate the two instruments tonight.*" Of course, I professed extreme penitence, but said I supposed I had to go in the same direction several days, and therefore it was no good lugging them backwards and forwards. This pacified him, and then he condescended to inform me that he was much pleased with my observations, which exactly tallied with his own. So, for the moment, I was safe and we went to the tents to have a *kümmel* before dinner.

After dinner I begged to be excused from further service that night, as I had a splitting headache, and must be up very early. This favour being granted, I turned in. I had previously received my instructions as to what I was to do the next day. Emilio and the Professor played *picquet*, another game invented by Satan expressly to floor thick-headed individuals like myself. I need not say I did not sleep much, or that at dawn I was in the saddle. I did not for a moment anticipate success: anyone can imagine how difficult it is to pick up a small article which you have lost in a run of a couple of miles; but I determined not to stop searching all day, and if I had no luck, to go home and make a clean breast of it. However, today Fortune really favoured me.

As I was not hunting, I had allowed all my puppies to come out with me for a treat; I think there were 17 in all: two litters, 1 of 8 months, and 1 of 4. These little wretches raced all over the place, puppy-like, poking their noses into every hole and corner. Getting nearly to the hill where I started my unlucky hunt, they suddenly all rushed to one place and began to drag about an object, which I soon recognised as my lost saddlebags. All my *amour propre* returned immediately: I was again the embryo scientist destined with my profound knowledge to shake the civilised world. Calmly, deliberately, I picked up the bags and proceeded to lash them to my saddle with every strap and thong I could lay hands on. It was still very early, and I had not to observe till 12 o'clock, so I tied up my horse, and had 3 or 4 hours sweet sleep; after which I calmly ascended to the top of the hill, and carried out my orders to the best of my ability. I then returned quickly home, feeling a virtuous man, at peace with all the world.

On arrival, I handed in my notes to the Doctor with his aneroid. I thought he looked at me rather curiously and humorously. After examining my notes, he said they were very creditable; and then, turning sharp round, he said: *"Now tell me how you lost my instruments yesterday? And how you found them today?"* I asked how on earth he knew I had lost them, and he replied: *"By your face last night, and the high hand you took when I asked for the aneroid."* *"The loss would not have been irreparable,"* he added, *"as in that new portmanteau you are always so inquisitive about, I have a duplicate set of instruments, precisely similar to those I am using. I am sorry you have worried yourself so much; it would have been better to have told me at once."* After this there appeared to commence a deep and sincere friendship between us: he was always patient when trying to teach me anything, except *skat*; then his nature changed, and the most trifling mistake he punished with the usual sarcasm and abuse.

The days were now drawing in very fast, the nights were never without sharp frost, and the tops of the mountains were covered with snow. The boat was at last finished, covered and oiled; we had made a mast and sail and 4 oars. She was well made but, owing to the green wood employed, tremendously heavy, and it took us nearly 2 days to get her down to the lake and launch her. She was perfectly watertight, but was like a bladder in the water, and would require a pile of ballast. We made a little trial trip with 6 men in her, and then found she worked exactly right.

We removed the same day with all our gear to the little bay which we had selected as a harbour, our intention being for some of the men, with all the heavy cargo, to embark in the boat and sail down to where the River Santa Cruz joins the Lake; then, pass all our horses, follow the shores of the Lake to Río Leona (of course taking the boat with us), and then up the Leona into Lake Viedma, and so on with all the succeeding waters till we got to Sierra Gigantes and the surrounding country. These plans were never carried out, for reasons which I shall explain.

Poor Doctor Steinmann's time was growing very short and, although I knew it would be a terrible disappointment to him not to cross the river, yet it was easy to see that he could not possibly explore these lakes. And yet, as he had arranged to meet all his *confrères* somewhere near the Pass of Mendoza[15] on the other side of the Andes, I did not see how he could possibly undertake even this lake exploration. One thing was, he could not go back to the Colony alone: I should have to go with him. I knew none of the other men would give up this expedition, about which they had the wildest and ridiculous anticipations. That night we had a long *confab*, and I finally arranged to start back on the next day; and when I had deposited him in the Colony, return to my party. I think the men were rather glad of this arrangement, as they thought there would be more pickings for them.

[15] Pass of Mendoza — Located 1,200 miles N of Lago Argentino, linking the central regions of Chile and Argentina.

Return to civilisation

Delayed by fog—Recovering a cache of fossils—The horse rejects the ammonite—Bivouac on high ground—Wind, rain and snow—Useful compass bearing—Safe arrival—Grand feast—Two rest days— Photographs—Farewell at Morro Chico—Final gifts and instructions

We started in the morning[16] — the Doctor, myself and my Chilean boy, named Juan. I had to take nearly all my horses as there were 3 of us, and the Doctor had 5 or 6 cargoes of fossils and gear already, besides what we had to pick up on the road. The journey did not appear tempting; we did not dare to cling to the *Cordillera* as we had done coming out, because we might any day be caught in the first heavy snow storm which always precedes the winter; and we should have to pass a stretch of at least 40 *leagues* without a stick of wood, except what we could carry with us. The Doctor was cheerful and game enough, and said he could put up with anything — only, he must be in the Colony in a fortnight, and sooner if possible.

We made our first two marches all right, and on the second evening arrived at the headwaters of a small branch of Coy Inlet, exactly in front of where I had left the Doctor's big ammonite and the other fossils (viz. in the canyon of the Vizcachas which, as will be remembered, we had ascended to pass the *Cordillera* on our way up to Lake Santa Cruz). Leaving my companions camped in the little canyon, the next day I started to fetch the fossils, a distance of about 3 *leagues*; unfortunately, before midday, it shut in a dense fog, and I had to wait till it cleared before I could strike the place I wanted.

I packed up all the fossils carefully in a pair of large canvas saddlebags I had, and carried the ammonite in front of me. I suppose I had not put enough grass when I packed the saddlebags; at any rate, I had no sooner started than the fossils began to rattle — this quite disturbed the equanimity of my horse, who was always given to be a little skittish. I therefore got down, took the wretched fossils off and packed them well this time; and besides, lashed them both to the saddle and synch rings, so that they could not possibly move. I then tried to mount, but the

---

[16] Return to civilisation — Steinmann's biographer says: "*At the end of March, Steinmann came to Lake Santa Cruz ... where he stayed until the 10th of April.*" (Wilckens op. cit.: 391).

beast of a horse evinced a rooted objection to the ammonite, and reared and plunged, and finally pulled the reins out of my hand, turned round, and trotted off to join his chums. Luckily, his reins were dangling about his hoofs, and I hoped he would soon get foul of them and stop. Anyway, I shouldered that accursed ammonite[17] and followed in his track.

To make matters more pleasant, a drizzling mixture of rain and snow began to fall, and I was soon wet to the skin. My horse, meantime, went steadily on, only stopping where he came across a particularly tempting patch of grass, when he would wait to have a feed. On two occasions I got within a yard or two of him, and addressed him by every endearing name I could think of. No good. He would look at me, shake his head and, holding it — with a demoniacal forethought — on one side, so that the reins trailed alongside of him and he could not by any possibility tread on them, proceeded on his course rejoicing. So we went on till it was just dark, and then I could distinguish the glow of our campfire a few hundred yards distant. I now threw down the ammonite, meaning to fetch it in the morning. I really don't know how I had carried it so far, but suppose rage gave me strength. To annoy me more, what does that confounded quadruped do? Why, he no sooner saw the gleam of the fire in the distance than he stood stock still, and waited for me to come and catch him. I did so, and from that time till we reached the tent he did not have a pleasant time.

The Doctor and the boy were having supper of roast *ostrich* when I arrived, all wet and tired, and looked most easy and comfortable. This made me (why I know not) madder than before: so I got off, chucked the fossils and gear on the ground, hobbled the horse, and lashed him to a big thorn bush so that he could not move an inch; then went into the tent and threw myself on the bed. The Doctor saw there was something wrong and did not make any remarks, but cut off some of the best of the meat and passed it to me; then he said I must be bitterly cold and wet, and reproached himself with having let me go on such a day. Moreover, he fished out another flask of *kümmel* from his saddlebags, which he had evidently been keeping in reserve, and gave me a big drink, recommending I should get into bed, and let the boy dry my clothes. This I did, and was soon recounting my adventures. Warm, snug and well fed,

---

[17] Large ammonite — Greenwood says earlier that it weighed as much as 100 pounds.

I now thought of my wretched horse, and told the boy to let the poor brute go, but with his hobbles on. He really deserved some punishment. During the evening they cooked the remainder of our *ostrich*, as I was not at all certain we should strike any wood till we arrived at Gallegos Range, where we had left our provisions. The Doctor passed the rest of the evening in arranging all his treasures, wrapping every individual piece in guanaco skin.

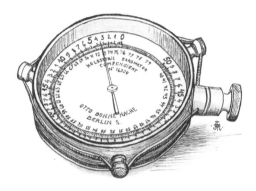

Very early in the morning we started, made a splendid march, and arrived at the long ridge, from the top of which the long desert plain I mentioned extended eight miles to Gallegos Woods. There was no shelter, except one big boulder, which we left for the horses. Passing a long rope round the rock, we tied the poor animals together, fastening them to it. It was hard on them, but we had no other means of holding them; at any rate, they had good shelter, and were all in good condition. We then made one big bed in a guanaco hole, which we covered with the tent, held down by the heavy packets of fossils. Then we crept in, had *ostrich* meat, and a little *kümmel*, and although it was one of the bitterest nights I ever experienced, slept as snugly as possible — a process which the dogs, by the warmth of their bodies, materially assisted.

The morning dawned snowing and raining, and the south wind would be blowing straight in our teeth crossing the plain; but there was no remedy, we must go on or starve. Out of the tent poles and pegs we managed to make a fire, and boil the kettle to make some *pampa tea* which, mixed with a little *kümmel*, warmed us up, and gave us energy to put on our cargoes. I had made up my mind not to stop any more till we arrived at the first *point* of *monte*. I dreaded being caught in the snow, which might fall at any moment. I told the Doctor this, and he said he would follow on as long as he could sit on horseback.

On getting up above on the plain, we were glad to find there was not much fog, and the wind was not exactly in our faces, but on the right cheek; bitterly cold, of course, at that altitude. We took the compass bearing of a point of *Cordillera* on the other side of the Gallegos, and which we could fortunately just make out. This point I knew to be almost in a line with the Dos Morros: only, steering for it, we should tumble almost on top of the place where we had left our provisions, etc. cached.

It was lucky we took this bearing, as it was very foggy during the greater part of the day. The plain was only covered by 2 or 3 inches of snow, just sufficient to make it good soft travelling for us. The horses seemed to know we were going to a land of plenty and travelled finely, almost too fast for cargo horses but, luckily, the packs were equally weighted and well lashed on, so gave no trouble. By midday we had crossed the 4th branch of Coy Inlet, and there we stopped for a quarter of an hour, tightened up all the cargoes, finished the Doctor's *kümmel* and whatever scraps of meat we could find, and then pushed on. By 4 o'clock we were in the wood, and by 5 under the trees where we had left all our gear, having made a most satisfactory march.

I note that on some days everything goes well, on others nothing — this was a good day. The Doctor had felt the cold terribly as he was thinly clad in light German clothes, but all the road he had been not only cheerful but merry; every time we stopped he would call out: "*Don Guillermo, tonight, whisky, cigars, soup, tortillas, chocolate and big, big fire*"; this he repeated at intervals, and with variations until we arrived.

Steinmann was soon up in the tree where we had stowed our things. Juan and I had the horses unloaded in a minute; here we could let them loose with safety, of course hobbling the bell-mare. We then built a big fire and put on it a big iron pail, which we had left behind us as too heavy to carry. Into this I crammed the best part of an *ostrich*, which we had caught in the woods close by. Meantime, the Doctor was raining down good things from above: flour, sugar, rice, a big skin of rum, a box of cigars, vegetables, etc., etc. Verily, we were in the land of plenty again.

It did not take long to cook the supper; when the meat was boiled we put in rice, vegetables, dumplings, etc., and there apparently was enough for a dozen people — certainly, in civilisation, there would have been. The Doctor was looking fearfully hungry (I believe he always was hungry), so I filled him one of our tin washing-basins full to the brim with the savoury mess, never thinking he could get through it all; however, he set to work stolidly, and soon emptied the basin. He then took a deep draught of wine, and peering into the pail again asked if he could have another plate full. Juan and I had finished by this time, and had had more than enough, but there still remained about a quarter of the bucket, which I promptly poured into his basin; and he as promptly devoured, drank some more wine and remarked, it was the only decent dinner he had had since we left Santa Cruz. After this he served us our cigars, and filled and lit a huge German pipe, which must have held at least an ounce of tobacco; and looked perfectly happy. We were all too tired and stiff to sit up late, so we soon turned in and needed no rocking.

A lovely day, after the bad weather we had experienced, found us out of bed pretty early. We had arranged to remain two days here, as the Doctor wanted to photograph the Morros and all the other interesting bits of country he could find; and, besides this, he had to pack up all his fossils properly. We had left a lot in the Morros, and I reckoned these would be about as many as we could manage. We passed a very quiet, nice day; everything that could be photographed, including ourselves, horses and dogs, was taken[18]. He also got a splendid view of a big flock of guanacos, which came feeding close to the camp. We had another grand banquet in the evening, and afterwards I was initiated into the mysteries of another German game called *pinocle*, very amusing and not complicated like *skat*, so I got on all right.

By the following morning, all was fixed up neatly and ready for the march. I was going to remain where I was and look after the horses, sending Juan in with the Doctor, only accompanying them across the 3 branches of the river as far as Morro Chico, from whence they could not possibly miss the road to Laguna Blanca and the Colony. I confess

---

[18] Photographs at Dos Morros — Unfortunately, Steinmann's Patagonian photographs have been lost.

I felt sad at the idea of parting from my kind though eccentric friend; and when, after crossing the 3 rivers safely, we arrived at the Morro Chico and camped together for the last time, I think we both felt quite sad. I helped them lash on their cargoes, and said goodbye early in the morning.

The Doctor's farewell was characteristic; he said in a mixture of English and Spanish: *"Friend Don Guillermo, I hate de English, all are stupid, all are proud, all are useless, but I luv (love) you and always shall."* Here he turned, grasped my hand once more, and galloped after the cargoes.

When Juan returned, he brought with him in good order all the provisions, etc. I had ordered, and an entire cargo of presents from the kind Doctor: long boots (each of which contained a bottle of champagne, and a bottle of whisky), warm clothes of every description, also biscuits, German sausages and sweets, not forgetting a quantity of chocolate for drinking. Besides these, there was a box containing the aneroid I had lost, thermometers, and other simple instruments, and a long manuscript of instructions explaining exactly what observations I was to take during the winter months. I had promised him to do this before we said goodbye and I kept my word for two years, sending results to Strasbourg at the end of each of my journeys. Although he has both written and also, until lately, sent me some present every year, I have never seen him again[19].

---

[19] Additional exploration — During his time in Southern Patagonia, Steinmann also visited Mount Tarn, Otway Water, and the channels of Tierra del Fuego. He embarked for central Chile in June 1883. (Wilckens op. cit.: 391). His name is honoured by a promontory (Punta Steinman [sic]), located on the S shore of Otway Water (LAT. 53° 06' S, LONG. 71° 26' W).

᎐᙮ 13 ᙮᎐

Volcano of the Giants in Eruption

Return to Santa Cruz valley—Rumbles and flames in night sky—Dense cloud of ash, difficulty breathing—Horses disappear—Fresh-water spring—Huge volcanic plume—Shifting winds—Seven suffocating days—Horses found emaciated—Companions nearby, suffer worse

I must return to my companions exploring, or supposed to be exploring, on the north side of the River Santa Cruz[1].

Having deposited Doctor Steinmann in the Colony, Juan returned punctually to the day in Laguna Blanca, where I met him according to promise. One thing did not quite please me, and that was that he had picked up another boy to help him on the way out — no less a person than Angel Brunel, the son of that ill-fated and vicious family, of whom Ascencio[2] was the brightest jewel. This lad had been employed with Englishmen all his life, and was better than the rest of the family; he had no means of living at the time, so I gave him leave to accompany us. I am glad I did so: our cargoes were many and heavy, and the roads, at the commencement of winter, very bad — the lad proved both useful and willing, and was of the greatest assistance on the trip.

We marched therefore directly for the north, hoping even yet to find some means of crossing the Santa Cruz and joining our party. The weather

---

[1] Date of these events — The narrative begins in or about June 1883, directly after the Steinmann expedition.
[2] Brother of Angel Brunel — See 14, Ascencio Brunel, Horse Thief.

187

was against us — in violent gales, snow squalls and thick fog — so that
we could only march about one day in three; and then had literally to
plough our way along in some places. I think it must have been fully
twenty days before we arrived at the most northern branch of Coy Inlet,
only a short distance from where we had parted from our companions.
We could not camp near the stream as the whole valley was one bog, but
we found a little lake on the top of the *pampa*, north side, and camped
where there were plenty of bushes, but very little grass; however, as we
intended remaining only the night, it did not matter.

The night appeared unusually dark and dreary, but was occasionally
lit up by big rumbling reports, sometimes lasting minutes, and sounding
like cannon shots. At times the whole northern horizon was lit with an
unearthly glow, from which spurts of flame occasionally shot out, apparently to an enormous height. We did not pass a very comfortable night
in the midst of all the strange phenomena; and the next morning did not
reassure us, as a dense cloud covered the entire country, and you could not
see five yards before you. Moreover, the entire atmosphere was impregnated with a fine white ash, which soon covered the entire country to a
depth of more than an inch and a half.

The tent was literally covered with these ashes, and we had to keep
shaking it to prevent the weight bearing it down. Breathing became
extremely difficult; we were parched with thirst, and had a horrible bitter taste from the lead and copper atmosphere we were inhaling[3].

The horses had disappeared altogether, and we could not go and look
for them. On trying the water of the lake, we found it was bitter as gall;
but, luckily, there was a small spring bubbling out under the bank, which,
being protected, was beautifully sweet and fresh. From this we filled all
our available utensils, and took them under the tent (covering them up
carefully), where we all three retired as soon as possible, closing up every
aperture, so that this death-giving air could not enter.

We passed a wretched time half-stifled for some hours, till about mid-
afternoon, when a strong breeze sprung up from the south, driving back
the dense ash clouds to the north. I shall never forget the relief when we
could again go outside and breathe fresh air; we all climbed the nearest

---

[3] Airborne ash — Greenwood further adds: "*I took into the Colony a bag full of these
ashes; Dr. Fenton analysed them, and he told me there was nothing but lead and copper
represented in them; for this reason, I term them 'Lead and Copper Ashes'.*"

hill to see what we could. The horses had completely disappeared — no wonder, poor things — with neither water, nor grass, that they could swallow, they had to clear out or die.

From behind Chaltén rose an immense pillar of dense black smoke from which, at long intervals, shot out bright flames accompanied by loud reports. The deep muttering, rumbling or throbbing sound (I know not how to describe it) was certainly more awe-inspiring than anything I ever heard.

This column of smoke apparently rose to a height of some hundred yards[4], and then spread out into a huge fan-shaped mass, more like a huge ostrich-feather *plumero* than anything else I can think of. There was evidently some strong current of air up above, which swept the masses

---

[4] Height of volcanic plume — Greenwood's figure of *"some hundred yards"* is insufficient, given the great distance from his point of observation.

of smoke down to the earth again. The wind now shifted again right to the northward, and in a few moments we were again enveloped in the dense, sickening ash cloud. We had, however, stopped up all interstices in the tent and covered the doors with blankets, so that this infernal ash could not get in. As it was, our mouths were sore and our tongues and lips parched and blistered: no amount of water seemed to cool them, and a constant sick feeling on our stomachs did not tend to improve matters.

This kind of thing lasted just 7 days without ceasing; had it not been for the changes of wind — which occurred at intervals and gave us fresh air and life — we could not have lived. The 4th day of the eruption was the worst of all, but after that the south wind blew more constantly and strongly, giving us longer intervals to breathe every day. On the eighth morning there was a hard frost, and the sun rose bright and clear, and no more smoke ascended from the volcano. Were it not for the extraordinary grey appearance of the grass and bushes, and the bitterness of the water, none could have imagined what an extraordinary convulsion of Nature had taken place.

The first thing was to recover our horses, so we all set out in different directions to look for them. I soon found tracks in the valley of the Coy Inlet just below us; no trouble to follow them, owing to the quantity of mud in the valley formed by the previous heavy rain. I caught up with them about three in the afternoon, feeding on short tufts of grass amongst a quantity of large boulders, which had protected the pasturage from the deadly ash fall. No one who did not witness it can imagine the difference there was in these poor animals in only a few short days. Eight days ago, when we let them go, they were all in good condition and fit for a long trip; now they were as thin as laths — in some, the bones appeared almost sticking through their skins. We drove the poor wretches down close to the camping place, and left them on the edge of the river where they could always pick up a few mouthfuls of washed green grass, and get a good drink of running water, although even that was bitter.

We were most anxious about our companions, but need not have been so. It seems they had passed the river safely, losing one horse (belonging to me of course), had then left the boat, and marched on horseback up Río Leona to Lake Viedma. They found game very scarce, as there were signs of a large body of Indians having been recently camped there, and they had completely cleared the *camp*. In fact, our friends were almost entirely destitute of provisions, and had to pass their time in hunting, and did no exploring at all. Finding it quite impossible to get meat, they resolved to return to the Santa Cruz and meet me. This they did, and re-crossed the river the very day the eruption commenced.

When this took place they were simply terrified, and made tracks for the south to escape from the ash fall, which, being nearer to the volcano was, of course, far worse than with us. They must have passed close to where we were, and during all the time we were prisoners, were camped down the Coy Inlet branch, about two miles from our tent. Here they suffered even more than ourselves, as they had nothing but meat to eat, and very often not even that; and they had no nice spring (as we had) and were obliged to drink the bitter river water. We, of course, plentifully supplied with provisions — even to wine and rum and various tinned meats — were, compared to our poor companions, in comparative clover.

Seeing that the horses would never be able to carry our heavy cargoes in their present state, I took the best one and rode down to the Santa Cruz, where we had left our companions when we went south. Here I found the boat hidden in a big bush, and a letter telling me they had had to clear south again. I returned home immediately, and the next day we were all together again.

"Catch me, who can!"

༷ 14 ༷

Ascencio Brunel, Horse Thief

Formative Experiences

Employed as a lad—Good-looking, but inveterate liar—Captain del Castillo accuses Ascencio of stealing his horses—Hired as del Castillo's guide—Sent to steal another man's horses—Greenwood disgusted, leaves expedition—Ascencio is denied his reward

Perhaps it is not right to call attention to a person of this description and might do harm, not only to the man himself — by making him consider himself a hero — but also by encouraging others to follow his bad example. However, Ascencio Brunel is, or was, such a well-known character in our part of the world (Southern Patagonia), and caused so much excitement during the period in which he was carrying on his depredations, that I think he deserves some mention ... if only to point out what a thoroughly unprincipled young scoundrel he was and, if alive, probably still is — unless he has (as is reported) come to an untimely end.

Ascencio was working for me as a lad of all work for nearly three years, and I know all his family and their antecedents, from the time they first arrived in Punta Arenas[1]. I can't say the stock was a particularly good one. I forget the exact number of the family, but their name was

---

[1] Brunel family — It is estimated that the Brunel family arrived in Punta Arenas from the Falkland Islands between 1885 and 1890. (Martinic 1980: 198–202).

legion, and both boys and girls, with the exception of the eldest son, who is a steady well-principled man, were a wild, unprincipled lot. Having made the Falkland Islands (whence they migrated to Sandy Point) too hot to hold them, they commenced to work on the same scale in their new country; others, I think, broke even their own record, which is saying a good deal. The boys of the family, being all first-class *gauchos*, and understanding all about sheep and farm work, soon found employment on different farms — and better workmen would not be desired — but they never, by any chance, remained long in any one place: they were rolling stones, and consequently gathered no moss.

As I wanted a handy lad to assist me in my hunting and exploring work, I employed Ascencio (then a lad of eight or nine years old) as a kind of general servant. I found him a very fair little servant, as far as handiness and general intelligence went; but a more consummate little liar and thief never existed. I tried to educate him and one of his brothers but, although they were particularly bright and clever, it was impossible to drive anything really into their heads — they would learn a thing one day and forget it the next — and, as for instilling anything like principles of truth and honour into them, that was an utter impossibility.

After being with me for several years, the lad left me and joined some of his brothers, who were leading a wild life in the *camp*, sometimes hunting and sometimes trading with the Indians. From that time, I think, the boy's gradual descent from bad to worse commenced. Living amongst savages — or, what is worse, semi-savage white men, utterly uneducated, with no principles of honour, and whose every other word was an oath or an indecency — what wonder that the poor boy contracted evil habits, and received the slight impetus which was alone wanting to assist him in his downward career. It was some time before I met him again: from a boy, he had sprung up into a man, well-made and very good-looking in exterior; as to his morals and general character, the less said the better, as subsequent events fully proved.

Still, I do not believe that, even then, he was past reclaiming. Had he met with some really good man, to help him to an honest livelihood and assist him with good advice, I really believe he could have become a useful member of society; but, as is invariably the case, there was not wanting a man of influence and position to give him the evil lesson — that he was only too ready to receive — and to materially assist in launching him on the evil career he finally adopted.

⁂

An expedition was organised by the authorities of Gallegos for the exploration of some of the interior *camps*, with a view to their colonisation. The chief of this party was the late Captain Agustín del Castillo (Commander in the Argentine Navy). Captain del Castillo was, at the time I refer to, carrying on his explorations at the headwaters of the river Gallegos. Ascencio Brunel was hunting in the same district but was not, I believe, aware that any other party were camped in his vicinity.

One morning he found several strange horses mixed up with his own. He did not steal them, as was reported — I know for a fact that he did not even know that anyone was camped in his vicinity. Anyway, in the usual way, he took charge of the animals, intending no doubt to claim the usual amount per head, which is always given to a man who recovers lost animals: he made no attempt at concealment. Captain del Castillo, who was looking for his animals, discovered them in Brunel's possession. It appears that he accused the man of having stolen them but, nevertheless, he invited the young man to join his party, and act as *campañista* and guide. Ascencio willingly accepted the offer, and became a member of the expedition.

At this time, I must mention that a great deal of ill-feeling existed between the two Republics (that is, between Argentines and Chileans). A short time previously, some horses belonging to Captain del Castillo were stolen by an Argentine soldier deserting to join the Chileans, and were sold by him to one of the provincial farmers named Dacquet, who owned a large establishment in Cape Negro. Certain it is, that M. Dacquet had no right to purchase these animals without the necessary certificates, but he did so. The news, of course, arrived at Captain del Castillo's ears, and he vowed reprisals. I must mention that there was no question as to the ownership of the horses, but the Frenchman declined to give them up unless the money he had paid for the stolen animals was refunded to him: it was only a nominal sum, not worth the trouble of quarrelling about, but so it was. Captain del Castillo paid for his horses and got them back, but he did not forget the affair and vowed reprisals.

When he met with the ill-starred Ascencio, he found the very man he wanted. Partly by threats, and partly by the promise of a reward of two hundred dollars if he succeeded in doing what he was told to do, he persuaded Ascencio to go in to Cape Negro and steal one of M. Dacquet's *tropillas*. Of course, the lad (only too ready to follow any evil advice) readily consented. He set off for Cape Negro, and in about ten days returned with the pick of M. Dacquet's horses, which he had, according to orders, stolen in the night.

I joined the expedition two or three days previous to Ascencio's return, intending to act as guide to the expedition[2], and take them to Lakes Santa Cruz and Viedma, and to other places well known to me. On my arrival, I missed Ascencio and, on enquiring for him, was told by the Commander that he had sent for him to Cape Negro to carry off some of the Frenchman's horses, as return or reprisal for what he (Captain del Castillo) had suffered at M. Dacquet's hands. I can assure my readers that I did not believe this statement, but thought it was only a joke. It appeared to me a deed of this sort was quite out of the question: this was only a private question, nothing whatever to do with the Republics of Argentina and Chile. There was bad blood enough between the two nations as it was, without increasing the amount by private feuds.

However, a day or two afterwards, Ascencio appeared with the stolen horses, which, of course, I immediately recognised. This was very early in the morning, and I immediately told my servant to disarm my tent[3], pack up and prepare to march. Whilst this order was in preparation, Captain del Castillo strolled over to my camping place and asked what I was doing. I simply replied that I did not care to accompany the expedition any further, and was going to clear out. I gave no reason for so doing; nor, I imagine, was it needed.

---

[2] Prior expedition — William Greenwood and François Poivre had previously accompanied Captain Agustín del Castillo as guides during a short exploration in 1887. In his official report, the Captain recognised Greenwood's valuable contribution. (Del Castillo 2007: 63 et. seq.).

[3] "Disarm my tent" — The intended meaning is "disassemble"; Greenwood may have inadvertently used the equivalent Spanish term "*desarmar*".

I never saw the Captain again, or heard that he did anything very wonderful in his exploring work. He only arrived as far as Lake Santa Cruz, where he camped in a well-known valley in which I had passed six previous winters. After hunting all the winter, and making the best collection of skins and feathers possible with a view to profit, the expedition returned to Gallegos, where they were received with much enthusiasm. They deserved it, as there is no doubt they had done what so many other expeditions have done, viz. spent the largest possible quantity of money in doing the least possible good. If this remark appears severe, it is at least absolutely correct.

To return to Ascencio: on arriving at Lake Santa Cruz, there was some misunderstanding between him and some of the others, and he determined to clear out — not surreptitiously, but in a straightforward manner. He therefore went to the Captain, and asked for the money he had earned for stealing Dacquet's horses, according to order. He was laughed at in reply and told that, if he was not careful, he would be sent to prison as a horse-stealer! This was the last straw: the one thing which was required to launch him on his reckless career. The next morning he was missing, together with his brother Ricardo and a Chilean named Anacleto and his wife, whom Captain del Castillo had picked up on his road and induced to join the expedition. It is now necessary to state that they did not go without horses: in fact, they took some of the best animals belonging to the explorers.

They passed the *Cordillera* surrounding Lake Santa Cruz in a place quite unknown to anyone except myself and one or two others, amongst them Ascencio, who had passed there with me on two previous occasions. No attempt was made to follow Brunel and his companions: of course, it would have been useless to attempt it, because there was not a single man amongst Castillo's party who knew anything about the *camp*, far less about the dangerous passes in the mountains. The exploring party remained on Lake Santa Cruz, hunting and generally enjoying themselves, and in October returned to Gallegos. From thence, Captain del Castillo went to Buenos Aires, there to receive the praise and general ovations, which he so well merited[4].

Murder and Imprisonment

Ascencio and brother Ricardo form party with Anacleto, wife and child—Anacleto murdered—Ascencio and widow denounce Ricardo—Both brothers arrested and detained—Doctor Arthur Fenton examines corpse at scene of the crime—Fenton's disappointment—Prison in Río Gallegos

Well, we will follow the fortunes of Ascencio and his party and recount — as far as they are known — the circumstances of the tragedy that followed. They crossed the *Cordillera* in safety and, striking the headwaters of the Coy Inlet River, determined to winter there. The Chilean Anacleto had with him, as I believe I mentioned, his wife, also a young child; the former, a very prepossessing young woman, who had been an old sweetheart of both the brothers Brunel.

It appears that, very soon, bad blood arose between the husband and his two companions. It is not necessary to say this was caused by the presence of the woman, with whom both the brothers Brunel were, after their fashion, in love. At any rate, affairs arrived at such a pitch that the brothers determined to kill the husband and take possession of his wife. Therefore, one (or both) of them took him by surprise, and before he could defend himself smashed his skull with their *boleadoras*, leaving him exactly as he fell — no trouble about burying, or anything of that sort. They then saddled up and returned north again, by another route, intending to travel to Chubut or Río Negro and so avoid justice.

By forming a boat of their tent and tent poles, they got safely across the River Santa Cruz, and might have got clear away, had they agreed. As it was, they quarrelled (probably about the lady) and one day, when the elder brother Ricardo was away, Ascencio very quietly saddled-up and cleared out with the woman, tent and everything else. Instead of going north, they went straight down to Santa Cruz, and reported the whole affair to the authorities there, accusing Ricardo Brunel of the murder. They were, of course, immediately arrested and conveyed to

---

[4] Events in Buenos Aires — Del Castillo died in January 1889, shortly after completing this new and longer expedition, before he was able to deliver his official report.

Gallegos, where they reiterated their statements. Personally, I do not doubt that Ricardo Brunel was the instigator and prime mover in the affair; but, without doubt, both of them were mixed up in it. Anyway, both the brothers were taken to the headquarters, and confined there pending further enquiries.

On receiving the news of the murder, and the exact place where it took place being discovered to them, the authorities in Gallegos sent out a Commission, headed by Dr. Arturo Fenton, the resident medical officer, to inspect the place and the remains of the victim. They found everything just as it had been described by the brothers Brunel.

A curious, and rather ridiculous, circumstance took place when the Doctor was examining the remains. Of course, the body was in the last stage of decomposition, but it was necessary for the Doctor to make a thorough examination, so he set to work on his repugnant task without the smallest hesitation. The skull of the victim being quite unrecognisable, and moreover full of black beetles and other insects, Doctor Fenton came to the conclusion that the best way to thoroughly examine it was to make a fire, singe the skull thoroughly, and then examine the fractures. He therefore severed the head from the body and, a good fire being made by his Indian guides, he proceeded to singe and 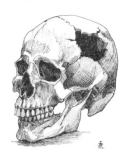 clean it, doubtless in the most approved medical fashion. The guides stood open-mouthed watching his proceedings and, finally, one of them asked Doctor Fenton what he was doing this for. He, being full of fun and doubtless quite in his element, replied laughing: "*What am I doing, boys? ... Why, you don't suppose I am going to lose this opportunity of having a good breakfast, do you?*" The men stared at him and then turned and fled from the presence of the cannibal Doctor.

This story he told me himself in his office, being engaged at the same time in cleaning and polishing the before-mentioned skull, before sending it to the authorities for inspection. He evidently considered this occupation a most entertaining and amusing one, and remarked that he was going to keep it amongst his collection of curiosities. I think he was nearly heartbroken when the Judge declined to return it to him, as it was required by the authorities as one of the proofs of the crime.

Shortly afterwards, Ascencio, who in company with his brother Ricardo was confined in a small zinc shed[5] close to the Government house, managed to escape.

Escape   *

Greenwood visits the prisoners—Horrible conditions—Brothers obtain files—Ascencio escapes—Forced to live by stealing—Arrives at Dos Morros—Frightens Greenwood's horses under cover of darkness—Steals the two best ones—Greenwood would have stood up for him

I happened to be in Gallegos when these two poor wretches were confined in their zinc prison, and by special favour obtained permission to visit them[6]. Being born in the Falkland Islands, all the Englishmen had an interest in them, although — heaven knows — they did not deserve it.

It was a broiling day and, on entering the little shed (about 8 feet by 6), I thought I was in an oven!! What the poor, wretched confined were suffering I cannot bear to think; but it must have been terrible — verily their sin had found them out, and with a vengeance. There was a tin of lukewarm water placed between them, but they were so heavily ironed that it is difficult to say if they could reach it. I tried to say a few kind and encouraging words to them, but it was in vain. The younger brother said nothing. The elder (Ricardo) broke out into a torrent of imprecations and curses, principally directed against his brother. He told him that he was a d—d fool, but for whom they might at that time be passing a jolly time, with everything they required at their fingers' ends. He also, before me, cursed his brother and told him he would cut his throat if ever he got the chance. Then Ascencio turned his head, smiled, and said to me: *"Two can play at that game, can't they, Don Guillermo?"* What could I say to men like these who, so far from regretting what they had done, seemed to glory in it?

I left them, promising to ask the commanding officer to relax their discipline a little. It appeared to me that useless torture was only calculated to fill evil minds like theirs with more terrible ideas than they already

---

[5] Zinc shed — Built of galvanised corrugated iron.
[6] Greenwood's visit to the jail in Río Gallegos — This probably occurred during 1889, since the Brunel brothers had been held prisoners that year. (Correspondence 1889).

possessed. The Lieutenant in charge of the prisoners, Señor Rivadavia, promised to do so; and not only that, but released a poor wrecked sailor (who was in prison for some trivial offence) at my request.

As usual, a parenthesis: this same sailor, George Wheeler, hearing three years afterwards that I was in the neighbourhood, walked 15 miles to thank me for what I had done for him. I had done nothing, just a few words said kindly. Never say, then, that there is no human kindness or gratitude to be found in anyone. I make this remark because a man said these words to me, a few days ago.

To return to the prisoners: their discipline was slightly relaxed, chains loosened etc., and they were allowed to hobble about outside their prison and converse with the soldiers. They appear to have both of them picked up friends; at any rate, they got files somehow, and started on the difficult task of filing off their irons. Ascencio appears to have been the best hand at this work, for he was all clear long before his brother. One night he suddenly threw off his fetters, rushed to the sentinel's horse which was picketed close to the little prison house, cut the *cabestro* and, leaping on horseback, cried out *"Catch me, who can!"* and cleared out. Of course, no one could follow him, as it was a dark night, and there was no other horse saddled.

Well, this young scamp, it appears, did not go away at all, but took a double round the back of the Government house and hid himself in the bushes (or in some corner of the beach), where he remained till the following night — receiving, of course, assistance from some friend in the vicinity. He then quietly came back to the town, and actually stole the favourite horse of the Governor. Mounted on this, he made straight for the *Cordillera* and his old haunts. He visited Laguna Blanca *en route*, there broke into several *camp* houses occupied by shepherds, and provided himself with all he needed; but he was so cunning that no one even saw or even heard him.

At this period, I was camped in the Dos Morros, at the junction of the rivers Turbio and Gallegos; and, as my evil fortune would have it, Ascencio came straight to my place. It was a pitch-dark night and raining hard, so I turned into my tent unusually early. As usual, my dogs were in the tent with me, most of them sleeping under the bedclothes, the others probably dreaming of future *ostrich* hunts. At any rate, none of them heard or suspected anything — neither did their master.

I had my two best horses tied up close to the tent, and meant to have a good hunt in the morning, having seen a *point* of *baguales* in the vicinity. Ascencio must have been watching me, or he could not have acted as cleverly as he did; anyway, he crept up and cut the ropes of the two guard-horses (a *moro* and an *azulejo*), and led them off. I could see the tracks in the morning as the *camp* was full of mud (as is nearly always the case in the month of September) and could therefore trace his proceedings exactly.

What happened was this. In the night, the first thing I heard was a stampede of the whole *tropilla*, and the dogs rushed out *en masse* and started barking. Of course, I turned out, but it was pitch-dark and raining and I could do nothing at all — I could not even see that my two guard-horses were missing. In the morning, at daylight, I was up, and at once saw that all my animals were gone, even down to the two I had tied up. The only animal near the camping place was a poor little *petizo* horse, standing with his head down and looking disgusted with life in general. He had reason, as he was not only terribly spur-marked, but had a hole in his back as big as a cheese-plate. I saw at once what had happened, and started off to look for and follow the tracks, which were only too apparent in the wet state of the *camp*.

It is not a pleasant thing to be left in the *camp*, even if you are near your own house; far less so when you are 200 miles from any civilised place, and all the rivers are swollen and overflowing. In the summer it would not matter, but in winter or early spring it is no joke. Anyway, I took my rifle and a pair of reins and followed steadily on the tracks. It was very fortunate for me that the ground was so muddy, as it rendered my task much less difficult than it would have otherwise been. Moreover, two of the mares had young foals and, of course, would hang behind, so I was almost sure to find some of my animals. So it turned out for, exactly at the junction of the two rivers, there were the whole lot of animals, quietly feeding; I very soon had them back at my tent. Of course the two best horses, which I had had tied up, were not to the fore. With these two animals, Ascencio commenced his horse-stealing career.

Now, I dearly loved my two stolen horses and, had anyone else robbed me, I would have got them back or died in the attempt. But, this young ruffian had been taught by myself all I knew, and had learned a great deal more than I could teach him. I was quite alone at the time; how could I tell but that, if I left my tent and followed in his tracks, he would not double on me and come back and loot my tent and take away my *tropilla*? I had a heavy cargo of skins and feathers, a little gold, and my general outfit: to lose these would mean to me absolute ruin. I therefore determined to put up with my first loss, and trust to Providence to find my two favourite horses later on. (In this case, Providence failed me, and I never saw them again.)

Please let everyone remember that I do not believe this lad would have robbed me in cold blood. I am sure he would, at any time, have risked his life for me; but he was pressed, the bloodhounds were on his heels, so what could he do? I confess frankly (and am not ashamed to do so) that, had he come to me — like a man — and told me the whole story (as I fully believe it took place), I would have assisted him to escape to the north. He was not bad by nature; but evil companions and worse advice had brought him down and trodden him into the mud.

✿ 15 ✿

Sheep, Shepherds and Sheep Farmers

Warning to Shepherds

Valuable part of local economy—Sheep neither docile, intelligent or amiable—A stressful occupation—Isolation—Management of flocks— The art of swearing

A s these *"intelligent, useful, docile, and affectionate animals"* are now the mainstay of our Patagonian prosperity, I am quite sure that the flocks, their owners and their shepherds deserve a long article to themselves. As both flocks and owners are mixed up together, I will give them my very best attention, and only trust I shall not offend any of my old friends or acquaintances by my criticisms. I hope any of the farmers or shepherds in the south who may read this will remember that for many years I lived with them and was, like themselves, completely wrapped up in the business of sheep-farming.

Of course, all I write must be taken *cum grano salis*; I want to amuse people, to criticise a little, and to give those who know little or nothing about our doings in the farming way some idea as to how we work and how we progress.

I am sorry to say I have no experience as to how farms are managed in other parts of the world: all I learned came from men who had had much experience in several countries. Many of my instructors had profited by their years of work and knew that there was always something to learn; others, on the contrary, with perhaps less experience, considered that they were perfect and thought they knew everything. From the former I learned much, from the latter I learned nothing, as I soon found that many of their ideas were radically false and wrong.

204

The expressions I commence this chapter with, on the intelligence, etc. of sheep, were used by a friend of mine — one of our principal and most experienced farmers — in a conversation I had with him some years ago. Of course, no one would ever dream of denying that sheep are most useful and invaluable animals; but, as to their docility, intelligence and general amiability, I am afraid I must differ most totally from my friend.

The Good Shepherd mentioned in the Bible must have been endowed with extraordinary quantities of goodness, patience and endurance if he really loved his flock; and the sheep themselves must have been pattern sheep — not to be compared with ours in Patagonia. I am quite sure that none of my animals would ever follow me or come to my call: on the contrary, whatever they could do to annoy me they invariably did. As a rule they resent kindness, scorn affection, and do all they possible can to drive their owners and their shepherds into raving lunacy.

The only really comfortable time I personally experienced in the course of the year's sheep work was when I had seen the flocks shorn, dipped off the shears, the shearers paid off, the wool all baled up, carted sixty-five miles and shipped — and when I had the Bills of Lading and Insurance in my pocket. Then I felt I had done my duty and could enjoy myself for a week or two. This was not, however, as a rule, very easy for, go where I might, or do what I could, the old cares followed me. I was always wondering: *"How are the sheep doing? How are the shepherds working? Are the flocks scabby? Are the lions killing?"* etc., etc., and I was really glad when the time came to return home again.

After ten years' absolute devotion to my flocks I was really tired out and could stand the worry and anxiety no longer, so I sold out and went home to spend the money. This pursuit I must confess was very much more to my taste; and it appeared, by the way in which my really hard-earned gains melted away, that I had quite a talent in the way of spending money. At least, I know it disappeared in a most extraordinary manner: in fact, it vanished just as the sheep used to vanish, in a moment almost. Only, the worst of it was that none of the money I had spent ever came back again, while some of the lost sheep used — as a rule — to turn up again. However, it is no good grieving over spilt milk, so I must try and make some use of the experience I gained in these ten long years.

I shall commence, therefore, with a few comments on, and a general sketch of, the way we manage — or mismanage — our flocks and herds, which may be interesting to sheep owners in the north; and, if I do no other good, I may perhaps, by writing this article, assist some one going to try his luck down south with some ideas.

I should strongly advise anyone who starts on this venture to be prepared to pass a very lonely, monotonous life. There he will find no amusement (except hunting and shooting), no church, no theatres and very little society of any kind — and what there is, a long way off. It is utterly useless even to think of becoming a real, genuine, typical Patagonian farmer unless you can make up your mind to give yourself up entirely, body and soul, to the sheep and their wellbeing.

When you arrive at the stage of being able to *"think of nothing else, dream of nothing else, eat nothing but mutton, sleep on nothing but sheepskins, and begin not only to feel like a sheep but look like one,"* then you can begin to entertain some hopes of — eventually — becoming all a shepherd should be.

Besides this, you must thoroughly learn the art of swearing. If a sheep is sworn at in an ordinary way, he does not take the least notice of it. It is absolutely necessary to combine the talents of a Thames bargee[1], a sailor before the mast, a London costermonger[2], and two or three years' experience as a Patagonian shepherd, before you can hope to talk to your flock in a sufficiently explicit manner, and to convince it that you are a Patagonian shepherd, and worthy of being a sheep-owner in the future.

---

[1] Bargee — Crewman of a barge (traditionally, with a reputation for cursing).
[2] Costermonger — Person who sells fruits and vegetables in the street by shouting about his wares (hence, someone loud).

I remember, when I first took up the business under the tuition of a dear old friend of mine (who is certainly one of the most quiet and gentlemanly men I ever met), that we were (in company with half a dozen shepherds) trying to drive a refractory lot of *hoggets* into the pens. They were a particularly obstinate lot, and every one of the men was doing his level best (in his choicest language) to convince them that into the pens they must go. Several of my friend's children came out to watch the proceedings; it appeared to me it was hardly the place for them, and I said as much to my old chum. He replied: *"Really, G., I have not heard anything wrong."* At this moment a *point* of the *hoggets* tried to break out close to us and … you should have been present to hear how their owner talked to them. The air was absolutely blue for five minutes as it was absolutely necessary for the owner to set a good example, and in this case — I must say — he excelled himself. When the excitement was over, I quietly remarked to him: *"I say, old man, I thought there was no swearing going on!"* He immediately realised the situation and vented his wrath on the children, whom he told, in the clearest possible terms, to clear out and not come near the pens again. This is really a fact, and told just as it occurred.

The previous story carries out what I said before, viz. that sheep are not the most amiable, intelligent and affectionate animals in the world, as my enthusiastic friend declared them to be; and indeed, in my opinion, a more than ordinary amount of good temper is necessary if a man wishes to make what I consider a good shepherd.

Of course, like everything else, sheep farming requires a lot of learning. For example, one of the great mistakes is in using so many dogs, and dogging the sheep incessantly. Moreover, dogs should not be allowed in the pens, as it leads to so much crushing and mauling; and, in a country where so much inflammation is prevalent, it is most important that your flocks should be neither over-heated nor bruised. I have noted that the death rate from this disease is generally doubled after a badly arranged gathering. Especially at the last dip before the shearing, and at the lamb-marking season, the greatest caution should be taken in handling the sheep. Lambs are particularly liable to die of this complaint if they are at all hurried or bruised. On one occasion we lost no fewer than six hundred lambs out of two thousand which we had marked: all died within thirty-six hours from the time of marking. This was in the first season I ever had charge of a lamb-marking; after this I was more careful, and we did not, as a rule, lose more than 3 or 4 per cent. — sometimes not that number.

A really good man, who understands his work, will easily find employment and receive, at the rate of £5 or £6 per month, a house free of rent, a *tropilla* of seven or nine horses according to the nature of his work, a piece of garden ground and meat *ad libitum*. He will, of course, have to keep himself in provisions, which will be sold to him at a very cheap rate by the master of the farm. Every large establishment keeps a store for the benefit of the men, and also to avoid the employees having to go to Santa Cruz or Punta Arenas for their stores, which entails a loss of five or six days' work.

Some of the principal farmers on the Straits of Magellan and vicinity commenced as mere shepherds, and in a few years saved enough to commence business on their own account. The principal farmers are always willing to assist one who has served them well and, if the man is trustworthy, will sell him sheep to start with at very reasonable rates.

The Problem of Scab

Scabby flocks—Dipping and other precautions—Prevention is better than cure—An obstacle to prosperity—Intervention by the authorities

To any newcomer who wishes to start a farm, I should recommend extreme caution in purchasing his stock. Some of the farms are completely impregnated with scab and, although the flocks may have been most carefully tended and dipped again and again, and appear perfectly clean, the disease invariably breaks out again — if not in the old sheep, then in the lambs, which are very often born scabby, a sure sign that it runs in the blood.

The greatest possible care should be taken at every dip that no stray sheep are left out. Any sheep that is not strong enough to reach the pens should be killed and the carcass burned; any exceptionally bad cases had better be parted out and kept in a paddock, if possible, and should be dipped two or three times in succession, at intervals of not more than 12 or 14 days.

I managed, by the use of two invaluable dips, to keep my flocks very fairly clean; and, I believe, should never have had occasion to dip the sheep more than once a year, had it not been for the constant stragglers coming in — either from neighbouring farms, or from passing flocks arriving from the north (of which the shepherds would carelessly leave any tired or diseased animal behind, without taking the trouble to destroy it).

The sheep farmer must bear in mind that prevention is better than cure; don't let him think that because the sheep appear clean they are clean. If once scab has got hold of a flock, it is almost impossible to eradicate it; but a judicially timed dipping may save hundreds of pounds and the loss of many sheep. I should also recommend to all managers and shepherds the most urgent necessity of keeping their *camps* absolutely clean; let any old wool or dead sheep found be burned at once, and any bush which has wool hanging to it or signs of the sheep rubbing against it should also be burned. Also the posts of the fences and *corrals* should be painted or tarred from time to time. No precaution should be omitted to reduce the probabilities of scab getting hold of your sheep.

Everyone knows that the best and the most careful man may get scab amongst his flocks; but, if the precautions I mention are taken, the chances are a hundred to one that, although you may not be quite clear of this terrible pest, you will be far better off than your more careless neighbours. It must be remembered that it is not only the loss in deaths that you have to encounter: it is the terrible expense of dipping, the reduction of your wool-clip by perhaps 40% or 50%, the constant increase of expenses by the necessary employment of more hands — let alone the trouble, anxiety and general wear and tear suffered by masters, men, horses and dogs. Therefore, sheep farmer: above all things, avoid the scab, or at least counteract it as much as possible.

Still on the topic of scab: as I mentioned previously, the great prevalence of scab amongst the flocks is one great drawback to the prosperity of the colonist and farmer in Santa Cruz and the vicinity. It is only for the last few years that any sheep farms worthy of the name existed there, and dipping was a thing almost unknown — the results can be imagined.

The original colonists were not more than a dozen altogether; none of them possessed more than a few hundred sheep, and never even attempted to dip them. As long as they had a sheep to kill when they wanted it, and managed to get half a dozen bales of wool from their flock, by the sale of which they could keep themselves in the few clothes and provisions they required, they were happy enough. This was all vey well for them, and they did not care whether their sheep were rotten with scab or not; but, when the *camp* began to change hands, and men came who thoroughly understood sheep-working, and meant business, one and all found their *camps* literally impregnated with scab.

Now, everyone with any experience as a sheep-farmer knows that it is perfectly easy to get your flocks diseased, but it is a very different matter to cure them when the pest once gets hold of them; and, moreover, it is a disease which advances with gigantic strides. If the *camp* has had unsound sheep on it for years, as was almost invariably the case in Santa Cruz and the neighbourhood, it is certain, sooner or later, to break out amongst the clean animals the newcomer brings onto his land. It is almost impossible to avoid this: no matter how many precautions are taken, still, some germs of the disease are certain to remain; and, although you may check it, yet, when you least expect it, it will break out again. This has happened again and again and, what is more, will continue to happen as, in my opinion, these *camps* have been so neglected, and got into such a fearful state, that ever to cleanse them properly is a perfect impossibility.

No one who did not see it can imagine the fearful state some of the sheep round Santa Cruz were in at the conclusion of the winter of 1899, which was unusually severe. At our house in Pescadores, it was quite the rule (not the exception) for us to find every morning ten or a dozen sheep, all thin and diseased, crouched alongside our garden fences. Many had not a particle of wool on them, or even strength to get up from the ground. It was quite a common occurrence for some of the poor devils to come into the courtyard in front of the house, looking for shelter; and, if any of the doors happened to be open, they would go right into the house, and make themselves comfortable. As for the *league* of *camp* I purchased, I don't believe that on the whole of it there was a decent-sized bush that had not one or more dead sheep lying under it, besides the bones and remains of numerous animals that had died in former years.

Our next neighbours, the Messrs. Richmond, holders of the concession of land granted by the Government to the late Captain Luis Piedra Buena, were constantly dipping their sheep, but to no purpose: the land not being fenced in, nor even measured, there was nothing to stop all the diseased sheep of the neighbourhood from boxing with theirs, which (as this particular *camp* appeared to be a favourite spot and general *rendezvous*) they invariably did. It is a thousand pities that when the colonists commenced work in these parts, there were not the same laws and regulations which are now supposed to exist (and should in any case have been in force there from the commencement); but now it is too late, and I do not believe that these *camps* can ever be properly disinfected.

During the last year before I left, the authorities were getting very particular. On several occasions, when they were advised that certain people had not and would not dip their sheep, they sent up a *comisario* and some men and did the business themselves, or tried to do it — which was certainly a good thing, and taught people that they must and should dip their flock. But, as for the process of dipping as carried out by these Commissions, the members of which understood nothing about the matter, I don't suppose that the animals dipped received the smallest benefit; however, the good example, and teaching people that if they did not obey the law they would be forced, was a very wise proceeding.

At the same time, I should be the last to recommend such a course on the part of the authorities, except in exceptional and very bad cases of neglect, and where such a neglect is doing harm to the neighbours. Then it has a good effect: the very fact of anyone daring to interfere with his sacred sheep and sheep work ought to drive any decent and civilised sheep man either into an asylum or his grave. I am sure they would far rather cure their flocks ten times over, than that any stranger, who did not understand and appreciate the beauty, intelligence and numerous virtues of the animals in question, should defile them with the touch of his unfriendly hands.

Gathering and Marking

A picturesque sight—Don't use dogs—A well-managed gathering—Breeds of sheep —Shepherds become obsessive—Greenwood, the worst culprit

I think I have said more than enough about all the drawbacks we have to encounter and can now go on to something more cheerful. I think a description of a general gathering (say for lamb marking) would be interesting; at any rate I will try it, although I am afraid it will be impossible for me to picture the scene in all its glory.

The great event of the year on a farm is "the marking day". The flocks have not been gathered or in any way disturbed for about six weeks and no one can really calculate what kind of a season he has had. The increase may be small or large; the sheep sound and in good condition, or excessively thin and scabby — no one can really tell.

The night before the eventful day is generally a very lively one. Some say one thing and some another as to the condition of the various flocks. Bets pass constantly between the men, as to who can show the best increase for the season; and, as a rule, instead of preparing themselves by a good sleep for an unusually tiring and eventful day, everyone sits up half the night smoking and talking. Then you turn in for an hour or two and have just had enough sleep to make you wish for more, when the cook rouses you out to take your coffee. This will be about three o'clock on some morning about the end of October or beginning of November.

As a rule it is a drizzly, cold and miserable morning and you turn out feeling far from "at peace with all the world". If the *tropillas* have come in, you first catch your horse (unless you have had sense enough to catch and tie him the night before), then saddle up and take your coffee; after which all hands mount and take the directions indicated to each one by the manager or shepherd in charge of the particular portion of *camp* which is to be gathered. This start ought to take place about three or half past three o'clock, it being absolutely necessary to get the flock in before the heat of the day commences: it is a well-known fact that, to ensure the minimum of loss at the marking, the sheep should be brought in as cool and quiet as possible. Well, if the shepherd in charge of the particular portion of the *camp* to be gathered is a careful man and has kept his flock well turned the night before, this first gathering should not give much trouble. If the man has been careless, it may cost hours before the sheep are all well in hand for, remember, this work must be accomplished without dogs, and be entirely and most deliberately carried out by the shepherds.

Dogs on this occasion are a nuisance and only mis-mother the lambs, which are still very small, and if at all hurried or frightened are most apt to lose their mothers. This means a most serious loss in a broken *camp* like ours, which is not only full of hills and valleys more or less covered with *mata negra*, but is also intersected with deep *zanjas* or *grips*: each one of these is capable of concealing a *point* of sheep so effectually that even the cleverest shepherd and the one most used to the ground is liable to miss them — unless he is extraordinarily careful. Therefore, the lambs, if once they miss their mothers, are very apt never to encounter them again.

Well, when all has been done that is possible to ensure a clean gather, and the sheep are in a focus on some plain or clear spot, a halt is called to let the ewes pick up their lambs, and to cool them all down. Meanwhile, the men refresh themselves. I shall never forget the delight of those feeds: it was so delicious to cut a lump from the meat or the bread, which a dozen dirty knives had been hacking at before, or to take a drink from the big *camp* bottle of rum, which the same number of mouths had previously sampled. But, what of that? The sheep were well together and, *"hunger being the best sauce"*, the viands and liquor disappear in a marvellously short time. By this time, the sheep are rested and beginning to scatter again, so pipes are lit and everyone goes to his post.

The main point now is to drive them very carefully and slowly to the pens and get them in without the lambs breaking — by no means an easy task in this latter case, for the little ones have never seen a house or a pen before and take fright immediately: they all get into a bunch behind the ewes and try to escape. The best plan to avoid this is to plant two lines of nets, each running from either side of the entrance to the main or gathering pen at an angle, so forming a wide entrance of two or three hundred yards. The sheep, once well inside this wide entrance, naturally follow on down the gradually narrowing space until they arrive at the gate of the main or gathering pen where (if the manager has been prudent) a small *point* of tame sheep will be shut in as a decoy. Seeing these quiet and peaceful, the others enter the pens with all confidence and there is no loss or trouble whatever.

This is how the gathering for lamb marking should be managed; but, unfortunately, on very few farms is this system carried out, and consequently many of the unmarked lambs break away, get lost and die. You would imagine that, as these precautions are so simple and give so little trouble, they would be universally adopted, but this is far from being the case. In fact, on one of the principal farms on the Straits of Magellan (where every kind of work is supposed to be carried on in the most superlative manner), a short time before I left, I saw the proprietor gather about six thousand sheep, bring them to the pens (with the aid of untrained dogs, stupid men, and screams and shouts, instead of absolute quietness) and finally have to let them all go again to pick up the lambs which broke out, and one third of which probably never saw their mothers again. It is really a fact that the longer some of these men are working sheep the less they seem to know about them.

However, when all is said and done, I think that sheep farming in general has proved a wonderful success in South Patagonia. No one who saw the various flocks a few years ago would recognise them now. Numerous first class Lincoln, Leicester and Romney Marsh rams have been imported, and all (especially the Lincoln stock, which is in my opinion especially adapted to the country) have given a magnificent result.

I confess that I was getting rather sick of the animal when I left Patagonia. I used to have quite enough bother and trouble with the farm during the day, without having sheep crammed down my throat at dinner time, and dinned into my ears from after dinner till bedtime. In vain would one try to turn the conversation on some different subject: the discussion invariably drifted back to … sheep!!

Once, I was driven nearly crazy by a man whom I invited to sleep in my room: he had talked on the everlasting subject all the afternoon and evening without cessation. When he went to bed, the last thing he did was to look out of the window and remark that it was a bad night for some rams we had shut in the pens. During the night, when he was not moving, I could hear the words "*hogget, ewe, ram* …" muttered at intervals; in the morning, his first move was to dart out of bed and gaze longingly at the pens in front of the window, to see what kind of a night the beasts had passed. This is rather an exceptionally bad case of "sheep fever", but I have known many others nearly as bad.

Mind you, in accusing other people I do not exonerate myself; on the contrary, I think I was rather given to this weakness myself, but it used to annoy me in other people. Once, I even declared that a fine of a plug of tobacco should be paid by every man who said *"sheep"* between dinner and bedtime. Balancing up accounts at the end of the week, I found I owed about double as many plugs as any of the other men, so I decided to let the matter rest and things go on as before. After all, in the wilds of Patagonia we had not much else to talk of, and farming was our trade, so it was not to be wondered at, if we turned again and again to the everlasting subject.

Unneighbourly Disputes

Silly quarrels caused by trifling matters—Incident at Coy Inlet—Impractical laws—Comisario takes action—Undeserved imprisonment—Peaceful solutions are needed

Before concluding, there is one thing I should wish to comment upon: that is, the great ill-feeling that exists between many of the settlers and farmers. A little of that sort of thing is sure to occur in every community, however large or small; but, it really seems as if the Patagonian climate in some measure turned the milk of human kindness into gall. You would imagine that, where there were so few foreign settlers, they would try and hang together and act and think towards one another with the utmost consideration and kindness; but, I am sorry to say, this is very far from being the case with us. I do not speak personally, because I can never be sufficiently grateful to one and all of my neighbours for the many acts of kindness I have received from them, but it is far from being generally the case: in fact, it is difficult to find two or three men holding adjoining farms who are on really good terms.

These silly quarrels are generally caused by the most trifling matters — a sheep being killed by mistake, a few lambs marked by accident, etc. — in fact, things which must occur in any country where large numbers of sheep are kept without sufficient fencing to keep them from straggling. It would be far better if, instead of having constant quarrels and lawsuits, the farmers named a committee to "enquire" into and adjust these matters. In some cases the causes are grave, but in others so trifling and silly as to render quarrelling about them both childish and ridiculous. I have no hesitation in saying that many of the farmers would be far better off now if they had avoided these ridiculous disputes; and if they would also avoid all scandal and gossip, and go in generally for *"peace on earth and good will towards men."*

One justice I must do to them all, and that is to testify to their general and complete devotion to everything in the way of sheep and all connected with them. It is really quite touching sometimes. I really do believe that if some of them saw a human being and a sheep drowning in the same hole, they would pick out the sheep first, and let the man take his chance.

Regarding this ill-feeling which so often exists between the neighbouring farmers, I must mention one little incident which happened in Coy Inlet, as an example of the feuds which we sometimes find among sheep-farmers. There were certain rules or laws or something of the sort made by the authorities, and placarded all over the country, which rendered it quite impossible for anyone to undertake any kind of sheep work without infringing one or other of them, or doing some injury to his neighbour.

It was supposed to be obligatory to advise anyone of your neighbours as to your proceedings, and to mention exactly the day and time when you expected to commence work. Any strange sheep found amongst your own were to be parted out into a separate pen, and kept there until their owner or owners appeared. If no one put in an appearance at a certain time, the sheep had to starve there, or be turned back into your flock, or else be herded out by the proprietor of the farm, who could charge the owner of the sheep (when he appeared) with the expenses. Any dispute about ear marks was to be decided by the Government Officer, who was supposed to be present at every sheep gathering or, if none were present, by the Judge in Santa Cruz or Gallegos.

Of course, in 99 cases of 100, no authority was present, and all disputes had to be decided by the farmers themselves; which, as in several cases they were at daggers drawn, was not an easy business and often had to remain in abeyance, thus making matters worse.

The amusing incident I referred to in connection with this subject, took place as follows[3].

As at this time there was no fencing to speak of in Coy Inlet, at each gathering, the proprietor of the farm found several of his neighbours' sheep mixed up with his own. The case in question took place on the farm of an Englishman who had, perhaps, as much (or more) experience in every detail of sheep work as any man in the district. Coming straight from New Zealand, where he had been born and bred on a large sheep run, carried on by his family for many years, he perhaps expected too much from the new country in which he was settling. Be this as it may, he was certainly the kind of man who was wanted out there, and had he had English neighbours, there would probably have been no dispute worth mentioning. But, unfortunately, the farmer nearest to him was not an Englishman, and moreover he knew nothing about sheep, but he thought he did, which everyone can understand is the worst kind of ignorance.

The result was what can easily be anticipated: the flocks of the ignoramus (who by the way was a Frenchman) got into a fearful state; and, not being properly turned in every day, were constantly mixing with the Englishman's animals. In vain did he part them out and drive them back, well into their *camp*; and, on several occasions, when dipping his own sheep, he also dipped those belonging to his neighbour after separating them. But, on finding he was not grateful for this favour but, in fact, rather resented it than otherwise, he wisely discontinued the practice, and contented himself with parting them out, and advising his neighbour of the fact. Surely, there was nothing in this proceeding to occasion a deadly feud between the parties; but so it was, and it did not take long for the Frenchman to find an opportunity for showing his teeth.

A good many of his diseased animals died on the Englishman's *camp* and, as the latter was (as all good sheep-farmers should be) most particular in keeping his *camp* clean, his shepherds (by accident) skinned some of the strange sheep; the skins were brought into the shed in due course, and mixed with the others belonging to the farm. When baling them up ready for transmission to Gallegos, no one noticed the few odd

[3] Incident at Coy Inlet — These events occurred in June 1896. The "Englishman" was Henry Jamieson, the "Frenchman" Auguste Guillaume.

skins belonging to the other farm. There was no attempt at concealment: nothing could have been easier than to cut off the ears from the skins, and no one would have been any the wiser. When the bales arrived at Gallegos, they were as usual left on the beach, pending the arrival of the vessel in which they could be shipped. Naturally, there was not wanting a busybody to examine the bales, and to note the marks on the ears, which were visible to everyone. He noted the two or three skins bearing the Frenchman's mark for, as I said before, there had been no more attempt at concealment than at robbery. A *comisario* was promptly called, and the marks indicated to him, and he immediately gave an order to summon the Englishman to Gallegos to answer for his mistake, or robbery, or whatever it might be considered.

It is not necessary to say how glad they were to be down on a man who had certainly not cultivated their acquaintance or, perhaps, deferred sufficiently to their authority. On being examined, he could not account for these few wretched pelts being mixed with his: all he could say was — what was quite true — that the fault (if such a trifle could be so called) rested with the men who had gathered the skins and baled them up. But this was all of no avail: it was such a splendid chance of making a public example of an intelligent man who was rapidly making his mark in the country. He was therefore told to confine himself to his room pending enquiries: that is to say, consider himself under arrest.

Of course, his friends soon heard the news and rallied round him. I believe for a day or two there was a regular jubilee held in the prisoner's room, and the price of champagne and whisky rose considerably. He was then liberated and was free, after paying a fine, to return to his farm and embezzle more scabby skins, if he felt so inclined. After this, however, strict supervision was maintained over the criminal: he was not going to gather his sheep, or carry on the usual routine of his work, without someone to look after him.

Now, he had bought the nucleus of his flock in Río Negro or the vicinity, and they had probably passed through a number of hands before; and so, the new owner had some difficulty in finding a corner of an ear on which he could place his own mark. Indeed, some had no ears left to be marked. Therefore, when Mr. *Comisario* _____ came on one occasion to inspect the flocks, he was completely nonplussed; but, being a man of genius, he selected about a dozen of the most doubtful cases — whose marks were perfectly indistinguishable, either because the number of their marks was legion, or because they had no ears to the fore — and, hobbling them fore and aft, packed them down to Gallegos in a cart (something like sardines in a tin) so that the brighter lights could decide the knotty question, as to whom they belonged.

Now, I consider it an insult to the whole race of sheep that any of their fraternity should be ignominiously packed into a cart, and not allowed their usual privilege of giving all the trouble they possibly could to their drivers; and the animals probably looked at the proceeding in the same light; for, when they found themselves in this position, they gave up all hope from God or man, and promptly succumbed to their semi-starved state, and the bruises received from the jolting of the cart; so that all that was presented at the *Gobernación* was a dozen dead carcasses, not pleasant to inspect or deal with, after being under a blazing sun for many hours. Who was the proper owner of them was not discovered; certain it is they belonged to someone, and that someone was the loser.

It is easy to understand from this occurrence that no particularly good result ensued from the intervention of the authorities. It would have been — and always will be — far better for trifling disputes of this kind to be arranged between the interested parties, without outside interference. I daresay at present things are very different: now that the boundary and other fences absolutely necessary for the well-being of a sheep-farmer are in most cases finished, there will be no more of these absurd quarrels; and yet, whether it is that there is something peculiar in the owner of the sheep, or their shepherds, or in the sheep themselves, which constantly occasions numberless rows, I know not; but, what I do know is, that these quarrels constantly occur, and are a great detriment to the progress of some farms.

⚜ 16 ⚜

Bosom Pals

Hunting Dogs

*Pedigree hounds imported by Piedra Buena—Essential for hunting—
Incident with pumas—Final days of "Bosun"—Deserving burial*

I certainly cannot leave off my scribblings about Patagonia without
writing something about our dogs. Most people are, I think, fond
of them, and therefore will not be annoyed with one who is literally a
dog-worshipper for spinning an extraordinarily long yarn about them.

Of one thing I am quite certain: that, were it not for the dogs, both
collies and hounds, our part of Patagonia would not be as prosperous
as it is now.

When I first landed in the Straits of Magellan, I had only one dog, a
setter whom I found utterly useless, as there were no partridges to be
found near the Colony; and I therefore exchanged him for a bulldog
named "*Jack*", about whom I could write a book — only I am afraid no
one would care to read it. At the time I mention, dogs of any value were
scarce. The only decent breed of hounds in the country belonged to the
late well-known Captain Luis Piedra Buena, who had imported the parent stock (Irish greyhounds) from the Río Negro — and splendid dogs
they were. By degrees, some of their descendants found their way to
Punta Arenas and were considered, and indeed were, of extraordinary
quality. These, however, were crossed with the Indian curs, and very
soon only two or three people had any of the real old stock.

But this was soon changed when Europeans began to arrive, as several of them brought well-bred hounds with them. The first to do this was the late Mr. J. W. Dunsmure, the first vice-consul, whom some of the readers of this article will remember as an old Buenos Aires resident. He imported a Crystal Palace prize-dog, a Scotch deerhound named "*Brenda*", and crossed her with the Piedra Buena breed[1]. Years afterwards, other Englishmen brought out or imported hounds, but the best stock sprang from the original source, and exists till the present day; and, as far as I know, no other has ever equalled them for speed or staying powers. I think I am somewhat an authority on this matter, as for many years I used no other breed, and one time and another have had no less than seventy of them.

People say hounds have not half the intelligence of retrievers and other dogs, and are only useful for the chase. I admit this to be the case in the ordinary course: that is to say, when they are used as hunting dogs, confined in a yard and only taken out for exercise or on the days they are on active service. But, if a man breeds and brings them up quite above and without interference from other people, it is quite incredible how intelligent they become and how faithful they are: they will do almost anything but talk.

Why, the best retriever I ever had was a half-bred Scotch deerhound: it did not matter whether the game was in the water or on the land — it was all the same to him. And not only this: if I wounded a *deer, ostrich* or guanaco, or any animal too large for him to fetch along, he would remain by the carcass till all hope of my finding him was over, and then come back and fetch me — unless one of his brothers, who seldom left him, was with him; in which case he would send him to look for me, and remain guarding the animal himself from the birds of prey. Once he remained alongside a big *ostrich* he had killed no less than 38 hours, without so much as touching a feather of the bird; nor, so far as I know, had he taken any water, as there was none within half a mile of him. I shall never forget his delight when I found him, or mine either, for I fully thought some *lion* had snapped him up.

[1] Deerhound "*Brenda*" — Animal mentioned in 11, DESTINATION LAKE SANTA CRUZ.

This dog ("*Bosun*" he was called) was singular in many ways; he loved to commune with his own thoughts and, with the exception of his brother "*Smut*", he absolutely declined to mingle with other dogs, or come anywhere near the camping place, except after his rations of meat. He would generally take up his quarters under some bush, not less than a hundred yards distant from the camp, and burrow a deep hole there, to which he would convey his meals. Moreover, if I went out hunting, he absolutely declined to follow me if I had more than two or three dogs with me, and one of these had to be his brother "*Smut*", or he would not budge an inch. If he had not finished all the meat I had given him the previous day, he, being a far-seeing dog, and well knowing that his domicile would be searched during his absence by the hounds who remained at home, to avoid robbery and general unpleasantness, would convey whatever remained in his mouth, always taking care to keep a long way behind me and the other dogs, till he got an opportunity of burying it unobserved. Coming back from *camp*, he would never omit to call at the place where he had left his treasure, unearth it and carry it back to his cave again.

One night he made me very angry, perhaps for the only time in his life. I was camped on the banks of the Río Centinela. The old dog absolutely refused to retire to his bush, but wandered up and down the banks of the river near the tent, every now and then giving vent to a single bark or howl. There is, by the way, nothing I hate like a dog barking without rhyme or reason, and I have frequently killed good dogs for having this defect. I went to where the dog was wandering about and scolded him, and drove him away at least a dozen times.

I could not see a sign of anything to account for his conduct nor, although there was deep snow all round, could I see any tracks whatever. However, he invariably returned to the same place after a little time, and finally squatted himself down right on the edge of the river (which at that spot had a very high perpendicular bank), every now and then looking at me and giving a bark. I now thought it was time to see what he wanted, so I clambered down to the river with some difficulty and walked along the frozen surface till I came in front of where the old dog was seated. Well, what did I find? The bank at this spot was very overhanging and formed a deep cave, in which were reposing no less than four pumas; hearing us move about, they had been afraid to clear out, and had not the old dog smelt them from above, I should never have known they were there. They would probably have waited till night and then sneaked away, perhaps previously killing one or two of my hounds; for, as it is known, the puma is very partial to dog-meat. As it was, I fetched my carbine from the tent and potted all four of them. After this I trusted *"Bosun"* implicitly and left him to pursue his own course of study[2].

I hope my readers will excuse me for this long yarn about my poor old friend, but he was a special favourite and followed me faithfully for nearly 12 years. For the last six months, as he could not travel, I carried him on horseback in front of me on a pillow; and when he died I took the trouble to bury him: a special honour of which he was well worthy.

Collies or Scottish sheepdogs

Story of "Tom"—Every shepherd has his favourite, better than the rest—Kindness rewarded—Devotion to work—Tracking ability—Absurd case of pampering

Perhaps I may have offended my friends the sheep devotees by having placed my special pets (the *ostrich* dogs) before the collies, and must beg their pardon for so doing. But, you see, the hounds gave me my living for so many years that, although I do not attempt to deny the utility, intelligence, amiability and numerous virtues of sheepdogs, yet my acquaintance with them was neither so long nor so intimate as it was

---

[2] Behaviour of *"Bosun"* — Here, Greenwood makes a comparison to *"Mr. Dick"*, a character in Charles Dickens' novel *"David Copperfield"*.

with my hunting dogs; for which reason I am apt to evince a partiality, which is not just for the latter.

At the same time I must mention that I, even I, once possessed a collie named "*Tom*" — in my opinion certainly the handsomest, cleverest and best dog that ever existed. I have not the slightest doubt that every shepherd in the neighbourhood had, in his opinion at least, one dog possessed of twice as many good qualities as my dear old "*Tom*". I can say this quite calmly now but, at that time, if anyone connected with sheep or sheep-farming had visited me, and ventured to compare any one of his dogs with mine ... Why, that man should have left my house that very moment ... Why, I should as soon thought of eating beef when I could get mutton, or have got rid of my cherished sheepskin bed and taken to a mattress, as of admitting such a comparison.

Year after year has passed since I left my farm but, even now, the very idea of such a breach of good manners makes my very blood run cold; and I am sure there is not one of my shepherd friends who will not, if he be true to his profession, back me up in these ideas.

No — even although I prefer hounds, and confess to the crime frankly — Yes, I loved my old "*Tom*", and rank him after my old friend "*Bosun*" in affectionate remembrance and regard; so much so that, even at the risk of boring people, I must write a special memoir of his numerous good qualities and eccentricities.

"*Tom*" was given me by my oldest and best friend, owner of one of the largest and most prosperous farms on the Straits of Magellan. If ever a man entertained a really passionate regard and respect for a dog, my friend was that man. It was really touching to watch his efforts to induce the dog to carry out every item of his duty. He had previously had several masters, each one crueller than the other; so, when he fell into really kind hands, he did not know what to make of it. After long and careful meditation, he came to the conclusion that at last he had met with a good kind master, and from that moment he determined to mend his ways. This could not be done all at once, more especially as he regarded the gentle *lickings* he now received as caresses; but, it is wonderful how docile and good he became in those kindly hands. Now, there was no one to howl at him, or throw stones at him, or insult him and the memory of his mother, and keep him without food for the smallest error of judgment. His work was explained to him with kind words and signs, and he soon plucked up courage and learnt all that was taught him.

When he was given to me, the *Old Adam* was still strong in him but, in a very short time, he learnt all his duties thoroughly; nothing could exceed his devotion to my interest, as far as sheep were concerned, and a more faithful and obedient dog could not be found.

When I first started, I only brought up about 600 sheep, including the necessary rams, and a few *wethers* for meat, and at first they gave no trouble at all; but, directly the green grass began to sprout (just before the lambing commenced) there was no holding them: they would keep steering for their old home in the south. Without "*Tom*", I could never have kept them, and the dog worked night and day, looking after them: I believe he knew every sheep amongst them.

Of course, we had to pen the sheep at first. After a few days "*Tom*" took entire charge of them, and remained with them all day, but generally came home at dinner time; even then he was not altogether happy, and would frequently go to the top of a hill close to the house, from whence he could see where his charges were feeding. On one occasion he made a mistake, and brought back 50 sheep short, amongst them 1 black one (there were 3 black ones in the whole lot). He found out his mistake himself when he got them in the pens, and immediately returned to look for them; it was long after dark when he came back with the stragglers, so they must have been some distance off.

He was a splendid *lion* dog and, if once he got on a track, would never leave it until he had located his prey. It was great fun if he got a *lion* in the open *camp*: he would then watch his opportunity and grab hold of the extreme end of the brute's tail — sometimes the two would go round in a circle, but I never knew him get even a scratch. Sometimes he would go into the caves in the *barrancas*, when he knew a *lion* was there, and follow it into the bowels of the earth, so far that you could barely hear his bark. When he returned after some time underground, as the entrances were too small for us to get in, we used to stop up the holes with stones and mud, and by so doing were perfectly certain we were killing one or more *lions*. Indeed, on several occasions, in our spare time, we opened up some of these same holes, and almost invariably found dead *lions* inside.

In one word: it is impossible for me to describe the services he rendered me; had he been younger, I would have taken him home with me (to England). As it was, I left him in charge of a man who — I thought — would take real care of him, the result being he was poisoned within six months of my leaving. As the old dog never by any chance stole anything, or ate anything that was not given to him, he was probably half-starved before he was reduced to eating meat which had been poisoned in the *camp*. Thus died the only collie I ever cared for; and on my return to Patagonia after a short absence, all my favourite dogs were dead, or had disappeared.

You see, I render praise where praise is due, and yield "*Tom*" all the encomiums which are his; nor do I for one moment doubt that there are, and were at that time, 100 other dogs equally as intelligent. Also, I am certain that, if some of the shepherds in training their young dogs exercised a little more patience and a little less cruelty, they would obtain a better result than most of them had attained.

On the other hand, it is useless to be too kind and let your dogs do what they please. I have seen men who carried their kindness to such an extreme that it was absolutely absurd. I knew one man who would always put a skin or a piece of carpet for each dog to feed on, and prepare their dinners each in a separate plate, with as much care as he did his own. On one occasion, this man made two or three long marches with me, and took eleven or twelve half-grown puppies with him, capable of making long marches and generally taking care of themselves. This did not satisfy my friend, who got down every five minutes to catch one or other of them, and carry him in front of him on the pommel; the puppies strenuously objected to this, but the man held on like grim death, despite howls and struggles. Once, his horse showed his dislike to being scratched, reared up, and over went man and puppy to one side, whilst the horse cleared out to the other. After this, he left his pets to their own devices till he came to the River Gallegos.

It was a hot day, and all the dogs promptly went into the water to refresh themselves. This did not suit my companion, who said that they would never have strength enough to swim the river; he therefore captured two and requested me to carry one across. I absolutely declined the office, whereupon he mounted himself, and I handed him his two treasures. He then proceeded to cross the river with them, let them go on the other side and returned for another cargo. His two former passengers, finding themselves abandoned, promptly swam back after him; so, he desisted from his labours. All passed in safety, except the two first, who thought they had done quite enough fooling around and declined to do anything but sit on the bank and howl. I camped in some *robles* on the other side of the river and, after spending about an hour in trying to capture his pets, he joined me; and, seeing there was no help for it, and probably smelling the supper, the deserters promptly came too. After this there was no more trouble with them as, thank heaven, the man had sense enough to understand that puppies of six months old can take care of themselves.

✺ 17 ✺

South American Lions (Pumas)

The Nature of the Beast

Patagonian pumas don't deserve the name of "lion"—Northern type are fiercer—Zamora tells of the violent death of two young girls—Greenwood knows of only three attacks on humans—Kelly dies as a result of a scratch from a puma's paw

Why on earth this animal has any claim to be called a *lion*, I do not know. Fancy calling a cowardly, mischievous, ugly cat like this, *lion*! He is no more to be compared to the noble African lion, or to the other numerous wild beasts found in other parts of the world, than a toy-terrier to a bulldog. I refer, of course, to the Patagonian *Lions*, with which I made an intimate acquaintance. I do not think that out of more than 1,100 of these animals which I have killed, I have seen more than two or three that had courage enough to attack anything beyond a poor, harmless sheep or guanaco. But, so he is denominated, and will probably retain his name till the end of time, without the smallest claim to the honour.

However, this is not the question; all I have to do is to tell you all I know about him and his habits; and, to sooth my feelings, I will speak of him as "puma" for the future.

✺

I believe that this animal is found in every part of South America, and I have heard that in the northern provinces of the Argentine Republic, Brazil, other South American countries and Mexico, the character of the animal completely changes: it will attack anything from a man down-wards, which is certainly not the case in S. Patagonia. The cause of this, I should imagine, is the enormous quantity of game, guanacos, *ostriches*, *deer*, etc., which abound there. In all my experience of *lions*, I have only known three persons injured by them, and on each occasion they had been driven into a corner, and acted in self-defence.

I have been told by several persons, old residents in the northern provinces, that the pumas there are of a very different temper, and not so easy to tackle. My old friend Zamora, who has appeared so many times in these sketches, often told me of a circumstance that happened under his own eyes (he also stated that he knew of various cases of a similar nature, but not quite so tragic.)

On one occasion, two young girls from Mendoza were placed in his father's charge, to convey to some town in Chile. After passing the *Cordillera*, it appeared that the mule-train was camped for the night in the plains, about 200 yards from a spring of fresh water. One of the girls took a pitcher and went to fetch water from the spring; as she was a long time gone, her sister went to look for her. Some time passed, and she also did not return; therefore, Zamora (who was then a child) and another man went in search of them.

On arriving at the spring, what was their horror to find both girls lying dead; one close to the spring with her skull smashed in, and her face terribly lacerated; the other, who had evidently been killed close to her sister, dragged about 20 yards distant, also with her skull frac-tured. This last one was practically covered with leaves and grass; all the upper part of her person, including her face, had been devoured. This, Zamora recounted, was the work of a man-eating puma, which was in the habit of killing women and children when found in solitary places. After the slaughter of the two young girls, all the neighbourhood turned out, bent on destroying this pest, but could never find him, although he was in the vicinity; for, whilst the men were away, he entered one of the villages and killed two children. The brute had never been known to attack a man, and though the authorities had offered a large reward to anyone who would kill him, no one had even yet seen him; nor, as far as Zamora could tell, was he ever found. This is the only authentic account I have had of a man-eating puma. I have no reason to doubt the truth of his statements — quite the contrary, as I know the man well.

"*The Standard*", with its long experience of all that passes, can doubt-less inform the readers whether they have ever received any details of cases of this sort occurring. All I can say is that, in Patagonia, the only three cases of anyone's being hurt by a puma (that I know of) are the ones that follow: in each case, it was the man's own fault.

In the first case, the man was foolhardy and started to kick the bush to drive out a *lion* that had taken shelter there; naturally, the animal got hold of his foot, which it chewed up through his thick *camp* boot. Had he not had these boots on, he would have lost his foot: he was lame for life.

The second case was that of my very old and valued servant, James Kelly, who lived with me before I turned hunter, and followed my fortunes when I went to the *camp*. Being alone in the tent, one dark winter's night, a puma came close to the tent, and the dogs smelt and went for him and drove him into a thick bush. The old man turned out, tied his long knife to a stick and, taking a lighted firebrand dipped in grease in his hand, went to the bush, with the intention of sticking the brute. He could not see the *lion*, but the *lion* could see him, more especially as he had a torch in his hand; and, as he was peering into the bush to see where to stab, he suddenly received a gentle pat in the face, just below the left eye. He was no coward, and killed his enemy with repeated stabs of his improvised lance; but, nevertheless, that little gentle pat in the face cost him his life. I came back the next day and found him with his face much swelled, but all you could see were five small punctures from the claws of the *lion*. It did not appear serious but, as he seemed in great pain, I took him to the Colony as soon as I could; but it was no good, and although he had a skilful physician, he grew worse and worse; finally cancer set in, and in two or three months he died. An English vessel came in at the time and, knowing him to be an old British sailor, they very kindly gave him a sailor's funeral.

In the third case (my own), I had just shot a puma in a bush and believed I had killed him, so I laid hold of one of his fore paws to drag him out. Not being quite dead, he resented this, and in his death-struggle drove his claws into my hand. It appeared nothing at the time, but in a short time my whole hand and arm swelled up, and it was a long time before I got well. To this day, I feel pain in that hand in cold or bad weather. The scratch was nothing, so I should imagine that the claws of the *lion* are like the horns of a deer, more or less poisonous.

Habits of Pumas

Mistaken ideas about their breeding habits—An average of four cubs per pregnancy—Move in groups in winter-time—Sometimes one or more found killed by own kind—Confirmed cannibals

In general, I have noted that many people (who ought, after many years' residence in the country, to know better) have a rooted idea that the female only bears one or two cubs at a time; and I heard one well-educated man, supposed to be an authority, declare that they only breed once during their lives. I would it were so, for the sake of the poor sheep farmers, who would (in that case) at this time be more or less free from these pests.

I can assure you that, unfortunately, it is so far from being the case: the puma always breeds twice a year, never less than three (3) cubs and very often five (5), but I think the general number is four (4) — at least, in all the nests that I have found, this has invariably been the number[1].

It is a very rare thing to find more than 5 or 6 *lions*, big and small, together on the coast, or where game is plentiful; but in the winter months, when the central *camps* are almost deserted by the guanacos or *ostriches*, the pumas get almost frantic with hunger and, like wolves,

[1] Patagonian puma — Greenwood's observations on cannibalism and rate of reproduction need scientific corroboration.

seek for their prey in packs. I have never seen more than 26 together, many of which were young cubs, but I have found tracks in the snow of at least 40; these were all travelling in the direction of the coast, and were evidently half-starved as, wherever there were any old bones or dead carcasses, they had always (to judge by the tracks) stopped and had a free fight over them. This lot must have come from a long distance, or over a lot of ice or rocky ground, as all the tracks were bloodstained, and many had lost their nails. Where they had come from it seems impossible to say, but I should imagine somewhere from the recesses of the *Cordilleras*.

I have killed or poisoned between 1,100 or 1,200 pumas and, amongst them, of course, many females that have recently given birth to their young. These I always examined, and almost invariably found portions of one or more cubs in their insides. I will even go further than this and state, with perfect truth, that if the mother is hungry she will, without the smallest compunction, kill and devour one of her cubs, even if it is three or four months old. I am also of the opinion that the female almost invariably eats one or more of her offspring when they are born; otherwise, the increase would be enormous, and the country uninhabitable. I have had two absolute proofs of this, which it may be interesting to my readers to hear.

One was in upper Coy Inlet in 1879, where I was hunting *ostriches* in the winter months. One morning I heard a row, as if about fifty cats were mewing and fighting at the same time; of course, off went all my dogs in a moment. I mounted and followed and soon found them with a large *lioness* in a bush, and some of the dogs were barking at two cubs of three or four months in another bush. Having dispatched them all, I returned to skin the mother, taking the cubs with me to eat. (I had been wanting some pork for some time and knew these young ones I had killed would be delicious.) On going to the bush where I had killed the old one, I was much surprised to find a half-eaten, freshly-killed cub close to her; it was the same size as the others and was no doubt one of the same family. This proves that, if pumas are hungry, they will go for any mortal thing.

On another occasion, near the same place, I was in bed one morning, having camped out the night, not having been able to find any game the previous day. The ground was so hard we had to take the greatest care not to work all of our dogs together, for fear they should all get lame at once — luckily, I had only 2 or 3 dogs with me at the time. (I had plenty of dogs, but in this season of terribly hard frost, it was hardly possible to take a dog out without breaking some of his nails.) We were again awakened by a caterwauling, just as if there were a regular cohort of huge cats fighting, or arranging some domestic difficulties, or something or other. I speedily turned out (I won't say dressed, because we always slept in our *lion* skin suits), and started in the direction of the noise, which came from a patch of thick *mata negra* about 200 yards distant. Luckily, the dogs I had with me were all *ostrich* hounds, and as each when young received more or less scratches from pumas, they had (as is usual with this class of dog) a holy horror of them, and kept a respectful distance behind me. It was really strange to see how well they knew what was up. We no sooner began to move than there was dead silence. On arriving at the bushes, all the snow was covered with tracks, going in and out. The whole patch was only about 100 yards in circumference, in the middle of which this amiable family had taken up their quarters, probably with a view to holding a cannibal feast. Some of them were lying down, others were feeding in the middle of the enclosure. I discharged all the cartridges I had in my Winchester (unfortunately only 3 or 4 in number) pell-mell into the lot of them. Every bullet must have taken effect, but only one large female remained, shot through the head — the rest cleared out as if ten thousand demons were after them.

On examining the ground, I found ample proof of what I had stated to many friends before, viz. that these animals are absolute cannibals: not only do they devour their young on the smallest provocation, but do not object to sacrifice one of their number for the good of the crowd. Whether the victim or victims are selected because they are fat or weak, or because there has been some private misunderstanding amongst the members of the community, I cannot tell. All I know is they do eat one another, and on this occasion they had had a regal time: the remains of two cubs, with their bones picked clean, and those of a large female, half-eaten, were left on the ground. My readers can draw their own conclusions; I only state what I saw.

On several other occasions, I have killed *lions* and found portions of others in their stomachs. I think that there is little doubt that the whole race of pumas are cannibals. I daresay they don't eat one another if they can find anything else, but in the event of their being hard up, I fancy they would stick at nothing.

Encounters with Pumas

Infuriated cow avenges its dead calf—Puma attacks Greenwood's horse— Cub scares Greenwood as he sleeps—Like two cats beside the campfire— Pumas enjoy dog-meat—Almost one embrace too many

In Patagonia the pumas rarely touch either cattle or horses, so long as there are sheep or game to be had; failing these, I have known them kill both horses and cattle — such cases are exceptional.

I remember a puma killing a calf in Coy Inlet, but he did not get off scot-free, for the old cow took revenge into her own hands and tossed, mauled, and stamped upon the puma until it was hardly recognisable as a puma. Also, in Punta Arenas, there were two or three *mountain lions* who did a great deal of mischief, constantly killing young mares, foals and heifers. In hunting the wild horses, we constantly found mares and foals killed by the *lions*. On one occasion, one of them sprung upon the back of a favourite *alazán* mare of mine, but could not get hold of her; the skin, however, was ripped in five or six places, right from the rump to the hocks, and she bore the marks to the day of her death.

Once, whilst hunting *ostriches*, a *lion* sprang at my horse from behind a bush, but fortunately missed us; and then actually followed us for about

200 yards; and, although I was going at full speed, ran me pretty close. When he found he could not catch us, he jumped on the top of a big rock — I then summoned up sufficient courage to return and shoot him.

Please let the reader remember that what I recount are exceptional cases; as a rule, the Patagonian puma only attacks animals incapable of defending themselves.

For sure, I have often seen them kill horses, cows and sheep, as every-one else has, but I should like to know if anyone knows of a really authenticated case of a man-eater amongst them. They have certainly had every chance of killing me, and many others, whilst sleeping on the *camp*.

On one occasion, I was camped in the Dos Morros, Upper Gallegos, hunting *deer*, which are very plentiful in the vicinity. I used to find their favourite watering places, and then go with my rifle and watch for them, either in the early morning or late in the evening, as I found at those times they came to water. One very sultry evening, I took my rifle and a book, and went to watch at one of my favourite places. By accident, I left the cleaning rod (a heavy hickory one with a large knob) in the rifle, which was a heavy one, carrying a 1½ oz. bullet. When I got to my destination, I quite forgot to remove the rod; and as, I am sorry to say, was very often the case, after watching and reading for about 10 minutes, I fell asleep.

I must have slept some time, and I should probably have gone on for an indefinite period, but I suddenly felt something sniffing my face. I thought it was one of my dogs who had followed me from the tent, and turned over impatiently. Presently I felt sniffing again, and this time started up in a rage: well, there, right alongside me, was a puma who had evidently been inspecting me with a view to his supper. I think he was as frightened at my sudden move as I was at his appearance; anyway, he turned round and jumped over to the other side of the stream which I was watching, and then stood looking at me. I grabbed hold of my rifle and, quite forgetting the cleaning rod, let him have both barrels in his chest; he did not want any more, as you may imagine, and moreover my shoulder was black and blue for a fortnight, with the recoil of the rifle. On examining the puma, which appeared to me to be as big as an elephant when I woke up, I found it was only a cub about half-grown, still quite large enough to throttle me in my sleep — if he had chosen — although he had probably been examining me solely out of curiosity.

On another occasion, I was sleeping near Skyring Water, but without a tent. I had made a huge fire, which had burned about half-down; waking up, I saw two very large ones, sitting just like two cats, on the other side of the fire. I had no gun and no dog with me but, directly I moved, they turned tail and fled. It was slightly different one very bad night when I was camped on the banks of the River Santa Cruz, with all my dogs round me. It was just daybreak, and I was thinking of turning out, when suddenly a large puma came and looked right into the tent. The dogs spotted him, however, and soon had him at bay in a bush where, of course, I shot him.

On another occasion, near the same place, in the night, one of my dogs was killed close to the tent and dragged about thirty yards away and eaten. We did not see the *lion* nor, although there were five of us present, did we hear any disturbance. Pumas have doubtless a taste for dog-meat, at any rate there is hardly one of the old *camp* men (I mean *ostrich*-hunters) who could not narrate some experiences of the sort.

The time I was in the greatest fright was in Cañadón de las Vacas, shortly after I had descended into a Patagonian sheep owner, when I was pursuing my usual employment of … hunting *lions*. I had got a *lion* into a cave, at the foot of the *barrancas*. The cave had a very narrow entrance, and took a sharp turn to the left, so I could not shoot the brute from the outside and it was impossible to get the beast out. As this animal had done a great deal of harm, I was down on him, and resolved not to let him go. I therefore took my revolver in one hand, and a lighted *mata negra* bush in the other, and crawled through the narrow passage to see if I could pot him inside. He apparently did not approve of the smell of the fire, for I had got about half way up the narrow passage when he made a dash for the opening. Meeting me on the road, he tried to pass me but, the passage being very narrow, we actually got stuck together (his head where my feet were) for a few seconds. I let go of my revolver and bunch of bushes. Being in a mortal funk and not quite understanding the position, I just stuck as close as I could to the side of the cave and did not move an inch. After a moment's struggle, which appeared to last about two centuries, we got clear of one another. I daresay the beast was as much frightened as I was. The *lion* gained the mouth of the cave, and there he encountered my *peon* and all the dogs, who soon made short work of him.

I mention these few anecdotes just to show what a puma might do with such chances as these, if he liked; but he is too cowardly to take advantage of them, far less to begin an attack himself. I daresay many of your Patagonian friends will bear out my words, and have had more or less the same experience as I have had. I don't think I need say much more about the South American *lion*, but only reiterate that, in ninety-nine cases out of a hundred, he is a consummate coward, and always a mischievous, ugly, ill-conditioned beast.

Strong, harmful and ... delicious!

Puma's strength underestimated—Greenwood's guanaco stolen—Refuge in the caves—Pumas kill thousands of sheep—Trapping and poisons—Cub meat makes a good roast—Practical joke on breakfast party

Do not for a moment suppose that because the puma is cowardly, he is not possessed of enormous strength; but, either he is not aware of it, or only uses it on rare occasions. We have only to dissect the body of one, and note the extraordinary muscular development, to know what they could do if they liked.

A male guanaco will weigh very often 300 or 350 pounds, and it is certainly a powerful animal — not, of course, able to fight, as Nature has not provided him with the means of so doing, but it would and does require a couple of very strong dogs to hold him; and if these are not quite *baquiano* in their work, the guanaco is going to get away from them. And yet, I have seen a little puma spring from the long grass at a full-sized buck guanaco, catch him behind the ears with his two fore paws, fix his teeth in his throat and hold on till the guanaco dropped dead; after which he dragged the carcass to a bush about 10 yards distant, stepping cautiously backwards. A big *lion* will work in a different manner: he just throws the long neck of the guanaco across his shoulders, turns his head round, takes the nose of the victim in his mouth, and drags away until he finds a convenient place for his meal.

I remember once, when first I went to *camp*, I was most egregiously mistaken. I had only just begun to wander, and had managed to get as far as Laguna Blanca, which in those days was quite uninhabited; owing to the broken nature of the ground, and enormous quantity of game found there, it formed a splendid hunting ground. The very first day I shot a large buck guanaco, very fat; but, instead of putting him on my horse like a man, and taking him home, I covered him up with a blanket, which I lashed on with a brand-new *lasso* (worth 20 dollars) and went back to *camp* to fetch my man to help me carry him home. As it was very late, we thought we would leave the business till next day. Well, in the morning, away we went to fetch our meat. We got to the place where I had left the animal, and found my tracks, and the marks where the guanaco had lain, plain enough; but, devil a sign of guanaco, *lasso* or blanket: the ground was very hard and we could not find a trace of anything. My man stuck to it: I had come to the wrong place, or left the guanaco alive, and he had cleared out, blanket and all; and we had quite a row over it. Anyway, we gave it up and started for home. We had gone about 400 yards, when out of a bush started a great big *lion*, which was quietly feeding on my guanaco. We soon killed him, and on examining the remains of the guanaco, found all the best of the meat eaten, my *lasso* bitten in a dozen different places, and a few stray pieces of my best red blanket strewn about in various directions. Considering the guanaco had been dragged uphill fully 400 yards, you can imagine the strength required to do it.

After this adventure with the guanaco, I became more cautious and took care not to leave my game in the *camp*, unless I could find a convenient tree to hang it on; but, on several occasions, I lost *ostriches* and nests of eggs, which I had for the moment no means of carrying. I only mentioned the instance of the guanaco to show what strength the puma has, if he liked to exercise it.

As in the case of the guanacos, which become more numerous as one gets more to the south, so it is with the puma; and like the guanacos, which seem to get into a focus in South Patagonia, so is it the case with the pumas.

The coast of Patagonia, from Gallegos to the far north, has a tremendous lot of cover; all the *barrancas* are full of large caves, and the canyons are full of dense undergrowth. Even with good dogs, you can rarely find a *lion*: you only come upon them by chance. So, the only plan I could think of was to blow up the caves with dynamite. I applied to several influential people here to see if they could get me some, but none of them could obtain permission to ship any.

Anyway, we killed a great many by watching for them near the caves, early in the morning and late at night; but, when I left[2], they were still doing a great deal of mischief; and, although every bit of the *camp* was poisoned and every precaution taken, they did not seem to be decreasing in numbers. I refer, of course, only to certain parts where there are unlimited covers, shelter caves, etc. for the brutes to hide in.

One thing very extraordinary is the very long time a puma can live without either food or water. A friend of mine had one shut in a cave in the *tosca* rock for more than a month; at the end of that time he opened the cave and found the animal alive, although very much emaciated. I fancy they must, like bears in winter, sleep and suck their paws for sustenance. I myself have had them shut in for a week or two, and at the end of that time they were as lively as crickets. This appears terribly cruel, and were there any other mode of killing them, no one but a brute would resort to such measures; but the farmers must protect themselves, and when once the pumas get into the caves or cracks in the *barrancas*,

---

[2] Departure from Patagonia — Greenwood left Cañadón de las Vacas around 1896.

it is your only course, if you wish to exterminate them — although, of course, a great deal can be done by poisoning the *camp* constantly. Sooner or later they are bound to eat the poisoned meat, and even if they don't eat it, the hawks and foxes, which are very destructive amongst the lambs will, so your work is not thrown away.

Perhaps my readers will think that I am exaggerating the mischief done by the pumas, and the quantity found in this part of Patagonia. I think none of the oldest residents will be of this opinion, but the readers have not had any experience whilst living in the *camp*.

They are, in any case, most destructive on a sheep farm and, as I think I told you before, whilst I was managing the farm at Cañadón de las Vacas, they destroyed at least three or four thousand sheep in less than seven years. These were what I found; how many more they killed which I did not find, I cannot imagine. Certain it is that, at every shearing and dipping, we were short of sheep, which we could never account for. A great friend of mine said to me, only a short time ago: "*I would willingly give the pumas on my land a fat sheep a day, if they would only let me alone.*" This year he had 1,150 killed, which he knew of, but heaven knows how many more had been lacerated or driven off the ground.

I have seen one *lion* kill one hundred and seventy sheep before I could kill him. In vain, we rounded up the flock and kept guard over them: every other night he came in regularly and made a slaughter. He always chose the darkest hour, then made a dash and scattered the flock all over the country. When he had done mischief enough, he would eat the last one killed, and cover up the remains for a future occasion. He was so cunning in concealing the meat he intended coming back to eat that it was nearly a month before I could manage to poison him, and by that time he had done us hundreds of pounds' worth of damage — not only by killing, but by making the sheep quite unmanageable, and scattering them all over the *camp* for *leagues* around; beside this, many of the ewes lost their lambs. At last, however, we managed to dispose of him: but only to be succeeded by others — not quite so troublesome as the one I refer to, but quite bad enough.

It is very disheartening work for the farmer when he finds twenty, thirty and even fifty sheep killed in one night, and many others wounded or driven off the ground. The reader can imagine the quantity of pumas there are in Patagonia when I state (as I mentioned before) that I have killed myself during my residence there between eleven and twelve hundred (that I know of); how many more I have poisoned and not found, it is impossible to say. Other farmers have killed and poisoned large numbers, but I think my record is the best: of course, I had more time to make it in, and more experience in hunting than the more recently arrived settlers.

The meanest farmer ought to be content to pay his shepherds £1 per head for every *lion* they kill, and it would repay him well. This is the rule on nearly every English farm but, I am sorry to say, it is not so amongst the farmers of other nationalities: otherwise the damage caused by the pumas would be much less than it is at present.

It is quite certain that this pest may be much decreased by constantly poisoning the *camp*, and paying your men for killing; but I do not for a moment suppose that *lions* will ever be exterminated in Patagonia — at least in the parts I am acquainted with. Between the Atlantic coast and the *Cordillera* there are hundreds of leagues of uninhabited *camp* and, what is more, *camps* which can never be occupied because there is no water. Generally, these *camps* are covered with thick *mata negra*, which affords unlimited shelter to the enemy. They do not do much damage in the summer months, as there is plenty of game outside; but in winter they follow the game down to the coast where, finding plenty of fat mutton easy to catch, they consider it advisable to take advantage of it, and leave the lean guanacos for a future period; then we knew it was time to give up all other pursuits and track *lions*.

We used to have great fun in Cañadón de las Vacas on moonlit nights, when there was snow on the ground, when some of us would sally forth in quest of *lions*. They used to be out killing every night, and return to their caves just about daylight. One night we were very fortunate and

got five into one cave, which did not appear very deep; we blocked up
the opening with big stones and earth, and went back to look for tools,
then returned and dug the brutes out. When we had got the opening
wide enough, we saw there no less than seven inside; they were evidently frightened out of their lives, and made no attempt to rush out,
but stopped, all huddled together, snarling and spitting. We soon gave
them Winchester bullets galore, and afterwards fished them out; finding the smallest one was beautifully fat, I sent one of the boys back for
some grog, biscuits and salt; meanwhile, we roasted him whole and then
had a glorious feed.

By the way, I would just as soon have a young fat *lion* as pork; and,
what is more, I defy anyone to tell the difference — that is to say, if the
lion is cooked properly. In proof of this, on several occasions, being
rather annoyed at the horror expressed by some of my English friends
at the very idea of my eating *lion* meat, I resolved to take my revenge.

On my return to the Colony, I brought with me a particularly fat
young *lion*. This I delivered to the cook at the English house in which
I was staying, with directions to serve up pork chops in the morning; he was an old *camp* hand, knew exactly how to make them, and
thoroughly appreciated the joke. Well, the chops were duly served; the
English Dr. and his wife, and 3 or 4 of the swells in Punta Arenas, ate
and pronounced them excellent. They certainly would not have known
to this day that they had not been eating pork, if the fool of a cook had
not let it out. At first they would not believe it, and were only convinced
by seeing the remains of the *lion*, and then they all agreed that they
were delicious. Next day, however, the same dish was served to the
same company, and no one would touch it except the Dr. and myself;
and even he, I think, did it out of pure bravado. On another occasion,
the Captain of one of the steamers took some smoked hams (that I had
cured) home with him, and told me afterwards both he and his friends
found it excellent. I should advise anyone who goes to Patagonia, and
gets a chance, to try for himself; only, let him take care that the animal
he eats is young and a female.

From the Straits of Magellan to Gallegos, I am told that in some parts a puma is now seldom seen[3], and everywhere it appears to be the exception when one comes in and kills sheep, not the rule as before. It is quite certain that, the more fencing is done the less trouble there will be, as I note that the puma objects to fencing and particularly to barbed wire.

[3] Pumas seldom seen in some parts — By 1900, the puma was becoming scarce in the more settled parts of Southern Patagonia. Yet, even as late as the 1940s, it remained a menace to the sheep farmers of the Cordillera. (Madsen & Bertomeu 1956).

⚜ 18 ⚜

Ostriches (Rheas)

Well-known bird—Migration habits—Breeding male forms harem—
Females lay in common nests and elsewhere—Male bird incubates eggs
and raises young—Attacks by grey fox and puma—Trade in feathers—
Cheating—Greenwood's involuntary mistake

Perhaps, as the rhea is found not only in Patagonia, but in all parts of Argentina, its habits, etc., may be well known to most people; but, there are doubtless some who have not studied the habits of this bird. So, I will write a slight sketch describing its customs and great utility.

The habits of the *ostrich* are very similar to those of the guanaco. As far as migrating from one part of the *camp* to the other goes — where you find plenty of guanaco, as a rule, you will find plenty of *ostriches*. In the winter months, they all migrate to the coast of the Atlantic, or to the western *canals*[1], unless the winter is very mild, when many of them remain in the central *camps*; but, with the first sign of snow, they march to the coast, Nature teaching them that where there is a large body of salt water, the snow does not last.

About the middle of August, the male *ostrich* commences to select his harem, varying generally from seven to thirteen females. These he takes away with him to where he can find a convenient ground; he is not particular where it is, so long as there are water and green herbs close by for the young ones, when they are hatched. Two or three younger

---

[1] Western canals — Sea channels (fjords) of the Patagonian Pacific coast.

246

male birds generally accompany these little flocks, but there is only one real chief, who bosses the lot. As each female lays from thirty to forty eggs during the season, of course, they have to lay in various nests; but, the nests belonging to each particular mob are almost invariably found only a few hundred yards apart from each other. The females lay indiscriminately in any of these nests which may not be occupied by another bird; if all the nests are in use, they will lay their eggs anywhere, even on the bare ground. These are called *huevos guachos*[2], and will be found distributed all over the *camp*, both before and after the breeding season. It is difficult to determine the exact period when the breeding season commences: it depends in a great measure on the previous winter but, generally, it begins about the beginning of September, and the birds continue laying till the end of December or beginning of January.

Well, we will follow as far as possible the routine observed by the bands of breeding *ostriches*. First of all, as I said, the old male bird selects a convenient spot for his nests; he does not look particularly for shelter — on the contrary he prefers a place where, while sitting, he can see far and wide. There is no regular number of eggs found in any particular nest: the smallest I ever saw contained only nine eggs, the largest no less than eighty-seven (87). This is a very extraordinary circumstance, and I can only account for it by supposing that two or three lots of females had been laying in the same nest. At any rate, there were two male *ostriches* sitting on this same nest, and several more wandering about the vicinity. I never saw such an enormous nest as this: it was as big as a small cartwheel, and the eggs were piled up three deep. The top layer were beautifully green and fresh, the second layer had chickens (*charas*) in them, just ready to be hatched; the lower tier were half-buried in the earth, and were perfectly sour. Whether the unfortunate male birds would have succeeded in hatching even one-third of them, I should think very doubtful.

We will suppose each nest has been taken possession of by a male bird. The chief, or oldest bird, will probably occupy the largest nest and the best spot; the younger ones will fight for the privilege of the

---

[2] "Huevos guachos" — (Spanish) Literally, "orphan eggs".

possession of other nests. At the end of six weeks, the young birds are hatched — not all at the same time, as is the case with other birds, but sometimes extending over a period of three or four days. The youngsters do not leave their nests as they are born, but stick close to their parent, until such time as they consider all good eggs are hatched. During this time of waiting, the little ones are fed by the old bird with the eggs that are stowed away at the bottom of the nest. Moreover, they are constantly pecking and sucking at the breast of the parent bird, which is absolutely bare of feathers by this time; the breast is full of a yellowish-white substance which the little birds, somehow or other, manage to draw out through the pores of the skin. When the old bird considers there are no more to be hatched, he leaves the nest with the entire family at his heels, and takes them to some sheltered spot where there is a spring or lake, with short, crisp, green grass and flowers. His favourite food is the common dandelion or chicory, of which they are inordinately fond; but, directly the wild fruits are ripe, they feed on nothing else. It is extraordinary to note the affection that the male parent bird bears to his offspring; the female just lays the eggs, and there is an end to the matter. I don't believe the male ever sleeps: he is constantly on the *qui vive*, and cannot bear any of his family to stray far from him.

I once noted a curious circumstance whilst watching an *ostrich* and his young ones feeding. A grey fox had spotted the family and was

cautiously following them, with the intention of devouring any of the young ones that might stray from its parent, but he had reckoned without his host. The old bird saw him, pursued him and caught him in a couple of turns, and proceeded to pound and jump on him with all his might. The fox lay perfectly still and shammed dead, and I certainly thought there was an end of him, as did the old *ostrich*, who quietly returned to his flock. But, he no sooner got a little distance away, than the fox quietly lifted up his head, got up and followed in the tracks of the young birds. This time he actually succeeded in catching one — with which he was sneaking off in his mouth — when he was again observed, caught, and received another tremendous pounding: this time, more to the purpose, as both legs and ribs were broken. I walked up and dispatched him. Pumas are also great enemies to these birds, and very often destroy both parent and whole brood while sleeping.

In former years, numbers of families were destroyed by the *camp* fires made by the Indians and *Christians* alike. It is impossible to imagine how many young animals were burnt to death in these fires, and *ostriches* were getting woefully scarce. But, since making *camp* fires was strictly prohibited, they have increased enormously; the more so that there is little or no hunting carried on nowadays by either *Christians* or Indians.

Although perhaps not quite so useful or valuable to *Christians* and Indians as the guanaco, the *ostrich* has, for years past, been a great staple, both of food and commerce, to thousands of people. At one time, the price of feathers rose to $2.50 gold per pound, and for a long time was not below $1 gold. This was a splendid business when you come to consider that a full-sized male *ostrich* will give from two to three pounds of feathers, a female 1½ pounds and a *chara* something under 1 pound. Those were splendid times, but unfortunately did not last, principally because the Indians and traders used to put stones, blood and sticks inside the bundles of feathers to make them weigh heavier. These people cut their own throats completely, as the Patagonian feathers got such a bad name on this account that no one would look at them.

On this subject, I remember an amusing incident that happened to myself whilst in this trade. Two kind old friends of mine who bought my feathers for years, without questioning or even looking at them if I said they were good, continued dealing with me in the same way after these feather swindles were known. I went in with three heavy sacks of feathers, something over 300 lb. weight, and handed them over as usual to my friends, who promptly paid me 2 dollars a pound for them. They were put into the deposit without examination, as they were well packed and ready to be shipped to Le Havre (France), which was the principal market at that time.

I went away and returned in six months with more feathers, when I noted on the mantelpiece in the sitting-room 3 large, round *bola* stones, of a peculiar blue granite which is much appreciated by the Indians for this purpose. I said to my friend Mr. R.: "*Why, I have been looking for those stones a long time, the best I ever found.*" "*Yes,*" Mr. R. remarked, very drily, "*they ought to be good: they cost us 15 dollars, and were also returned to us from Havre as a specimen of Patagonian feathers.*" The whole thing struck me in a moment: evidently, I had been in a hurry to march and had shoved these 3 stones in the mouth of one of the feather sacks, forgotten all about them, filled the sack with feathers and sewn it up. There was a laugh against me for this for years, as I had always been the first to cry down and expatiate against the practice of mixing blood, gravel, etc. with the feathers to make them weigh heavily, and thus ruin the trade. Of course they knew it was a mistake, and we had a hearty laugh over it many a time.

⚜ 19 ⚜

Guanacos

Ugly in eyes of the uninformed public—Mainstay of the Indian economy—Seasonal migration for reproduction—Number of skins for a rug—Quality of the meat—Value of hides—Is there demand?

Whilst visiting the Zoo for the first time, after many years' absence from the old country, I naturally looked out, first of all, for all my old Patagonian friends; and, of course, amongst the first came the Guanaco. Whilst standing before the paddock in which the animals were enclosed, and thinking of the many services their species had rendered me for so many years, a party of visitors came up and, as usual, commenced to criticise them.

One lady remarked: *"What an ugly, uninteresting animal!"* It may be so, and probably another lady, over whose best blouse one of them had just discharged a mouthful of half-masticated grass in return for some affectionate demonstration on her part, had some reason to think so — more especially as she was  evidently most kindly disposed to all living creatures, and stroked the nose of this particular specimen with the utmost kindness and a blind confidence in his amiability; but still, I am sure she would not have made this remark, had she known all we Patagonians know about these most useful animals.

Ugly he is, uninteresting he may appear, but useless he is not. If any person, animal, or thing deserves notice, it is this particular atom of

251

nature; and, considering that from time immemorial he has been the mainstay of an entire race of people, has supplied them with food, clothes, shelter, weapons, shoes, etc., I think he deserves an article to himself, and a long one. I can, however, only afford him a few paragraphs, as I have at least twenty of his wild brothers and sisters to describe and comment upon before I have done with Patagonian Natural History.

Well, this animal exists in such vast quantities in Patagonia, and also all up the *Cordilleras*, even as far as Brazil, that it is difficult to determine what were his original headquarters; but, I should think, from the vast quantity found in all parts of Patagonia, that these were — as they are now — his principal haunts, centuries ago. The farther south one goes, the more plentiful they become; and, as in the northern districts they are only found in small flocks, so, in the south, they may be met with in enormous mobs — nay, in masses I might say; in fact (I repeat) they are, in some districts, a perfect nuisance.

It is only in the summer season that the coast and the numerous farms situated thereon are comparatively free from them: at that time they return inland to breed, and it is then that the Indians are in their glory and can fully calculate upon making enough, if not to keep them for the whole year, at least to most materially assist them. A hard-working Indian or *Christian* ought not to kill less than from thirty to forty young guanacos *per diem*, and this means three *rugs* (*capas*) of 13 to 15 skins each, and varying in value from $15 to $20 each. The breeding season commences about the 5th November, and lasts till the beginning of January; after that the young ones begin to run well and give more trouble to catch them; but, meantime, the hunter has made his harvest.

Well, now for the utility of the old animal: first, his skin is used by the Indians to make their *toldos* (houses): sometimes as many as 100 old skins are employed in fashioning a single house. They are fitted together in exactly the same fashion as the *rugs*, being also greased and softened before sewing. Therefore, you see our friend has already supplied us with a house and money for current expenses, independently of the clothes and bedclothes, constantly used by the Indians, in the shape of these *rugs*. No Indian would dream of being without one to wear by day, and to cover himself with by night.

The skin of the legs, taken off in the shape of bags, serves to hold the winter's supply of grease, so necessary to an Indian. The skin of the neck serves to make the *sogas* for the *bolas*, and the curves taken from the lower joint of the leg serve to *retobar* or cover the *bolas* themselves; all the plaited *lassoes* are also made from the neck of the female (those of the males are too thick to serve for plaiting). The Indian *monturas* are also covered with the same hide taken from the sides, where it is thinnest and most even. The *squaws* undertake the drying of the skins, the softening of them, and the making of the *rugs* (*capas*) — the men only attend to their hunting and gear-making. I wonder where they would all be without the poor, stupid, uninteresting Guanaco?

They cause great damage to the farmers, but I do not think that this can continue: as the population increases, the poor animals must seek other feeding grounds. Even now, I am informed by various farmers that the mobs of animals are much decreased in number and, unless in very severe weather, do not come down in enormous flocks as they used to when I first visited the country.

The meat of the Guanaco is not generally appreciated, but I think it is not at all bad, if well *carneado* and the best parts selected. I am quite sure that there is not an old resident in Patagonia who has not been glad to get a good meal of guanaco meat, many a time and oft.

It is a pity that the skin is not more valuable — at least, it used not to be valuable. I sent home 300 skins some years ago and, actually, they did not pay expenses. It seems a pity that there is not a good market for the article, as anyone who dedicated himself entirely to the work could make a really good thing of it (if the skins gave only a moderate result). I heard recently that they were in much demand in Germany, but do not know if it is true or not.

❧ 20 ❧

Seals and Sea Lions

*Large colony of hair seals at Monte León—Return to land from feeding
at daybreak—Pebbles provide ballast for swimming—Training the
pups—Beware of stampedes—Uses for hide and oil—If fur coats could
talk ...*

I don't suppose there are any animals more interesting, or whose habits
are more worthy of observance, than those of the seal.

I have not had many opportunities of studying the habits of the fur
seal, the smallest and most valuable of the various species found on the
Patagonian coast, Tierra del Fuego and the numerous islands adjacent.
I had, however, a splendid chance of observing a large rookery of hair
seals or sea lions, which had headquarters called Monte León, situated
only a few miles from our sheep station in Cañadón de las Vacas.

The herd consisted of about 2,000 head, big and small, and they
hauled up in a small cove nearly in front of the island of Monte León,
and in some large caves adjoining. By keeping to the edge of the cliffs
(only about 20 feet high at that point), one could get a splendid view of
all their performances, and very interesting they were; but, to make their
real acquaintance, and to gain an insight into all their habits, would have
required more time and careful attention than I had leisure to bestow.
I only state what I noticed, during the short visits that my numerous
duties on a newly established sheep farm enabled me to pay them.

❧

I can assure anyone interested in the Natural History and habits of
these animals that, if circumstances should call him to that part of the

world, a visit to the sea lion rookery at Monte León would amply repay
any little trouble he may experience in getting there. There is a farm-
house a short distance from the rookery (say 3 or 4 miles), where the
visitor would be most hospitably received by Mr. Roger Campbell, one
of our pioneers and principal farmers.

I should, however, recommend camping out close to the seals' home,
so that the seeker after knowledge can be on the spot at daybreak, to
catch the animals coming home from their fishing excursions. After
seeing the herd arrive and settle themselves down for a long nap and
digester, till the fishing hour arrives again, the explorer will find ample
amusement and occupation, either in hunting and shooting (as game
abounds in the vicinity); or, if he is not a sportsman, the neighbouring
hills and *barrancas* abound in fossils of every description. Some of the
best specimens existing at the present time in the Museums of La Plata,
Strasbourg and South Kensington[1], have been taken from the cliffs of
Monte León and the vicinity.

Well, to return to the seals: shortly before sunrise, the herd begins to
return from their fishing excursion, and to take up their quarters for the
day. A good deal of squabbling and grunting ensues, as each new arrival

---

[1] Museums — (1) La Plata: Buenos Aires province, Argentina; (2) Strasbourg: Alsace,
France; (3) South Kensington: London, England.

comes ashore, but each one eventually occupies, as nearly as possible, his usual quarters.

They have chosen a lovely spot for their morning siesta, a delightful little bay with no stones, but only soft dry white sand, and sheltered from all the most prevalent winds. There is plenty of room for ten times their number, but they appear to like company and lie all in a bunch — looking, for all the world, like a lot of black slippery rocks, shining as if recently uncovered by the water. They are not quite gentlemen in their habits, and are probably confirmed gluttons. They have certainly eaten more than is good for them, as each one, before settling down for his nap, proceeds to throw up a portion of the night's catch which has proved too much for his digestive powers; so that each one, when he goes to sleep, has a pile of half-digested fish beside him, and the atmosphere for some hundreds of yards round is not a pleasant one. Some old seals, for greater ease, throw up a portion of their ballast stones but, sleeping or waking, always retain sufficient to enable them to take to the water at a moment's notice.

Perhaps many people do not know that the seal is quite useless in the water without his ballast; he is so fat, as a rule, that, if he is not well weighted, he can neither swim nor dive, or pursue his trade of fishing to advantage — in fact, he would bob about in the water like a cork. The baby seals do not understand this necessity, and the mothers have the greatest difficulty in persuading or, I should say, forcing them to take in their ballast.

Strangely enough, more difficulty is experienced in getting them into the water; but, by dint of shoving, pushing, biting and even sometimes carrying them, the whole lot of pups are in their native element. One would think all the trouble was over for, once in, the youngsters simply revel in it. For some reason or other, the parents do not allow them to remain in the water long, at least for the first few days. Then there is a general rebellion: the youngsters refuse to come out; and their parents, who are dying to resume their nap, have to go after them, collect them and literally force them ashore. Once there, they get rid of their unaccustomed load of stones and resume their *siesta*, each pup beside the mother. There is a great deal of gaping and grunting before all are settled down. I am sure, however, there are always some few awake, or supposed to be so, to serve as sentinels. These lie generally in twos or threes, somewhat apart from the sleeping mass of seals (you can call it nothing else). If you wish to kill one, either as a specimen or to obtain his oil, you must be most careful in approaching them, and mind and see how the wind is: for, if they once wind you, there is a general rush and flurry, and all but the babies are on their way to the sea, and even some of these follow.

How they get on in the water without ballast I don't know, but I should imagine they always retain a portion in their stomachs; certainly the old ones do, as they are ready to take to the water at the first sign of alarm. Woe betide you if you get between the mass of seals and the sea, or you will most assuredly be rolled over and over, and may think yourself lucky if you do not get some of your bones broken, or a bite taken out of you by one of the big lions. Many a serious (and even fatal) accident has occurred to sealers who have incautiously got between the mob of seals and the sea.

If the visitor wishes to get a specimen, he can easily do so; first, by noting the direction of the wind and seeing that they are all more or less asleep; then he can crawl to within a few feet of the herd, and pick off what he pleases. The only safe shot is just behind or in the ear; wounds in any other part of the body do not seem to affect them — in fact they appear rather livelier with a shot in the body: once hit behind the ear, they are done for. The skins are of little value, except for cutting into *lassoes* for tying up your horses, as no fox will bite a rope of seal hide, and for this purpose the hide is most useful; also the oil is excellent for sharpening shears, and we always provided ourselves with a quantity before shearing time. For burning purposes, it is also very useful for outside *camps* or in the farm sheds; inside the house, as it has a very strong smell, it is useless.

With regard to the fur seals, I am informed by many old sealers that their habits are nearly identical with those of the hair seal. The fur seals seldom haul up to breed or shed their coats, except on islands generally most difficult of access: they seldom breed on the mainland. The general custom is for the sealing vessels to place two or three hands on each of the different rocks which the seals frequent, and leave then there till the season is over. In many cases, in former years, this custom has proved fatal to many of the poor fellows, as the rocks they imagine quite safe have been, at certain seasons, completely covered by the waves, and the men washed away; other poor fellows have literally starved to death before their vessels could find an opportunity to take them off. I believe that now great care is taken, and men are never left on rocks which are not known to be perfectly safe; but, 25 years ago, accidents of the kind I mention were very common, and scarcely a season passed without some tragedy occurring. I often think, when I see people wearing expensive sealskin coats and jackets, what sad stories some of these furs could tell if they could speak.

⚜ 21 ⚜

Lesser Game

The Huemul or Mountain Deer

Graceful, beautiful animals—Attractive eyes—Small antlers—
Valuable hide and meat—Easily tamed—Sad end of a pet—Innocent
curiosity makes them vulnerable to Man—Fighting bucks

If not the most useful or interesting animal found in the *Cordilleras*, the *mountain deer* (huemul)[1] will most certainly carry off the palm for both beauty and grace. Lady Florence Dixie, in her work "*Across Patagonia*" (Chapter XV), gives a very good description of their fine encounter with a herd of *deer*. She did not, however, see them at their best, as it was the shedding season, when their coats assume a mangy, brownish-yellow colour. To see them at their best, go at the beginning of winter, when they are of a beautiful reddish-brown on back, sides and haunches, the legs of a lighter colour, nose and feet black, the former very wide with extended nostrils. They have, without exception, the most beautiful eyes I ever saw of any living animal.

I quite agree with Lady Dixie that it seems cruel to kill them. This is all very well for parties of pleasure, who have no necessity to do so. All they have to do is to admire the graceful forms, gazelle-like eyes and general beauty of the animals. Unfortunately, my living depended on what I could hunt, so all my sentiment went to the winds. First, the meat is splendid (by far the best found in Patagonia) and the skins used to be worth three dollars each. Also the heads, with their small antlers never

---

[1] Huemul (*mountain deer*) — Standing no more than 90 cm. high, the huemul is treated as "lesser game".

consisting of more than the short parent stump and two straight prongs, used to fetch three or four dollars each. So, you see, this animal gave a better result (to the hunter) than even the *ostrich*, only they are not so plentiful, and are difficult to find without good dogs.

As for the *"spreading antlers"* mentioned by Lady Dixie, I am afraid they are a creation of her Ladyship's brain as, amongst the many hundreds I have killed, I have only found the short stump and two prongs before mentioned; but, perhaps the specimens met with by this party were of some peculiar kind, which I had not the pleasure of encountering.

The skins are very useful to the hunter in various ways: the hair can easily be removed, and the hide softened with the hand until it becomes like chamois leather. For years, my whole clothing was made of *lion* and *deer* skins — the former with the hair left on and well softened, served for upper clothing, whilst the beautifully soft *deer* skins make capital drawers and shirts.

I have visited many zoological gardens but, strangely enough, never saw a specimen, at which I wonder, as they are so very easily tamed. I have brought up several young ones on mare's milk, with the intention of sending one or two home (to England) but, unfortunately, they have always come to an untimely end. One, in particular, I brought up till he was quite big, and we had a mutual affection for one another. He would always sleep at the mouth of the tent, close to the dogs, none of whom attempted to touch him; he would sometimes play with some of the puppies. He would follow me like a dog, whether I was on foot or horseback; indeed, I could not go out without his accompanying me, and this was the cause of his death. When I was going a long distance I had to tie him up, as he soon got tired on the level *camp*, although he would run up and down hills and steep places half the day for his own pleasure.

One day I went out early to hunt and, as usual, left my poor pet tied to a tree with a long rope, so that he could feed. What was my disgust, when I returned, to find that two stray Indian dogs had paid a visit to the camp during my absence, and killed him, and were quietly feeding on him. I shot the dogs as a matter of course, but that did not give me back my pet. I was so thoroughly grieved that, although I frequently came across young *deer* of just the right age, I never tried to tame another.

When I first went to the Straits of Magellan, these animals were very plentiful in the neighbourhood — indeed their meat formed one of the staple articles of food — but now I hear they are very scarce. Nowadays, if the hunter or explorer wishes to find them in any quantity and study their habits, he must seek the innermost recesses of the mountains where the foot of man seldom, if ever, treads. There he will find them plentiful: not in large mobs like the guanaco, but in small herds varying from six to ten.

If these poor animals have never known what Man the destroyer is, it is incredible how tame they are, and also so very inquisitive; this is, I believe, a peculiarity of all species of deer, if they see anything strange or unknown to them. They will generally walk round and round in a circle till they get quite close to you, staring at you with all their might; indeed, on one occasion, during that miserable time when I was so long on food, I actually grabbed a young doe by the leg, and devoured her afterwards.

In common with other deer, they shed their horns every year, the horn being, as they sprout, covered with thick moss[2], which does not peel off till they are quite hardened. While this process goes on, the young bucks have to abstain from fighting (a very favourite diversion of theirs, by the way); but, directly their horns are hardened, they set to with renewed vigour. I have often heard their horns clashing in the evening and early morning, and have killed them with their heads and

---

[2] Thick moss on the growing antler — This is known as "velvet".

chests covered with wounds. Very often the old bucks will fight the dogs, and on one occasion one of my favourite dogs was literally transfixed on the long prongs of a big buck, and I had to kill him.

Foxes: The Aguará, Culpeo and Little Grey

Aguará very scarce—Culpeo as large and fierce as a wolf—Little grey fox a threat to sheep—How to use strychnine—Furs fetch good prices

I have often wondered that there are no wolves found in Patagonia: only the *aguará* (which is more a jackal than a wolf), is found in the Río Negro *camps* and sometimes as far south as Chubut, but even those are scarce, and more than two are seldom found together. They never run in packs; if they did, it would be a bad thing for the sheep-farmer in the north, as I am told they are splendid hands at killing and worrying. In all my wanderings I only came across one, and he cleared out before I could get a shot at him. Had I not seen this specimen, and also numerous skins in Río Negro, I should regard the animal as a myth.

I don't know anything about the animal, except what I have been told; but I do know that the skins are very handsome, being, if I remember rightly, of a bright *bayo* or yellow, with a black stripe from the end of the tail to the tip of the nose. The hair on them is very slack and comes out in handfuls, unless they are properly cured, in which case they make very good house or dogcart mats. This is all I know about the *aguará*.

I will go on to the *culpeo* or big mountain fox, so common in the woods of S. Patagonia, and particularly so on the wooded coasts of the Straits of Magellan and the mainland of Tierra del Fuego and the numerous forest-clad islands adjacent.

You really might call the *culpeo* a wolf, as far as size and ferocity when brought to bay goes; and, from what some of the settlers in Tierra del Fuego have told me, they are most destructive when they get amongst a flock of sheep. I only go by hearsay as, except in Oazy and Pecket Harbours, where one or two occasionally sallied forth from the woods and killed a few lambs, they never did us much harm on the Patagonian side of the Straits. But I expect that in Laguna Blanca and the various corners of the *Cordillera*, which are now all occupied, they will be a great nuisance. In Tierra del Fuego, before the farms were started, they must have maintained themselves upon *cururos* (pampa rats), and dead seals, and fish washed up on the beach; they certainly had nothing else till the sheep came.

The *culpeo* is a very handsome animal, and yields a lovely greyish-red skin and *brush*; he is a really powerful animal, generally fully half as big again as an English fox. He is no coward, and I had only one dog which would kill one alone. During the battle, the dog was invariably badly mauled. I have frequently seen one thoroughly rout and put to flight 4 or 5 of my greyhounds, and I noted that when any of these dogs had had a taste of the animal's teeth, they were particularly careful to avoid a fight for the future.

Next we come to the little grey fox who, if he has not the power of strength, has certainly the will to do as much mischief as possible. They certainly prefer turkeys, geese, and fowls to other prey, but they are not at all averse to killing small lambs when they get a chance. Once I caught no less than 3 of them hanging onto the legs of a good-sized lamb, at least 3 months old, and the poor animal was completely hamstrung, and I had to kill it. I put some poison in it and retired; the foxes immediately returned and commenced feeding, of course beginning at the incisions I had made to put the poison in. I began counting very slowly, and when I got to 180, all three foxes were racing about and going into convulsions, and in less than five minutes were *toes up*.

I may mention here for the benefit of those who do not understand the use of strychnine, that although no poison is more deadly, its effects are very often in a great measure nullified if it is not properly applied. If possible, the meat should be poisoned when warm, then the strychnine mixes thoroughly with the blood, and even the very bones of the animal are impregnated with the poison. On many occasions I have seen foxes and *lions* die from gnawing old bones, poisoned at least six months before, and have lost many valuable dogs from the same cause.

This class of smaller foxes is excessively mischievous in many other ways. If you happen to leave a skin in the camp for a night, you may be pretty well sure it will be torn to pieces before the morning; and, if you are fool enough to tie up your horse with a *lasso*, it is 10 chances to one that your *lasso* will be eaten and your horse gone in the morning. Their quantity is enormous, especially near the coast or in any district where the *cururos* abound: to exterminate them will, I fear, be almost an impossibility. I think every farmer would find it advisable to pay his men so much for every fox he kills; this is done on many farms, but is by no means a general custom.

Little grey fox skins make very nice *rugs*, especially if all the tails are left on to serve as a border; they require very careful sewing, as the skin is very tender. 40 skins are required for each *rug* and, when made, it is worth from 40 to 60 dollars. A single skin is generally valued about 60 cents; the large *culpeo* skins are really valuable, and worth at least 3 or 4 dollars each, if taken in the season.

Sometimes these little foxes, like the North American species, turn to a pure white in winter. I killed 4 or 5 specimens who had not changed their coats, but this was always near or in the mountains, where the snowfalls are heavy and last many months. I have only seen 1 or 2 really white in the Pampas but, if there is much snow, many turn to a dingy yellow colour.

Skunks

Source of profit—Raised family of pups—Food preferences—Prone to sucking eggs—Christmas fury—Stench—Pets no more—Unexpected winter food-source and shelter—Attacks on domestic fowl—Skins for rugs—Good eating

Amongst the few of my Patagonian acquaintances whom I have not yet described, there still remains the skunk. I ought to have put him down one of the first on the list, instead of almost the last, as he was a particular friend of mine and a never-failing source of profit; and as far as killing, skinning and eating him went, I did my level best for many years to cultivate his acquaintance.

Also once, in my most enthusiastic days, I tamed a whole family of 4 (2 males and 2 females) as an experiment. These I took from their cave when very young; old Kelly's cat "*Jennie*", who had just had kittens, very kindly brought them up for us. She seemed just as fond of them as she was of the one kitten we left her, when we destroyed her newly born family to make way for the newcomers.

We found them most interesting little animals as long as they were young, and moreover scrupulously clean (which I am sorry to say the cat and her kitten were not), neither had they any smell whatever; but then, no one interfered with them when they were young, so they never got angry, which accounts for it. They passed most of their time in burrowing amongst the long grass, digging up a certain white root or bulb, which they appeared particularly to appreciate. We tried them with meat but, although certainly carnivorous, they did not care for it: I suppose having been brought up entirely on milk was the reason. Eggs they were particularly fond of; and, to make them more so, we were fools enough to give them eggs to suck when their adopted mother had no milk to give them. This fondness for eggs eventually proved their ruin, and also that of 2 or 3 young grey foxes which we were bringing up at the same time.

It was in this wise. We always had a great notion of keeping up Xmas the best way we could, not always an easy thing in the wilds of Patagonia. To facilitate this good old custom, we used to stow away a certain portion of all the good things we brought from Punta Arenas when we took in our winter catch of feathers, specially to celebrate the season. As egg season was finished at Xmas, we used to bury *ostrich* and other eggs for weeks before, so that we might have a decent pudding and plenty of egg-flip.

This year we had a whole lot of eggs (*ostrich*, geese, etc.) buried in the corner of the log house we were living in. I don't know whether the skunks or foxes were in fault, but certain it is that one or other of them discovered our egg deposit, which must have contained at least from 50 to 100 (large and small). Now, they were far too cunning to make an entry into the treasure house from the inside of the shanty, but they commenced operations from the outside. They were so successful that, when we opened the hole on Xmas morning to get out eggs for our pudding and take our first cocktail, the wretches had not only sucked all the small eggs, but smashed all the *ostrich* eggs (less about half a dozen), on the usual foxy plan of rolling them one against the other. I laid the blame entirely on the foxes and, being in an awful rage, set the dogs onto them, who soon annihilated them.

I did not think the skunks were in fault, and even if they had been I don't think I should have killed them just for stealing, as I really was attached to the little animals; but, on going to the remaining eggs, I found the 4 of them busily engaged in trying to break the rest. I promptly kicked them all away, and put them in a furious rage; their entire nature seemed to alter, and for the rest of the day we could not get near the house with any comfort for the disagreeable odour, which increased and intensified every time anyone went near them. I kept them, however, several days, hoping they would get over their ill temper; but that they never did, and whenever one of us or one of the dogs went near them, they exercised their skunk-like functions to the very best of their ability, rendering their neighbourhood unbearable — therefore I was forced to kill them. I was sorry for it, as it really was impatience which was the cause of their commencing to be a nuisance. Anyhow, I never tried to tame skunks again.

I do not think that the skunk prefers a meat diet, but he is certainly distinctly carnivorous during the winter months, probably because the ground is too hard for him to dig up his favourite roots. In summer and spring they have their caves to live in, and when there is a river or spring you will almost invariably find their little colonies near it. In or near damp marshy ground or bogs, where fowl are abundant, they are generally very plentiful, suck a great many eggs, and very often kill the young birds and sometimes the old ones.

In winter they will travel very long distances in search of food, and if they come across a dead animal, they often take up their residence, not alongside, but inside it; they generally bore a hole in the stomach of the dead carcass, and drag a lot of dry grass inside and make themselves thoroughly comfortable, till they have devoured all the meat they can manage to get at. When that carcass is finished, they move on till they find another dead body. I think this is a very convenient way of living: to get food and room at the same time, for nothing, must be nice.

Unfortunately, the skunk is not contented with the goods the Gods find for him, but must go further afield to look for luxuries in the way of fowls and eggs. It is extraordinary what an amount of damage a family of these animals will do if they take up their residence near or under a house, which latter proceeding is a very common one in these parts.

If this happens, as in the *camp* houses is frequently the case, you must expect no peace till you have exterminated every member of the community. Not only is the smell of the house unbearable but, if you have a henhouse, or keep ducks, geese or turkeys, these little wretches are bound to find them out and do a lot of mischief.

In Santa Cruz, just before I left, we had a terrible trouble to get rid of a lot, which had taken up their residence in some *barrancas* close to our home; they made a subterranean passage, both under the house and into the henhouse. The house was so unpleasant inside, when anyone passed anywhere over or near them, that it became almost unbearable; and, although we were constantly taking up portions of the flooring and killed several, we had no peace until we destroyed the whole colony. On two occasions, in the middle of the night, there was a tremendous disturbance in the henhouse, which was not far distant from the house. Of course, I rushed there at once, but it was too late to prevent the mischief, as on both occasions they had killed several fowls, and I caught and killed them in the very act of sucking their victims' blood. To avoid this very catastrophe, we had placed big stones below the bottom beams of the henhouse, but they had burrowed beneath them like rabbits. How on earth they got at the birds I cannot imagine, because all the big fowls roosted on crossbars or high shelves, and the sitting hens and all the young ones were in coops. It was invariably the pick of our full-grown cocks and hens that were killed. You can understand from these details that, although the skunk is a valuable little animal in several ways (which I shall presently mention), his virtues are more than counterbalanced by his vices.

The skin is in much request amongst the Indians and the *rugs* made by them are really valuable. Each *rug* contains 54 skins; if they are perfectly black they vary in value from 60 to 90 dollars in Patagonia, and in England are worth much more. A single skin is worth about 60 cents; they are much used for ladies' muffs, cuffs and toques.

If you wish to enjoy roast sucking pig to perfection, take a fat skunk unawares and kill him stone-dead before he has time to get angry; skin and clean him at once and sprinkle him with salt and hang him in the sun for several hours; then stuff and roast him and be happy, but beware of indigestion. N.B. If you happen to have a friend who is fond of hunting and eating skunk, ask him as a personal favour not to bring home a bag containing 6 or 7 specimens, only stunned not killed, because they might come to life again — and the result, as it happened in my house on one occasion, is not a pleasant one.

Patagonian Hares (Maras)

Hares or rabbits?—Methods of hunting—Social behaviour—Attractive skins and rugs

It is a pity there are no *hares* to the south of Santa Cruz, as not only do I consider them good eating, but they afford very fair sport, both for gun and rifle, also for your hounds. Indeed, I should say south of San Julián, for they are quite rare between that district and Santa Cruz. In the San Julián *camps*, if not plentiful, still they are to be found, if one knows where to look for them; this I have from hearsay, as it is about twenty-eight years since I travelled in the *camps*. We used to find them all along the coast in great quantities, especially near the Ovens and in Camarones Bay, and spent a lot of time in hunting them. They were a great change from the everlasting guanaco and *ostrich* meat. I don't think the Indians care much for the meat: it is not fat enough to please them.

I really don't know why this animal is called a *hare*[3] — nor do I know to what family it belongs, unless it is a relation of the jackass rabbit found in Mexico, California and other parts of the United States — but we

---

[3] European hare — (*Lepus europaeus*) The species has subsequently been introduced into Southern Patagonia and, escaping from captivity, is now widely distributed.

called it a *hare*, and *"custom makes the law"* in that part of the world. It certainly, however, has more the habits of a rabbit, as it has large burrows, which it makes for on the slightest alarm. I have no doubt they would be ferreted like ordinary rabbits but, unfortunately, ferrets did not exist at that time in Patagonia; nor, to the best of my belief, do they now.

We had several modes of hunting them, sometimes finding them sitting in their lairs, and running them down with dogs. Sometimes they would reach their earth before the dogs could catch them; and then, if we could not dig them out, we stopped up all the holes but the principal bolt-hole, then made a gunpowder squib, and smoked them out. The plan was generally very successful; at other times, the *hares* preferred to be stifled, and would not budge an inch. I found the best plan was to watch for them late in the evening, or early in the morning, and shoot them when they came out to feed or when they returned from feeding.

They generally choose some place for their homes where there is one of the small patches of short green grass so common near the coast; sometimes there is a spring in them and sometimes not, but water can almost invariably be obtained by digging. In Camarones Bay there were some extraordinarily large sets of burrows: I have often seen as many as fifty or sixty sitting outside their holes at one time and behaving (quite unlike rabbits, who would be always skipping about) in the most formal manner. Occasionally, two of the males will have a fight for the amusement of the assembled company; and when these two have finished, another pair will have a set-to, apparently without any just reason for a quarrel. At the smallest noise or fright their white tails disappear into their burrows like a flash of lightning and, once frightened, they are not coming out again in a hurry.

Their skins are very pretty, more like a young *deer's* than a true hare's; indeed, if you notice their form when they run, their movement is more like that of a *deer*. Thirty skins are employed for each *rug* which, when I last purchased some, were worth about 30 dollars each; the white fringe of fur edging the skins has a very pretty effect. They are not nearly as durable as the guanaco robes as, although much prettier, the damp affects them and makes the hair come out.

Cururos (Pampa Rats)

Widespread—Dangerous burrows—Disappear after arrival of sheep—
Mass death in times of flood—Tasty morsel—Useful tunnels—Apologies
to the reader

I must write a few lines about these little animals which inhabit in such innumerable quantities nearly all Tierra del Fuego, and a great part of S. Patagonia (particularly near the coast, both E. and W.), and also generally near the shores of all the large lakes.

Were it not for the terrible way in which they undermine the *camps*, so much so as to render them in some parts almost impassable except at a walk, they might be considered the most harmless little creatures in existence. As it is, in some places they are a perfect nuisance, besides causing innumerable accidents to travellers and *camp* men who are not careful and gallop, or try to gallop, over portions of what we call *cururo* ground. They injure the pasturage excessively by eating both the roots and seeds of the grass, so much so that, in many places, there are *leagues* and *leagues* of *camp* almost void of herbage.

One great thing is that, wherever a sheep-farm is established, *cururos* very soon get trodden out and in a few years disappear altogether. Some of the principal farms on the Straits of Magellan and to the north of the coast were, years ago, literally infested by them, and in wet weather became so boggy that to travel over them was an impossibility. Now, except in places where sheep and other animals do not feed, a *cururo* is a rarity.

I should think that, in the matter of increasing, rabbits are fools to them. For example, some of the *camps* infested with these animals are sometimes covered with water, and all those who cannot find refuge on some little hillock or tuft of grass must be drowned. After a flood I have seen thousands lying dead. I remember on one occasion, in wet weather, making my bed on a little mound in the middle of some *cururo camp*; and, as the water rose, the mound became quite covered with them and in the night many actually crept into and under my bed, which was not pleasant.

But even these little animals, like every thing created, have their utility. As I mentioned elsewhere, they form quite a staple article of food for the poor Fuegian Indians, and really, they might have worse food, for they are just like a very tender young rabbit[4]. I can answer for this, as I have many times eaten them when hard up; only you require about 20 to make a meal, and they are troublesome to skin and prepare.

Sometimes I have seen the little chaps do a great deal of good to the *camp*, in draining it after very wet weather. For example, as I said before, they are very partial to making their homes near large lakes, in the ridges of sand or loose earth round them. In the spring the waters rise and overflow the borders of the lakes and would perhaps, in some cases, cover large tracts of flat *camp*; but, they are checked, in a great measure, when they arrive at the *cururo camp*, which I know from experience absorbs vast quantities of water. How many millions of these little animals are destroyed in these floods, it is impossible to say.

Anyhow, you see that even these atoms have their uses, although every farmer in Patagonia who has them on his land hates the very name of them.

I think that these last notes about the little *cururo* will wind up all the remarks I have made about the various animals in Patagonia. I have endeavoured to depict them and their habits to the best of my ability. I only wish I had been naturalist enough to describe them better; but, failing that, I have simply recounted what I have seen, and that at least is correct. I wish some really practical naturalist would visit and make a long stay in the country, and we should then learn something worth knowing.

---

[4] Cururos as a staple article of food — See 6, INDIANS.

❧ 22 ❧

Advice to Visitors, Settlers and Investors

Profitable Pursuits

Excellent place for a summer vacation—Promising future in fossils—Potential for a gold strike—Disappointment at Cape Virgins—Prudent money management—Expected profits in coal—Room for new farms

Anyone who really wants to enjoy himself and to pass a good time, cannot do better than take his summer *paseo* in the Straits of Magellan; and, moreover, he will find everything there so cheap and good (on account of the Free Ports) that he will on his return growl more than ever over the exorbitant prices charged on most of the articles sold in Buenos Aires. Don't suppose for one moment that it is necessary to take a lot of stores, etc. with you when you go; on the contrary, it will pay you far better to purchase these at almost the same prices as you pay in England.

Not only can you obtain stores and every kind of luxury in Sandy Point, but also at every large farm on the coast, and in Coy Inlet, Gallegos, Santa Cruz and San Julián. Meat, of course, costs next to nothing. For that matter, you don't require to buy any at all, as you can always kill more than enough game to keep you going, and thus avoid the never-ending supply of repugnantly fat mutton.

Although the quantity of game has increased ten-fold since the cessation of the actual business of hunting, occasioned by the occupation of all the best land by sheep-farmers, a very good thing could be made by anyone who devoted himself entirely to hunting and collecting fossils and other curiosities, which can be found in quantities in all parts of the country. Were I a single man, and young and strong again, I would go straight away and ransack Patagonia from north to south, hunting, collecting curios and skins, and washing a little gold whenever I found a paying spot.

Last time I was in the south, I shipped home to the South Kensington Museum (London) a large consignment of fossils and other curiosities, and am only awaiting the reports from the directors to determine whether it will be advisable to organise a large expedition, which will be exclusively occupied in the collection of fossilised remains of every description. I think I know all the best spots where these remains are to be found. Most of them have been worked a good deal by the geologists *Sres*. Ameghino, Moreno, and Doctor Steinmann of Strasbourg University and others. But I also know of one district (which appeared to me very prolific in specimens of all kinds), which, to the best of my belief, has never been visited by anyone but myself. There you find large rocks literally full of fossil remains, also huge masses of fossilised wood and bones of every description. If I can organise the expedition I have in view, I shall devote a long time exclusively to this spot, which appeared to me most interesting and well worth more serious attention. The worst of it is that the place is most inaccessible, right inside the mountain ranges, and the transport of large specimens (except in sections) would be almost impossible. There might be a means of transport *per mar*, and vessels might come up some of the various *canals*, which intersect this portion of the *Cordillera*, and I have no doubt this will eventually be the case; but, hitherto, it has not been attempted.

Some of these days a great gold strike will be made in this country and very rich quality veins will be discovered and worked. Hitherto, only alluvial gold has been discovered. The richest spot yet found was in the Straits of Magellan, at Cape Virgins and the coast in that vicinity. This gold was cast up by the sea whenever there was a particularly high tide, mixed with coarse black sand. To the first two or three men who discovered it, it was a perfect El Dorado and, if they had only kept the thing quiet, each of the discoverers could have made a very large fortune. It is strange but true that gold, like murder, will out. I believe there is no case on record where a gold discovery has not eventually become public property. This was the case in Cape Virgins. No sooner did one of the men have necessity to go into the Colony of Punta Arenas to buy stores, than the news of the find was bruited all over the country; and in a month there was a rush of more than a thousand people to the spot from all parts of the Argentine Republic, also from the Banda Oriental (Uruguay), Chile, Peru and even from the United States. The little corner where the gold had been found was soon played out, and large quantities of machinery, stores, etc., which had been sent down by enterprising firms in Buenos Aires, Montevideo, and the Chilean Republic, were abandoned; and I believe a good deal of valuable machinery for crushing the quartz, which never existed at all, is still to be found distributed over various parts of the coast.

Of course, the discovery was exaggerated to the extreme limit of possibility, and many a poor wretch travelled hundreds of *leagues* to get to the new El Dorado, full of hope and anticipations, which were never to be realised. Only the first few men on the spot made a good thing of it, but these did really well; and, afterwards, those amongst them who were careful men invested their gains in stock, and are now in several cases very prosperous men. Others, and by far the greater portion, spent their money as fast as they had made it. It is strange how little thought a successful gold digger as a general rule takes for the future. The axiom *"There is plenty more where this came from"* is almost universal amongst them; and many a poor fellow, who with care had enough to ensure him prosperity for the rest of his life, literally threw his hard-earned gains away, and had to begin life again.

This was the case with many men I have known. I regret that amongst them I must include myself, despite several comfortable little sums made out of a small gold-strike, the discovery of the wild horses, and the never-failing resource of hunting *ostriches* and guanacos, by which any man could make a comfortable little income of at least one hundred dollars a month. I started two prosperous farms, but everything seemed to slip through my fingers in the most wonderful and incomprehensible manner; however, I hope next time (and I have several very likely affairs on hand at present) I shall gain wisdom by experience. This is possible but not, I fear, probable, and I think the betting is about ten to one that precisely the same thing will happen again, and all my present virtuous resolves will be distributed to the four winds of Heaven. Time will show.

The discovery of good coal in these districts would be the making of the place. Coal there is, and in very large quantities, and I know of numerous veins which crop out in various places all along some of the mountain ranges. I sent several samples, both to Buenos Aires and to Europe: it is declared to be too new to serve for getting up steam, but in the course of a few centuries it will be ripe. This is a very poor consolation to the discoverer and does not hold out a very lively prospect. I was, however, informed by Doctor Steinmann that without the least doubt, strata of really good coal and ripe existed; but, to discover this, shafts would have to be sunk to a great depth and the enterprise would have to be undertaken by a rich company as a speculation, which might bring a splendid return or lead to the ruin of the shareholders. You will probably remember that no less than three different companies were started about twenty-five years ago for the development of the coal leads in Sandy Point and Otway Water, all of which came to grief for want of funds to conclude their work. Had they been able to continue sinking, there is no doubt they would have eventually been rewarded with success.

There are still many tracts, in the interior of the mountains, which are untenanted but are quite suitable for the establishment of small farms; I do not doubt that in a very short time all will be occupied.

Some Inconveniences

Mail troubles—Postman drowned—Salary inadequate—Government steamer service short-lived—Regular mail ceased—Lack of land survey threatens security of tenure—Suspension of customs duties is a boon to all

I consider one great drawback to the prosperity of the district is, and has been, the extreme irregularity of the mail service between Patagonia and Buenos Aires.

For some years, when we had only the old vessels "*Ushuaia*" and "*Villarino*" to depend upon, many of the settlers subscribed to pay a postman to run between Punta Arenas and San Julián, calling at all the various stations *en route*. This went on for some time, till the postman was unfortunately drowned in passing the River Gallegos and, although we afterwards employed several other men, we found no one willing to continue the work; all complained, and perhaps with reason, that the constant riding long distances in all kinds of weather was too trying for them; and also that the pay of ten shillings per month from each person who employed him was not sufficient. Had all the settlers united, and agreed to pay this amount, all would have gone well; but, unfortunately, outside the English residents, very few cared to pay anything and consequently the postman's income was not a bewildering one.

Therefore, when no one could be found to undertake the job, everyone was delighted when it was announced that Government steamers would run regularly, and the mails be received and despatched once a month. As everyone knows, this arrangement only continued for a short time — that is to say, until the "*Villarino*" and another vessel were lost, and the "*Ushuaia*" taken off the service, and placed absolutely at the disposal of the missionary settlement after which she was called. After this there was no regularity: we constantly had to wait three (or even four) months to receive or despatch a letter, unless some stray vessel happened to call in, or we went to the expense of sending a man to Punta Arenas. This is a great pity and has proved a great drawback which, if not already remedied, ought to be so at once; for, if there is one thing more necessary than another to the prosperity of these new colonies, it is that regular postal communication should be maintained both with Buenos Aires and Europe.

Another great drawback was the great delay in the measurement of the land: for years no one knew whether he was working on his own land, or that of some other man, and I fear that even now the survey is not concluded. At any rate, those who were colonists should have had the exact position and limits of the *league* of land granted them by the Government indicated to them, which even to the present day has not, to the best of my knowledge, been done. This has caused many complications and disagreements, and more than one man has abandoned his work in consequence. Also, the exact limits of the concession granted by the Government to the late Captain Luis Piedra Buena should be understood; when I left, several of the colonists were in doubt if their land was not situated on the before-mentioned concession.

All the settlers are, and ought to be, grateful that both the export and import duties have, for the present, been remitted by the Government. This is a great point, and had it not been the case, they could not have continued their work, but would have had to abandon what they had already accomplished.

Land of Opportunity

Work is available—Be prepared to face tough conditions—Effort will be rewarded

Now that my scribblings are drawing very near their termination, and having looked over them carefully, I feel how unworthy they are of the subjects on which I have written. I regret this the more because, as is natural to a man who has passed all the best years of his life in this comparatively new country, I feel, and shall always feel, the deepest interest in its progress, and I should be much grieved if anything I have said should deter others from trying their luck there.

I would recommend anyone who cannot find employment in the cities to try his luck in Patagonia. He will at least find no difficulty in obtaining work there, whilst waiting for a chance to start for himself. I have already mentioned that all kinds of provisions are so remarkably cheap, owing to the Free Ports, that he will find it far more advantageous to work for a moderate salary, which will amply suffice for all his needs (one which in the towns and cities of the Republic would barely keep him in the necessities of life).

But, the man who makes a venture must fully understand that he will not always find ready to his hand the comforts and luxuries to which he has been accustomed. Moreover, he must be prepared on occasions to rough it, in the most extreme sense of the word "roughing it", and to submit to the circumstances cheerfully — in fact, rather to enjoy them than otherwise. When people see this, and find that you are not too delicate to turn your hand to any kind of dirty work, from cleaning

out the clip to skinning or plucking a sheep which died of inflammation three or four days before — and also that you are not constantly
growling at the indifferent food, strong wind, cold or bad weather, or
any little inconvenience you may have to undergo — you may rest well
assured that you will find no difficulty in obtaining good employment.
Also, there will not be wanting men who note all this, and will lend
you a hand when opportunity arises to advance yourself. The number
of men who have come out to Patagonia as shepherds or employees in
some store or other, and who are now, in not a few cases, rising and
prosperous men, vouch for the truth of my remarks.

Of course, the first-comers, like myself, had the best chances, but I
do not mean for one moment to infer that there is not a good opening
for every hard-working man at the present moment. If I have not made
a fortune there, it has not been from want of opportunities of every
kind.   Unfortunately, I never had the sense to grasp them, as others
without a *tithe* of my chances or experiences did, and who are now, in
consequence, prosperous men.

One thing, however, I wish to reiterate: that is, that there is still a fine
field open in Patagonia for anyone who is enterprising and prepared
to work. I have not done with Patagonia yet, and I fully believe my
fortunes or misfortunes will be mixed up with that country till I hand
in my checks[1].

⁂ ⁂ ⁂

---

[1]   Continued involvement with Patagonia — Despite his stated intention, Greenwood
returned to England in the same year as this article was published (1901); he died
there in 1923, without ever returning to Patagonia. See ANNEX TWO, KEY DATES AND
EVENTS.

❧ AFTERWORD ❧

Apart from this series of newspaper articles, did William Greenwood ever publish his Patagonia experiences in book form? He certainly had hopes of doing so.

In 1901, he wrote to Dr. Woodward, Director of the Kensington Museum, in London:

> " ... I trust also that you will excuse my troubling you on another matter in which I should be very glad of your advice. During and before my illness I have employed myself in writing a series of articles on Patagonia, which I published in the Buenos Aires newspapers, & which were very well received and criticised. I propose enlarging these and publishing them in England, either in book form, or in some periodical. Can you advise me as to the best way to set about it & to what Editor I could apply who would take them up? Everything is strictly true and dates from thirty years back up to the present time."[†]

We do not have Woodward's reply; nor have any publications by William H. Greenwood been found in Great Britain.

As late as November 1920 (less than three years before his death), Greenwood wrote wistfully to a son of his old ranching partner Henry Reynard:

> " ... Herewith I forward to you a quantity of my Patagonian articles, published some years ago. I am sure they will interest you. Keep them as long as you like and copy what you like but return them to me when you have quite finished with them; as, if I ever manage to get my own book finished, I may require them for reference. I doubt if I shall ever write all I want to — you know I am a very old feeble man now, and tho' the spirit is willing the flesh is weak."[‡]

To judge by this evidence, it seems unlikely that he ever completed his book. Learning of Greenwood's aspiration has provided a further incentive to republish his articles.

THE EDITORS

[†] Letter dated 29 March 1901. (Correspondence, 1899–1902, DF100/33).
[‡] Letter dated 14 November 1920. (Reynard Family Papers, p. 170).

Process of Discovery

When we began *"hunting the hunter"* (i.e. researching William Greenwood), the available information was scarce and, sometimes, confusing: for example, we found a variety of years quoted for his arrival in Punta Arenas. An Internet search for the appropriate time period revealed (in addition to William) two more "Greenwoods" in Patagonia — James and George.

> *Later we learned that George was William's nephew, and that they had worked together for several years. James does not appear to be related to them. That was all.*

FALSE LEADS AND TRUE

Searching for other sources, we next found additional information in the following old publications (see BIBLIOGRAPHY):

(a) The magazine ARGENTINA AUSTRAL. One contributor, Carlos Borgialli, stated that, after retiring to Britain, Greenwood had published the story of his life in Patagonia in English newspapers and magazines.

> *This assertion was ambiguous, and proved to be only partially correct: although the material was written in English, the supposedly "English" publication was actually printed exclusively in Buenos Aires.*

(b) The official report EXPLORACIÓN DE SANTA CRUZ Y LAS COSTAS DEL PACÍFICO. Its author, the Argentine explorer Agustín del Castillo, retold several episodes heard from his guide Greenwood; he also included some personal information, for example, that he was from a distinguished family of York.

Once again, this information was only partially correct: Greenwood's family was indeed well placed socially, but he had been born in the county of Essex (Southeast England) rather than the Northern city of York.

At another point, the author stated that Greenwood was 37 years of age (in 1887), implying that he had been born in 1849 or 1850.

This data was useful, but insufficient, because no fewer than 81 children had been registered as "WILLIAM GREENWOOD" in England during that 2-year period.

(c) The book, THE GOLD DIGGINGS OF CAPE HORN. Its author, US journalist John Spears, wrote that while visiting Santa Cruz in 1894 he had met a sheep-owner named W. H. GREENWOOD, who had killed over 1,000 "panthers" (pumas) single-handed.

This information is not as trivial as it might appear: it provided a second initial letter ("H") for Greenwood's name; plus, it identified the date and place where the two had met.

GREENWOOD, THE GODFATHER

Our first, unexpected, breakthrough occurred while reviewing the baptism register of the Cathedral of Punta Arenas: an entry for 1889 recorded WILLIAM HERRINGHAM GREENWOOD as godfather to Federico, the son of Juan Harvey and Manuela Sánchez. Both the place and the time-period were appropriate for the man we were "tracking". It was particularly helpful that the initial letter of his middle name coincided with the reference by Spears. Using the comparatively unusual middle name HERRINGHAM, we could identify the man unambiguously. Despite being unable to locate a civil birth registration, we were successful in finding his baptism record in the expected timeframe, allowing us to rapidly construct his genealogy.

This was good progress: the identity of our hunter was defined, but there was still no sign of his memoirs.

CRUCIAL DISCOVERY

From time to time, in the course of collecting information for our web page (*The British Presence in Southern Patagonia*, http://patbrit.org), we visit descendants of British immigrants who generously share their stories with us. Just such a visit led us, again unexpectedly, to our second and crucial discovery. While at a ranch in Santa Cruz province — *Cañadón de las Vacas*, originally owned by Henry Reynard — we came across a couple of surprises in some old family papers. First, there were letters by Greenwood explaining that, as Reynard's business partner, he had personally set up the ranch in the late 1880s.

This was promising information, because his presence in the area confirmed the name given by Spears for the panther killer.

Continuing our search, we were excited to find the transcript of a newspaper article describing the 1877 mutiny in Punta Arenas, written by no less a person than W. H. GREENWOOD! Fortunately, whoever had transcribed it had also noted the source — "*The Standard*" newspaper, Buenos Aires — plus the edition number and year of publication.

Finally, this was a solid lead to a specific document. Our confidence in the citation did not guarantee that we would locate the specific newspaper, but we now knew which road to follow.

SUCCESS BEYOND EXPECTATIONS

Using the Internet once again, we established that the University of San Andrés, in Buenos Aires, holds a full series of the former newspaper "*The Standard*"; so, armed with our reference, we paid a visit in April 2014 to their Special Collections Department and found the article in question — plus 58 more! All had appeared between 1900 and 1901, under the title of "Patagonia", and were signed by W. H. Greenwood.

These were the long-sought-after memoirs! Our "hunt" was over, and the task of compilation and diffusion was about to begin.

W. H. Greenwood: Key Dates and Events

1849	Born in village of Colne Engaine, Essex. Son of Rev. John Greenwood D.D. and Lucy Brown. The youngest of his 15 children.
circa 1870	Travels to Buenos Aires; (said to) work for an English-language newspaper.
1871	Visits Chubut with friend John Leesmith, hunting and prospecting unsuccessfully for gold.
1872	Settles in Punta Arenas (Chile). Operates general store, lodging house and bar. Hunts seals with his small cutter.
circa 1874	Goes bankrupt. Abandons Punta Arenas. Associates with Santiago Zamora, hunting and trading in skins and feathers.
1875-1888	Lives far from civilisation. Develops backcountry survival skills. Visits Santa Cruz valley and lake. Acts as guide to several explorers.
circa 1888	Associates with sheep rancher Henry Reynard, working at Oazy Harbour and establishing Cañadón de las Vacas (Argentina).
1893	Hands over management of the ranch to his nephew George.
1896	Returns to England in poor health.
1898	Marries Alice Shepherd. Shortly after, returns alone to Patagonia.
1900-1901	Publishes collection of articles about Patagonia in Buenos Aires. Serious illness. Wife travels out from England to care for him.
1901	Returns with wife to Britain. They move to Germoe, Cornwall.
1920	Writes more reminiscences of Patagonia for the Reynard children *in memoriam* of Henry, his great friend and former business partner, who had died in 1919.
1922	Death of wife Alice.
1923	Dies. Buried with his wife in Godolphin, Cornwall.

Persons in "Patagonia"

AMEGHINO, Florentino (1854–1911): Argentine; prominent palaeontologist; director of the National Museum of Buenos Aires

ANACLETO [surname unknown]: Chilean; joined DEL CASTILLO's 1888 expedition; murdered by the BRUNEL brothers, Ascencio and Ricardo

AUWERS, Arthur (1838–1913): German; astronomer at Berlin Academy of Sciences; head of German Commission that observed the 1882 Transit of Venus at Punta Arenas

BAYS, Emilio: Swiss; hotel-keeper at Chabunco (near Cape Negro); accompanied the Steinmann expedition in 1883

BIGUÁ, Casimiro (c1819–1874): Tehuelche; principal chief of all the Tehuelche; awarded rank of lieutenant colonel in Argentine army

BRIDGES, Thomas (c1842–1898): English; Anglican missionary at Ushuaia

BRUNEL, Angel: Uruguayan / Falklander; gaucho; brother of Ascencio and Ricardo BRUNEL

BRUNEL, Ascencio: Uruguayan / Falklander; gaucho; renowned horse-thief; brother of Angel and Ricardo BRUNEL

BRUNEL, Ricardo: Uruguayan / Falklander; gaucho; brother of Angel and Ascencio BRUNEL

CAMPBELL, Roger: British; sheep rancher at Monte León, Santa Cruz

CATTLE, Ernest: English; former naval officer; settled at Lago Argentino in 1894; partner of William GAME

DACQUET [or DARQUIÉ], Guillermo: French; settler at Chabunco (near Cape Negro), N of Punta Arenas

DEL CASTILLO, Agustín (1855–1889): Argentine; navy captain; led two expeditions from Río Gallegos to the Cordillera: in 1887 (with Greenwood as guide) and again in 1888

DIXIE, Lady: see Florence DOUGLAS

DOUGLAS, Florence (1855–1905): Scottish; Travelled from Punta Arenas to the Paine district in 1878–1879. Other members of her party included John and James DOUGLAS (her brothers), Alexander Beaumont Churchill Dixie (her husband) and Julius Beerbohm; author of the book "Across Patagonia".

DOUGLAS, John (1844–1900): Scottish; Ninth Marquess of Queensberry, and older brother of Lady Florence DIXIE; was one of the members of her party that visited Patagonia in 1878–1879.

APPENDIX ONE

DUBLÉ ALMEIDA, Diego (1841–1922): Chilean; governor of Magallanes Territory, 1874–1878

DUNSMURE [or DUNSMUIR], James Alexander Henderson (1847–1879): Scottish; one of the British travellers who arrived at Punta Arenas with Greenwood; later, British vice-consul at Punta Arenas

ELLIS, Honorable Evelyn Henry (1843–1913): English; fifth son of the 6th Baron Howard de Walden, made a private expedition from Punta Arenas to Lago Argentino in January–March 1877.

ESTUARDO, José Antonio; Chilean; army sergeant; ringleader in 1877 Punta Arenas mutiny

FENTON, Arthur [Arturo] (c1861–1942): Irish; medical doctor in Río Gallegos; brother of Thomas FENTON

FENTON, Thomas [Tomás] (1850–1886): Irish; medical doctor in Punta Arenas; brother of Arthur FENTON

GAME, William: English; former naval officer; rancher at Lago Argentino; partner of Ernest CATTLE

HOWARD DE WALDEN, Lord: see Evelyn Henry ELLIS

JUAN [surname unknown]: Chilean; young assistant of Greenwood

KELLY (or BROWN), James (?–1880): English; former sailor; resident in Magallanes as early as 1874; long-time companion of Greenwood in the interior of the territory

LEESMITH, John (1833–?): English; investor; companion of Greenwood

MAJOR, Pedro: Tehuelche; chief; visited Santiago in 1874

MANZANO, José: Spanish; settler, arrived in territory c1874; established farm near Laguna Blanca, raising pigs and cattle; sheltered Greenwood in winter of 1877

MORENO, Francisco P. (1852–1919): Argentine; man of multiple interests, as scientist, explorer, naturalist, geographer and politician; founder of the La Plata Museum of Natural History (Buenos Aires)

MUSTERS, George C. (1841–1879): British (born in Italy); former army captain; accompanied Tehuelche party in lengthy expedition through Patagonia, 1869–1870; author of the book "*At Home with the Patagonians*"

PALIQUE [surname unknown]: Tehuelche; chief; a hill carries his name

PIEDRA BUENA [or PIEDRABUENA], Luis (1833–1883): Argentine; sea captain and ship-owner; lieutenant-colonel in the Argentine navy; known by Greenwood as a merchant and temporary resident of Punta Arenas; later, awarded extensive tracts of land by the Argentine government

PLATERO, Pedro: Tehuelche; chief

POZO Y MONTT, Isaac: Chilean; army sergeant; implicated and condemned to death for his participation in 1877 Punta Arenas mutiny

PRICHARD, [forename unknown]: ship captain; perhaps the same person as Griffith Prichard, active in Punta Arenas

QUEENSBERRY, Marquess of: see John DOUGLAS

REYNARD, Henry Leonard (1845–1919): English; merchant at Punta Arenas; British vice-consul in Magallanes; sheep rancher at Oazy Harbour and Cañadón de las Vacas; great friend of Greenwood

RICHMOND, [forenames unknown]: Argentine; ranchers at Puerto Santa Cruz

RIQUELME, José A.: Chilean; army sergeant; ringleader in 1877 Punta Arenas mutiny

RIVADAVIA, [forename unknown]: Argentine; lieutenant at jail, Río Gallegos, 1889

ROGERS, Thomas: Chilean; navy lieutenant; Greenwood was his guide to Obstruction Sound, November-December 1877

STEINMANN, Gustav (1856–1929): German; prominent geologist and palaeontologist; member of German commission which observed the Transit of Venus at Punta Arenas (December 1882); guided by Greenwood, explored the Interior of the region in January–May, 1883

STIRLING, Waite Hockin (1829–1923): English; Anglican bishop; formerly, superintendent of the South American Missionary Society; first missionary to live among the Yámana (Yahgan) natives, at Ushuaia

TORRES, [forename unknown]: Chilean; peon employed by Greenwood

VIEL, Oscar (1837–1892): Chilean; governor of Magallanes Territory, 1868–1874

WHEELER, George: English; sailor; briefly imprisoned at Río Gallegos

WOOD, Carlos (1836–1905): Chilean; governor of Magallanes Territory, 1878–1880

YÁÑEZ, [forename unknown]: Chilean; member of ROGERS' exploring party, 1879

ZAMORA, Santiago (c1806–1892): Argentine / Chilean; famous hunter, explorer and guide ("baqueano"); Greenwood's friend, mentor and sometime business partner

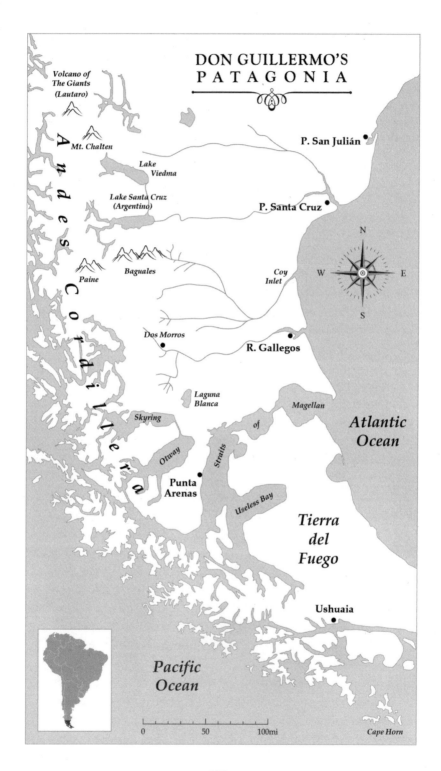

DON GUILLERMO'S
P A T A G O N I A

Volcano of
The Giants
(Lautaro)

Mt. Chalten

P. San Julián

Andes

Lake
Viedma

Lake Santa Cruz
(Argentino)

P. Santa Cruz

N

W   E

Baguales

Paine

Coy
Inlet

S

Cordillera

Dos Morros

R. Gallegos

Laguna
Blanca

Magellan

Skyring

of

Atlantic
Ocean

Otway

Straits

Punta
Arenas

Useless Bay

Tierra
del
Fuego

Ushuaia

Pacific
Ocean

0   50   100mi   Cape Horn

Locations in "Patagonia"

> Refer to accompanying General Map for locations of the principal features.

BAGUALES (Range): E of Paine; named by Greenwood and Zamora for the
quantity of wild horses discovered in this district

BAGUALES (Valley): S of Baguales Range

BLANCA, LAGUNA (Lake): 80 km N of Punta Arenas

CAGUAL: *see* BAGUALES

CAMARONES (Bay): coast of Chubut, between Trelew and Comodoro Rivadavia

CAR-AIKEN (Location): E shore of Lago Argentino

CENTINELA: *see* SENTINEL

CHALTÉN (Mountain): (also known as FitzRoy) N of Lake Viedma; highest
peak in region

CHICO (River): N of River Santa Cruz; drains SE into same estuary

COLONY, THE (Settlement): *see* PUNTA ARENAS

COY INLET (River): modern Río Coyle; multiple branches lie between Gallegos
and Santa Cruz rivers; drains E to estuary of same name on Atlantic coast

DESPUNTADERO (Bay): SW corner of Cabeza del Mar (N of Punta Arenas)

DIANA (Range): low hills bordering Llanuras de Diana, S of Puerto Natales

DOS MORROS (Hill): two prominent rock outcrops, named Domeyko and
Philippi, in upper reaches of the Gallegos–Turbio valley; a third outcrop
(Morro Gay) is close-by

DOS MORROS, LAGUNA (Lake): modern Laguna Cóndor; close to Dos Morros,
in valley of rivers Gallegos and Turbio

FAMINE, PORT (Settlement): site of failed 16th-century Spanish settlement on
Magellan Strait, S of Punta Arenas

FINADO ZURDO, CHORRILLO DEL (River): probably modern Río El Zurdo,
drains N, crossing border of Argentina and Chile, E of Morro Chico

FINADO ZURDO (Valley): modern Zurdo; N of Laguna Blanca

FITZROY'S CHANNEL (Strait): links Otway and Skyring Sounds

GALLEGOS (River): between Magellan Strait and Coy Inlet; drains E to estuary of same name on Atlantic coast

GALLEGOS, PORT (Settlement): *see* Río GALLEGOS

GALLEGOS, Río (Settlement): S shore of estuary of River Gallegos

GIANTS, VOLCANO OF THE (Mountain): modern Volcán Lautaro; located in the Southern Patagonian Ice Field, 55 km NW of Chaltén

GIGANTES: *see* GIANTS

ILL-LUCK (River): term is Greenwood's; probably, Río Calafate, S of Lago Argentino

ILL-LUCK CAMP (Location): term is Greenwood's; probably on the shore of Laguna Nímez, beside the city of El Calafate

KING WILLIAM THE 4TH LAND (Island): modern Isla Riesco

LEONA (River): drains S from Lago Viedma into Lago Argentino; named when the explorer Moreno was attacked by a puma

LEÓN, MONTE (Hill): Atlantic coast, S of Santa Cruz estuary

LION RANGE (Range): S border of Santa Cruz valley

MAGELLAN (Strait): links Atlantic and Pacific Oceans

MALO, CAÑADÓN (Valley): S of Laguna Blanca

MORRO CHICO (Hill): conspicuous rock outcrop, SE of Puerto Natales, beside Río Penitente

NEGRO (Cape): continental shore of Magellan Strait, N of Punta Arenas

OAZY HARBOUR (Bay): Magellan Strait, N of Punta Arenas

OBSERVATION, MOUNT (Hill): S of Puerto Santa Cruz

OBSTRUCTION SOUND (Inlet): S of Puerto Natales

OTWAY WATER (Sound): NW of Punta Arenas

OVENS (Inlet): Caleta Hornos (Chubut Province)

PAINE (Range): 100 km N of Puerto Natales

PALIQUE, CERRO (Hill): close to Río Vizcachas, E of Cerro Guido, and S of Cerro Pináculo

PALOS, LAGUNA DE LOS (Lake): close to Cabeza del Mar, N of Punta Arenas

PAVÓN, ISLA (Island): lowest crossing of River Santa Cruz; early trading station

PECKET HARBOUR (Bay): Magellan Strait, N of Punta Arenas

PESCADORES (Location): S shore of River Santa Cruz, close to its estuary

PUNTA ARENAS (Settlement): continental shore of Magellan Strait

PUNTA DEL MONTE (Location): Greenwood refers to a point between the River Gallegos and Laguna Blanca, near the Río El Zurdo. (N.B. There are several places with the same name.)

RAPID (River): [unidentified] in Paine district

ROBLES, PASS OF THE (Location): ford in upper reaches of the River Gallegos, near Dos Morros and Morro Gay

SAN JULIÁN, PORT (Settlement): Atlantic coast, N of Santa Cruz

SANDY POINT (Settlement): *see* Punta Arenas

SANTA CRUZ (Lake): modern Lago Argentino

SANTA CRUZ, PORT (Settlement): Atlantic coast, at mouth of River Santa Cruz

SANTA CRUZ (River): drains E from Lago Argentino to the Atlantic

SENTINEL PEAK (Mountain): (Sp. CENTINELA) N of Baguales range; named by Greenwood and Zamora

SENTINEL (River): (Sp. CENTINELA) drains N from Baguales range to Lago Argentino

SENTINEL (Valley): (Sp. CENTINELA) N of Baguales range

SKYRING WATER (Sound): NW of Punta Arenas

SOLO, CERRO (Hill): modern Cerro Frías; isolated peak on S shore of Lago Argentino

TIERRA DEL FUEGO (Island): extreme S of the continent, to S and E of Magellan Strait

TURBIO (River): westernmost tributary of River Gallegos; named by Greenwood

USHUAIA (Settlement): site of early Anglican mission station; N shore of Beagle Channel (Tierra del Fuego)

VACAS, CAÑADÓN DE LAS (Valley): between Coy Inlet and River Santa Cruz.

VIEDMA (Lake): N of Lago Argentino

VIRGINS (Cape): N shore of Magellan Strait, at its easternmost point

VIZCACHAS (Valley): SE from Baguales range

ZURDO, LAGUNA DEL (Lake): 4 km N of Laguna Blanca

Flora and Fauna in "Patagonia"

The names given are Greenwood's own terminology, influenced by his British background. We have provided the modern English and scientific names which (in our best judgment) match the species that he mentions or describes.

PLANTS AND FUNGI

Greenwood's name	Scientific name
BLACKCURRANT	*Ribes magellanicum*
CALAFATE	*Berberis microphylla* OR *Berberis buxifolia*
CALCEOLARIA	genus *Calceolaria*
CONVOLVULUS	genus *Convolvulus*
DANDELION or CHICORY	*Taraxacum officinale*
HOUSELEEK	genus *Sempervivum*
INCENSE BUSH	*Schinus longifolius*
JONQUIL or DAFFODIL	genus *Narcissus*
LEÑADURA	*Maytenus magellanica*
MANZANILLA	*Cotula scariosa* OR *Matricaria chamomilla*
MATA NEGRA	*Junellia tridens*
MICHAY	*Berberis ilicifolia*
MURTILLA	*Empetrum rubrum*
MUSHROOM	type not identified
PAMPA TEA	*Satureja darwinii*
PINATRE	genus *Cyttaria*
ROBLE	genus *Nothofagus*
ROMERILLO	*Chiliotrichum diffusum* OR *Baccharis patagonica*
WILD CELERY	*Apium australe*
WILD STRAWBERRY	*Rubus geoides*

ANIMALS

Greenwood's name	Equivalent modern name	Scientific name
AGUARÁ (Yellow Wolf)	Aguará Guazú	Chrysocyon brachyurus
BAGUAL	Wild Horse	Equus ferus caballus
CURURO	Magellan's Tuco-Tuco	Ctenomys magellanicus
DEER or HUEMUL	Huemul	Hippocamelus bisulcus
GREY FOX	Grey Fox	Dusicyon griseus
GUANACO	Guanaco	Lama guanicoe
HAIR SEAL	Sea Lion	Otaria flavescens
HARE	Mara	Dolichotis patagonum
LIZARD	Lizard	(type not identified)
PUMA or LION	Puma	Felis concolor
RED FOX or CULPEO	Culpeo Fox	Dusicyon culpaeus magellanicus
ROCK MARTEN	Mountain Vizcacha	Lagidium viscacia
SCORPION	Scorpion	(type not identified)
SKUNK	Patagonian Skunk	Conepatus humboldti
WILD CATTLE	Wild Cattle	Bos taurus

BIRDS

Greenwood's name	Equivalent modern name	Scientific name
BARKING DUCK	Crested Duck	Lophonetta specularioides
BLACK-NECKED SWAN	Black-necked Swan	Cygnus melancorypha
BRANT GOOSE	Upland Goose	Chloephaga picta
HAWK - small brown	Chimango Caracara	Milvago chimango
EAGLE	Eagle	(type not identified)
KINGFISHER - blue (very scarce)	Kingfisher	Ceryle torquata
LESSER RHEA; CHARA	Lesser Rhea; young Lesser Rhea	Pterocnemia pennata
PARROT	Austral Parakeet	Enicognathus ferrugineus
PICAZO DUCK	Picazo Duck	Netta peposaca
ROCK GROUSE	Ashy-headed Goose	Chloephaga poliocephala
WHITE GREBE (red head, most scarce)	Hooded Grebe	Podiceps gallardoi
WOODPECKER	Woodpecker	three types (not identified)

GREENWOOD'S LIST

*The following additional names appeared in a separate list, accompanying one of Greenwood's articles. Some of the terms are clear misnomers. He admits that the list is not comprehensive: one notable omission is the Andean Condor. Asterisks were used in the original edition to denote scarcity (where * = somewhat scarce, ** = very scarce, and *** = most scarce).*

OTHER WILD ANIMALS FOUND IN S. PATAGONIA

Wild Cat (Large Grey)	** Deer (Gama)
Armadillo (Mulita)	** Tiger Cat
* Pole Cat	*** White Fox

OTHER WILD FOWL FOUND IN S. PATAGONIA

	Curlew (Brown)
Flamingo	Curlew (Grey)
White Swan	Common Grebe
White Goose	Small Grebe or Dabchick
Falkland Island Goose	Quail
Kelp Goose	Common Bittern
Mallard Duck (common species)	Common Small Partridge
Widgeon (common species)	Large Crested Partridge (Martinet)
Widgeon Blue Winged	Dwarf Brown Partridge
Widgeon Grey	Large Black Woodpecker (red head)
Teal Green	Small Green Woodpecker
Teal Grey	Small Variegated Woodpecker (black
Steamer Duck	and white)
Grey Duck	Large Green Parrot (red wings)
Large Green Ibis	Small Green Parrot
Common Woodcock	* Rock Goose (male bird white, female
Dwarf Woodcock	black)
Common Snipe	* Small Grey Ibis
Sand Piper	* Jack Snipe
Green Plover	* Small Grey Heron
Curlew (black and white)	** Grey Plover
	** Pampa Grouse

❧ GLOSSARY ❧

AD LIBITUM: (Latin) at the person's pleasure or discretion (abbrev. *ad lib*)

AGUARÁ [GUAZÚ]: native South American mammal that looks like a long-legged dog; maned wolf

AIDE-DE-CAMP: (French) military officer serving as personal assistant to a senior

AMIGO: friend

AMOUR PROPRE: (French) self-esteem; self-love

AZULEJO: bluish-grey horse with white patches

BAD WAS THE BEST: (expression) "it was the best we could do"

BAGUAL (pl. BAGUALES, fem. BAGUALA): wild horse

BAQUEANO [or BAQUIANO]: (noun) person familiar with a given territory, skilled in wilderness travel and survival; guide; (adj.) competent; experienced; expert

BARRANCA: steep slope; bank; escarpment

BARRANCO: gully, ravine

BAYO: cream-coloured horse with dark mane and tail

BOLAS: from Spanish "balls", a throwing weapon made of weights on the ends of interconnected cords, designed to capture animals by entangling their legs.

BOLEADORA (V. BOLEAR): same as BOLAS; three-weight BOLEADORAS were usually designed with two shorter cords attached to the heavier weights, and one longer cord with a light weight (which was the one that wrapped around the legs of the hunted animal).

BONNE BOUCHE: (French) tasty titbit or morsel

BOSQUE: forest; wood; woods; woodland

BRUSH: tail of a fox

CABESTRO: halter

CALAFATE: shiny, small berry that grows on evergreen shrubs; the bush itself (Magellan barberry)

CAMP: (local usage) land, open country

CAMPAÑISTA: rural worker in charge of horses and cattle

CANAL: (local usage) sea channel; watercourse

CAÑA: sugarcane; hence, alcohol made from cane (*see* GUACHACAY)

CAÑADÓN: ravine

CANOE INDIANS: coastal natives of Patagonia and Tierra del Fuego; Alacaluf, Yahgan (modern names: Kawéskar, Yámana)

CAPA: cloak or cape of guanaco skin worn by the Tehuelche

CAPATAZ: foreman

CARGUERO: beast of burden; cargo animal

CARNEADO (V. CARNEAR): butchered

CERRO: hill; mountain

CHAGRIN: (French) embarrassment; humiliation

CHARA: young ostrich (rhea)

CHARQUEADO (V. CHARQUEAR): seared (meat)

CHARQUI: jerked meat (air-dried and salted)

CHASQUE (also CHASQUI): courier; (origin) messenger in the Inca Empire

CHIRIPÁ: sort of trousers consisting of a cloth passing between the legs and held at the waist

CHORO: mussel

CHRISTIAN(S): (local usage) generic term used to denote non-native people

COLLERA: horse collar

COMISARIO: inspector; commissary

CONFAB: private conversation

CONFRÈRE: (French) colleague; fellow member of a profession or fraternity

CORDILLERA: mountain range or chain; (Cordillera - leading capital letter) the main ridge of the Andes

CORRAL: animal pen

CUARTEL: barracks

CULPEO: species of wild fox

CUM GRANO SALIS: (Latin) (literally, with a grain of salt) not too literally

CURURO: a burrowing rodent. Greenwood uses this name for the Magellanic tuco-tuco

DEER: (local usage) huemul

DON (also D.): Mister

EN MASSE: (French) all together; in one group or body

EN ROUTE: (French) on or along the way

FIRE-WATER: (figurative) strong (distilled) alcohol

FUEGIANS: natives of Tierra del Fuego; specifically Ona (modern Selk'nam)

GAUCHO: cowboy of the pampas

GOBERNACIÓN: Government building / officials

GRASERÍA: fat-rendering works

GREASE: fat

GRIP: (English dialect) small ditch; trench; drain

GUACHACAY (= WACHAKAI): liquor made by the Tehuelche using CALAFATE berry and brandy; strong alcoholic drink of low quality

GUALICHO: (Tehuelche) evil spirit

GUSTO: vigorous enjoyment

HACIENDA: large farm

HAND: unit of measure for the height of a horse, equal to 4 inches (10 cm.)

HARE: (local usage) mara

HARINA: flour

HOGGET: sheep between one and two years of age

HUEVOS GUACHOS: (literally, orphan eggs); eggs of the rhea laid outside of the nest

INCENSE BUSH: (local usage) small tree of the Acacia family; popular name "molle"

INFRA DIG: (Latin) beneath one's dignity

ISLA: island

JERGA: woven blanket made by the Tehuelche, used as a saddle blanket

KÜMMEL: sweet liqueur (= kimmel)

LAGO: lake

LAGUNA: small lake

LASSO: rope with a noose at one end

LAZAR: (verb) use a lasso

LEAGUE: old measure of distance. As an approximation for Southern Patagonia, one league of distance is equivalent to 5 km; and one league of area (strictly one square league) to 25 square km or 2,500 hectares.

LEÑADURA: (literally, hard wood) small perennial tree native to southern South America

LICKINGS: (Scots) punishment by beating

LION: (local usage) puma

LIONESS: (local usage) female puma

LONJA: leather strip (literally, slice)

MACHETE: heavy knife used as a tool or weapon

MADRINA: (horse) bell-mare, trained to guide the members of a troop (TROPILLA)

MANANTIAL: natural spring

MANCARRÓN: old horse with damaged legs; "nag"

MANEA: leather hobble, attached to the front legs of a horse

MANZANILLA: camomile; camomile tea

MARA: type of large rodent

MARUCHO: boy who rides the guide-mare ("MADRINA")

MATA NEGRA: type of shrub native to Patagonia

MATE: a herb (*Ilex paraguensis*); common tea made with the mate herb (*see* YERBA)

MEET: (Archaic) appropriate; fitting

MICHAY: thorny shrub, related to the CALAFATE

MILCH COW: cow kept for milking

MODUS VIVENDI: (Latin) way of life

MONKEY JACKET: short, close-fitting jacket worn by sailors

MONTE: scrubland; woodland

MONTURA: saddle; mount

MORO: dappled grey horse

MOUNTAIN DEER: *see* DEER

MOUNTAIN LION: *see* LION

MURTILLA: native shrub, producing edible berries

NATIVE TEA: *see* PAMPA TEA

NIGGER: derogatory term for a Negro; nowadays, the term is considered offensive; "[worked] like a nigger" = with great energy

NON EST: (Latin) does not exist = dead

OLD ADAM: natural tendency to sin (biblical reference)

OLD NICK: The Devil

OSTRICH: (local usage) lesser rhea

OVERO: type of horse with large, irregular white spots; usually has a bald face and solid legs

PALM AND NEEDLE: sewing tool used by sailors

PAMPA (pl. PAMPAS): treeless plain; open land (Quechua)

PAMPA TEA: (local usage) low plant reminiscent of thyme

PASEO: walk; stroll; outing (figuratively, excursion)

PEON: farm labourer

PER DIEM: (Latin) daily

PER MAR: (Latin) by sea

PETISO (PETIZO): small horse

PICANA: part of the rump of a rhea, a favourite food of the Tehuelche (also a pointed instrument; or cattle prod)

PICQUET (PIQUET): card game for two players

PINATRE: (Tehuelche) type of parasitic fungus

PINOCLE: card game for up to eight players, popular in Germany (also pinochle, binokel)

PLUMERO: cluster of feathers; feather duster

POINT: (local usage) small group (such as sheep, trees)

PONCHO: South American cloak in the form of a blanket, with a hole for the head

POTRO BOOTS: footwear obtained by removing the hide from the rear leg of a colt; the custom is of native origin, originally using the hide of a guanaco

PRE-CORDILLERA: foothills or lower range preceding the main Cordillera

PUNTERO: leader

QUI VIVE: (French) on the alert; vigilant

QUILLANGO: cape made of pieces of young guanaco skins sewn together

QUINTA: vegetable patch; vegetable garden

QUONDAM: (Latin) that once was

RAKING: (of a horse) fast-looking

RAW-BONED: (of a horse) having little flesh on its bones; gaunt

RENDEZVOUS: (French) to meet; meeting-place

RETOBAR: to wrap something with leather or cloth

RINCÓN: corner; hidden or out-of-the-way place

RÍO: river

ROBLE: (literally, oak) type of Patagonian beech tree

ROMERILLO: low flowering shrub

ROSADO: type of light-coloured horse

ROSILLO: type of horse having red and white hairs (that turn white with age, except head, legs and tail)

RUG: cape, in the British sense of "travelling rug"

SANGFROID: (French) coolness and composure, especially in trying circumstances

SIERRA: mountain range

SIESTA: afternoon nap

SKAT: card-game for three players, formerly popular in Germany

SOGA: rope, thong

SQUAW: (by analogy with United States terminology) Tehuelche woman

STATION: cattle ranch (especially Australia and New Zealand; cf. Spanish term *estancia*)

TACHO: metal container used informally as a kind of kettle (Chile, Argentina)

TAPAPECHO: brisket

TEHUELCHES: natives of Patagonian steppes (modern name, Aónikenk)

THOROUGH-PACED: conscientious; committed; dedicated

TITHE: tenth part

TOLDO: temporary dwelling of hides, erected on poles, used by the Tehuelche

TORDILLO: whitish-grey horse

TOSCA: (literally, coarse); limestone

TRABA: animal restraint (*see* also MANEA)

TRISTE: sad

TROPILLA: drove or troop of tame horses

TWITCH: (of a horse) calming device, attached to the upper lip

VAQUERO: cowboy; cow hunter

VELD: (Afrikaans, Dutch) open country (term used in South Africa)

VIDE: (Latin, imperative) refer to

VULPES CANIS: (or *Canis vulpes*) (Latin) red fox

WACHAKAI: *see* GUACHACAY

WETHER: castrated ram

YERBA: herb, usually generic term for the popular infusion MATE

ZANJA: ditch

✳ BIBLIOGRAPHY ✳

PUBLICATIONS CITED IN THE TEXT

BROWN, Charles H. 1854. *Insurrection at Magellan: Narrative of the Imprisonment and Escape of Capt. Chas. H. Brown, from the Chilian Convicts*. Boston: The author. URL: http://patlibros.org/iam/

DEL CASTILLO, Agustín. 2007. *Exploración de Santa Cruz y las costas del Pacífico*. Buenos Aires: Continente.

DUBLÉ ALMEIDA, Diego. 1938a. "Diario del viaje al Río Santa Cruz, Patagonia." In *Revista Chilena de Historia y Geografía* 84: 208–231.

_____ 1938b. "Diario del viaje al Río Santa Cruz, Patagonia (Cont.)." In *Revista Chilena de Historia y Geografía* 85: 254–290.

GREENWOOD, William H. 1900–1901. "Patagonia." In *The Standard* (Buenos Aires): selected issues from Nº 11386 to Nº 11565.

IBAR SIERRA, Enrique. 1879. *Estudios sobre las Aguas de Skyring i la parte austral de Patagonia*. Ed. Federico Puga Borne. Santiago: Imprenta Nacional.
URL: https://archive.org/details/estudiossobrela00siergoog

MADSEN, Andreas & BERTOMEU, Carlos A. 1956. *Cazando Pumas en la Patagonia*. Buenos Aires: The author.

MARTINIC B, Mateo. 1980. *Patagonia de ayer y de hoy*. Punta Arenas: Difusora Patagonia.
URL: http://www.memoriachilena.cl/602/w3-article-10396.html

_____ 1988. *Punta Arenas en su Primer Medio Siglo 1848–1898*. Punta Arenas: The author.
URL: http://www.memoriachilena.cl/602/w3-article-10383.html

ROGERS, Juan Tomás. 1878. "Expedicion a la parte austral de Patagonia por el teniente 2.º señor Juan Tomas Rogers." In *Anuario Hidrográfico de la Armada de Chile* 5: 56–95.

_____ 1880. "Segunda Esploracion de la parte austral de la Patagonia." In *Anuario Hidrográfico de la Armada de Chile* 6: 97–150.

STEINMANN, Gustav. 1883. "Reisenotizen aus Patagonien." In *Neues Jahrbuch für Mineralogie, Geologie und Palaeontologie* 2: 255–258.

WILCKENS, Otto. 1930. "Gustav Steinmann, Sein Leben und Wirken." Berlin: Verlag von Gebrüder Borntraeger. Reprinted from *Geologischen Rundschau* 21 (6): 389–415.

UNPUBLISHED MATERIAL CITED

BAPTISM REGISTER 1866–1899. Church of the Sacred Heart, Roman Catholic Cathedral, Punta Arenas, Magallanes, Chile. Microfilm, FHL N° 1110478. In Family History Library, Church of Jesus Christ of Latter-day Saints.

CORRESPONDENCE 1889, ARCHIVES. Río Gallegos, Gobernación, Santa Cruz Territory, Argentina. (Refs. 1889/002, 3 pieces). URL: http://patlibros.org/sned/txt/SN001.php

CORRESPONDENCE, 1899-1902, LETTERS OF WILLIAM H. GREENWOOD. Palaeontology Archives, Natural History Museum, London, England. (refs. DFH100/24 and DFH100/33, 7 pieces). URL: http://donduncan.org/greenwood/nhm.pdf

REGISTER OF DEATHS 1892. Civil Registration, Magallanes Territory, Punta Arenas, Chile. Microfilm, FHL N° 1159821. In Family History Library, Church of Jesus Christ of Latter-day Saints.

REYNARD FAMILY PAPERS, ca. 1920. *A Life of Henry Leonard Reynard*. Unpublished biography, 187 typewritten pages. URL: http://patlibros.org/reyn/

OTHER PUBLICATIONS CONSULTED

ÁLVAREZ, José S ("Fray Mocho"). 1920. *En el Mar Austral — Croquis Fueguinos*. Buenos Aires: Vaccaro. URL: https://archive.org/details/3198803

BEERBOHM, Julius. 1879. *Wanderings in Patagonia OR Life among the Ostrich-Hunters*. London: Chatto and Windus. URL: https://archive.org/details/wanderingsinpata00beerrich

BORGIALLI, Carlos. 1935. "Galería de hombres ilustres de la Patagonia: Tte. de Navío D. Agustín del Castillo." In *Revista Argentina Austral* 69: 33–43.

BRAUN MENÉNDEZ, Armando. 1934. *El Motín de los Artilleros*. Buenos Aires: Viau y Zona.

CHILDS, Herbert. 1936. *El Jimmy, Outlaw of Patagonia*. Philadelphia / London: Lippincott.

COUVE, Enrique & VIDAL, Claudio. 2003. *Birds of Patagonia, Tierra del Fuego & Antarctic Peninsula*. Punta Arenas: Fantástico Sur.

CRAMER, Jorge A. 2006. *Por si Quede*. Buenos Aires: Photo Design.

DIXIE, Florence. 1880. *Across Patagonia*. London: Bentley.
URL: http://www.gutenberg.org/ebooks/42666

GAVIRATI, Marcelo. 2007. "Ascencio Brunel, El Demonio de la Patagonia." In *Todo es Historia* 47: 36–44.

HARRIS, Graham. 1998. *A Guide to the Birds and Mammals of Coastal Patagonia*. Princeton: University Press.

HERNÁNDEZ, José. 1968. *Martín Fierro* (6th ed.). Madrid: Aguilar.

HESKETH–PRICHARD, H. 1902. *Through the Heart of Patagonia*. New York: Appleton.
URL: https://archive.org/details/throughheartofpa00pricrich

HUDSON, W H. 1923. *Idle Days in Patagonia*. London: Dent.
URL: https://archive.org/details/idledaysinpatago00hudsuoft

LISTA, Ramón. 1880. *Mis Esploraciones y Descubrimientos en la Patagonia 1877–1880*. Buenos Aires: Martín Biedma.
URL: https://archive.org/details/misesploracione00listgoog

MAINWARING, Michael James. 1983. *From the Falklands to Patagonia*. London / New York: Allison & Busby.

MARTINIC B, Mateo. 1963. *Presencia de Chile en la Patagonia Austral, 1843-1879*. Santiago: Andrés Bello.

_____ 2000. *Última Esperanza en el tiempo* (2nd ed.). Punta Arenas: Universidad de Magallanes.

MORENO, Francisco P. 1879. *Viaje a la Patagonia Austral 1*. Buenos Aires: Imprenta de la Nación.
URL: https://archive.org/details/viajelapatagoni00moregoog

MUSTERS, George Chaworth. 1871. *At Home with the Patagonians: a year's wanderings over untrodden ground from the Straits of Magellan to the Rio Negro*. London: John Murray.
URL: http://www.gutenberg.org/ebooks/42483

PAYRÓ, Roberto. 1898. *La Australia Argentina: Excursión periodística a las costas patagónicas, Tierra del Fuego e Isla de los Estados.* Buenos Aires: Imprenta de la Nación.
URL: https://archive.org/details/laaustraliaarge00payrgoog

SEIBOLD, Eugen & SEIBOLD, Ilse. 2010. "Gustav Steinmann (1856–1929): Ein deutscher Ordinarius der Kaiserzeit." In *International Journal of Earth Sciences* 99(1): S3–S15, Springer–Verlag.

SPEARS, John R. 1895. *The Gold Diggings of Cape Horn: A study of Life in Tierra del Fuego and Patagonia.* New York: Putnam's.
URL: https://archive.org/details/golddiggingscap00speagoog

WILLIAMS, Ralph. 1913. "Life in Patagonia." In *How I became a Governor.* 50–62. London: John Murray.
URL: http://patlibros.org/clip/txt/CL064.htm

ᴥ ILLUSTRATIONS ᴥ

ᴥ SKETCH MAPS ᴥ

ᴥ PHOTOGRAPHS ᴥ

This first edition of
Patagonia Wild and Free
comprises 1,100 copies,
of which 100 are in hardcover.

Set in Minion Pro and reproduced on
ivory 80gsm Bond paper.

Printed by
Salesianos Impresores S.A.,
Santiago de Chile
November 2015.